P9-AFL-465

WITHDRAWN

Guns and Violence

Joyce Lee Malcolm

Guns and Violence

THE ENGLISH EXPERIENCE

Harvard University Press
Cambridge, Massachusetts and London, England
2002

Library of Congress Cataloging-in-Publication Data
Malcolm, Joyce Lee.
Guns and violence : the English experience / Joyce Lee Malcolm.
p. cm.
Includes bibliographical references and index.
ISBN 0-674-00753-0 (alk. paper)
1. Firearms and crime—England—History.
2. Gun control—England—History.
I. Title.
HV7439.G72 E546 2002
363.3'3'0942—dc21   2002020541

To my family

Acknowledgments

I T IS A PLEASURE to have an opportunity to thank those who have contributed to this enterprise with their support, advice, questions, enthusiasm, and friendship. David Wootton is perhaps most responsible for this book. His review of my earlier study, *To Keep and Bear Arms: The Origins of an Anglo-American Right,* pointed to the need for research into the impact of private arms on crime in England and the puzzling fact that the Victorian era managed to achieve an enviably low rate of violent crime despite numerous social problems and no controls on guns. We have had many discussions since, as I worked my way through the issues and materials. Thank you, David. Henry Neuburger, a distinguished economist and statistician and member of the British civil service, enthusiastically researched government tallies of the first English firearms licence act and constructed a regression analysis of gun ownership in England. Sadly, Henry died before this book was completed, but Professor Gary Mauser of Simon Fraser University has generously analyzed Henry's graphs and provided a commentary on them for me. Grateful thanks also go to Martin Wiener and Colin Greenwood, who have read several chapters and tactfully rescued me from error. Colin Greenwood's own book served as a pioneering work in this field. I also thank Robert Cottrol, Don B. Kates Jr. and C. B. Kates, R. A. I. Munday, and the faculty and fellows of the MIT Security Studies Program, above all its director, Harvey Sapolsky, for welcoming me into their midst, pointing me to important materials, and raising their customary challenging questions. Many thanks are due also to the anonymous readers whose excellent suggestions and corrections have strengthened this book. I have been fortunate to have in Kathleen McDermott and Ann Hawthorne excellent editors. My debt to the numerous scholars whose work I have drawn upon is clearly apparent in the notes. Those faults and errors that remain are mine alone.

Many institutions have also provided invaluable help. Bentley College awarded me the sabbatical leave that enabled me to undertake the initial research; Robinson College, Cambridge, welcomed me warmly during my research trips; the Earhart Foundation awarded me a generous research fellowship grant; and the Liberty Fund appointed me a visiting scholar for the crucial six months needed to complete most of the writing. Aïda Donald, former editor-in-chief at Harvard University Press, has been a friend and patron who has not flinched in her belief that controversial subjects deserve support. A special thank-you goes to my dear family for bearing with my preoccupation with unflagging grace and love.

Contents

Guns and Violence

Introduction

Discourage self-help, and loyal subjects become the slaves of ruffians. Over-stimulate self-assertion, and for the arbitrament of the courts you substitute the decision of the sword or the revolver.

—A. V. DICEY, *The Law of the Constitution*

BEHIND THE PASSIONATE debate over gun control and armed crime lie untested assumptions about the connection between firearms and violence. Conventional wisdom equates the number of guns in private hands with the frequency of armed crimes.[1] Contributing causes—poverty, unemployment, an unstable social environment—are acknowledged, but guns are viewed as an important, if not the most important, factor. Indeed some scholars claim that "the weapons effect on aggressive behavior is well established"—that is, the mere presence or sight of a gun triggers hostile action.[2] The removal of privately owned firearms therefore seems the easiest means of reducing violence. This logic undergirds the firearms policies of Great Britain and of most other developed countries. Further, it presumes that legislation is capable of reducing the quantity of guns available to those individuals likely to commit crimes.

The belief that statutes can actually deprive criminals of firearms has long been questioned. But recently the deeper question, the relationship between the number of guns and the number of armed crimes, has been vigorously challenged as well. One forceful argument turns that equation on its head, claiming that having more guns in private hands will decrease crime. Criminals are logical, according to this argument; therefore, when they weigh the cost of committing a crime, they will be more hesitant to prey on individuals who are armed. Thus, if many people are armed, violent crime will decline. On that theory thirty-three American states now have statutes permitting law-abiding citizens to carry concealed weapons. There is a third possibility, of course: the number of guns available to the public may have no appreciable impact on the rate of violent crime, and the solution, whatever it is, lies elsewhere. These alternative approaches deserve closer scrutiny.

History offers us the opportunity to test their validity, and this book does so by analyzing the impact of firearms and firearms policy on violent crime in England. There are sound reasons for focusing upon the English case. England currently has among the most stringent gun control laws in the world and certainly the most restrictive of any democracy. It has also had, until recently, a low rate of violent crime. This combination has made it the model most touted as proof that removing weapons from private hands does reduce violent crime.

From the historian's point of view the English example has several additional advantages. Government records of serious crimes extend back to medieval times.[3] And for more than a century the English government has been compiling national statistics on crime and on the numbers of licenced firearms. These two sets of figures provide data that go back fifty years before the imposition of gun controls and have continued for the more than eighty years since. This book focuses upon England and Wales, which government statistics have consistently paired, but does not include Scotland, as one set of data begins before the United Kingdom was formed, and, more important, Scotland has its own legal system. Although these official statistics do have serious flaws, they can at least indicate trends. In addition, in the past quarter century, perhaps because of increasing concern about crime, there has been unprecedented scholarly interest in the history of crime in England. The impressive body of research that has resulted covers the past six hundred years and includes broad studies of long-term national patterns of violence, close investigations into crime and criminal procedure, in particular regions at particular times, and thoughtful probes into the nature, causes, and prevention of crime.[4]

Comparisons can also be instructive. This book combines a close historical treatment of one country, England, with the modern experience of another, the United States. No two nations' firearms policies seem more at odds, or are more often compared by their peoples. England has strict gun control and a reputation for low rates of violent crime. America has permissive gun laws and a reputation for high rates of violent crime.[5] Most comparisons begin and end with this interesting but unexamined correspondence. Yet even a brief investigation of the history of each nation makes the comparison all the more intriguing and all the more instructive. Until 1920 the English and American peoples shared a legacy akin to the second theory described above, the use of an armed public to help prevent violent crime. England's reliance upon ordinary people to protect themselves and their community was a survival from medieval times.[6] In 1689 the English Bill of Rights elevated this customary duty into a right for the great majority of Englishmen "to have arms for their defence." By the time of the American Revolution English jurists such as William Blackstone had also come to see this right as a constitutional device by which the people, *in extremis,* might protect all their other rights.

Englishmen brought with them to the New World their habit of relying on civilians for peacekeeping and the right for these civilians to have weapons. Indeed, that practice seemed so crucial to the survival of colonists in a wilderness that most Americans still believe widespread dependence on firearms was a colonial innovation.[7] When the founders of the American republic drafted their own Bill of Rights they incorporated the right to be armed along with others culled from the English Bill of Rights. The American Second Amendment, however, broadened the language of an English guarantee that confined the right to be armed to Protestants and implied some regulation was permissible. The American language flatly asserts that "the right of the people to keep and bear arms shall not be infringed."[8]

In practice, the right of both peoples was similar. Whatever other differences England and America had, for three centuries they agreed upon the importance of privately owned firearms for self-defence, for the maintenance of public peace, and for constitutional stability. Only in our own century has a sharp divergence in policy and attitude occurred. The right of Englishmen "to have arms for their defence" has been effectively demolished by a series of ever more stringent parliamentary statutes and bureaucratic regulations. These culminated in a classified 1969 Home Office regulation that barred possession of a firearm for personal protection; the 1988 Firearms Act's tighter controls on shotguns, the last firearm that could be purchased with a simple show of fitness; and the 1997 Firearms Act's nearly complete ban on handguns. Firearms apart, English law now prohibits civilians from carrying *any* article for what is termed "private defence." Paired with this policy is a much-narrowed legal standard of what force is acceptable for personal protection.

By contrast, while American jurisdictions restrict specific types of firearms, and an estimated 20,000 state and local regulations control the use of guns, American citizens own approximately 200 million firearms. The National Rifle Association, with its 4 million members, is America's largest lobby group, and a majority of states now permit law-abiding citizens to carry concealed weapons. Starting from a shared legacy, the contrast between English and American practice and experience could not be more dramatic. The story of this common origin and modern divergence is informative. There are, of course, key cultural and legal differences to consider, but a thoughtful probe beneath the oft-repeated generalities can advance our understanding of the relationship between guns and violence.

The complicated task of placing the government and legal records of both nations in a broader context has been made immeasurably easier thanks to the work of scholars from a host of disciplines. They have tackled many aspects of the problem—statistics of international rates of crime, analyses of national crime statistics, studies into the backgrounds and motivations of criminals, the possible causes of crime—all in search of the key, or keys, to criminal behavior.[9] Surprisingly, although guns are continually linked to crime rates in the public arena, scholarly investigations of England rarely consider private possession as a factor in the level of interpersonal violence. In *The Growth of Crime: The International Experience,* for example, Sir Leon Radzinowicz and Joan King use England as their point of departure but never single out firearms or any other weapon as either causing or deterring crime. The same is true of Paul and Patricia Brantingham in their fascinating statistical study, *Patterns in Crime.* They detected basic patterns of violence that seem to exist irrespective of the availability of firearms. Among the most intriguing was their finding that countries with very high rates of crimes against property tend to have low rates of crimes against persons, and vice versa.[10] They categorized both England and the United States as countries with high rates of property crimes and low rates of crimes against persons. When Terence Morris turned from the impact of poverty, prosperity, and unemployment on crime in England to "the problem of firearms," it was only to consider the use of firearms by the English police, not as a cause of violence, despite the increasing use of firearms in crime during the period he was studying.[11] Morris and Louis Blom-Cooper, in *A Calendar of Murder: Criminal Homicide in England since 1957,* say nothing about guns as a factor in crime.[12] Robert Sindall's study of street violence in the nineteenth century led him to single out the media's role in fostering the notion that crime was a serious problem at a time when it was actually declining.[13] In Nigel Walker's efforts to explain misbehaviour, he doesn't mention firearms but finds that Durkheim's principle of "one effect, one cause" is nonsense. Walker argues that the quest for a general theory "which will account for all instances of crime or deviance or misbehaviour makes no more sense than would a search for a general theory of disease."[14] Two notable exceptions are Colin Greenwood and Peter Squires. Greenwood's groundbreaking book, *Firearms Control: A Study of Armed Crime and Firearms Control in England and Wales,* published in 1972, traces English firearms legislation and the impact of firearms on crime. Greenwood, then chief inspector of the West Yorkshire Constabulary, provided a wealth of information about English firearms controls up to 1968 and their impact to 1969 and discovered little direct relationship between the number of guns in private hands and armed crime. More recently, in *Gun Culture or Gun Control? Firearms, Violence and Society,* Peter Squires, a British social scientist, compares English and American attitudes toward what he terms "the sociology of the gun." The book's title makes a more simplistic distinction than the content itself, which provides a brief history of each country before focusing on its modern cultural and political clashes over controls on firearms. Unfortunately, since Squires's homicide figures for America stop in 1994, he is seemingly unaware of the plummeting rate of firearms homicide in the United States since then, or of the increasing armed crime in England, and concludes that "the most acute moment of the UK's handgun crisis has now passed." Whether recent trends would have altered Squires's conclusions is uncertain, for he sees no justification for a more permissive firearms policy in the 1980s, when firearms-related offences were rising while numbers of firearms certificate holders declined, and sticks to the same view when armed crime seemed to be falling after

1994, judging: "The fact that firearm offending now appears to be falling does not amount to a reason for reconsidering handgun prohibition."[15]

The American preoccupation with crime has focused more frequently on the relationship between firearms and violence. Even so it is only since the mid-1970s that this concern about guns has been reflected in journals "with scientific pretensions." Since then there has been an explosion of interest, with more articles published about firearms and crime between 1975 and 1985 than in all the years before.[16] In such a complex and emotional field of study, some authors, provoked into print by a deep conviction about who ought to have access to weapons, have accepted untested assumptions. Happily the results of many careful, scholarly investigations of English, American, and international crime provide penetrating insights that can lead to a better understanding of the relationship between guns and violence.

What we cannot know, of course, and what no historical work—or any other for that matter—can establish, is a counterfactual, in this case what would have happened in the absence of restrictions such as those imposed by modern English firearms regulations. But that is no reason to down tools. Available evidence enables us to set these restrictions in historical context and, by comparing patterns of violence before and after their passage, to assess whether they achieved the goal envisaged. Taking the long historical view makes this strategy all the more valid.

I begin this study with an examination of the customary common-law treatment of violence and popular attitudes toward crime and self-defence in the Middle Ages. This first chapter also provides a control of sorts for what follows by indicating the level and type of violent crime in England before the appearance of firearms. Chapter 2 focuses on the emergence of guns during the sixteenth and seventeenth centuries, the impact of these weapons on violent crime, and the establishment in 1689 of a right for English Protestants—then 90 percent of the population—to have weapons for personal defence. Chapter 3 takes up the events of the "long eighteenth century," an era of frequent foreign wars, draconian domestic legislation such as the Black Act, with its 200 to 350 new felonies, heavy reliance upon the transportation of felons, and easy access to firearms. Chapter 4 examines the relationship between guns and violence in the nineteenth century, when the aftermath of the French Revolution and the full emergence of the Industrial Revolution provided new challenges to public order. Yet as this century, replete with all those usual suspects of disorder and crime—poverty, dislocation, absence of "safety nets," and cheap guns—came to an end, England boasted extraordinarily low levels of violent crime. The next two chapters treat the English experience in the twentieth century in detail, from the imposition of the first general restrictions on gun ownership just after World War I to sweeping controls on firearms and imitation firearms, and on carrying anything for self-defence. The impact of a government strategy intended to reduce crime by removing any article that might deter it is carefully examined. Last, Chapter 7 examines and assesses the American use of guns, its multiplicity of firearms policies, and their impact on violent crime in the past few years.

Such a complex subject necessarily involves considering

a variety of factors that may have affected the crime rate, among them dearth, war, and demobilization, long- and short-term changes in criminal law and in the criminal's weapon of choice, fluctuations in cultural attitudes toward interpersonal crime and its punishment, and attempts at deterrence. With all this in mind Chapter 8 draws conclusions about the relationship between firearms and violent crime. This ambitious agenda is necessary to set the problem in its historical context.

"It is difficult to analyze the state of crime," England's chief investigator of prisons complained,

> because the statistics obtained by civil servants, and
> used by ministers, almost invariably mislead. It is
> easy to suggest crime is up or crime is down by
> looking at a single variety of crime, or a single loca-
> tion such as a big city . . . Much crime is not re-
> ported. Much crime, where there is no trial, is
> falsely reported . . . It is in the interests of politi-
> cians to show that their political measures have
> been effective. They have waved the wand and crime
> is no more.[17]

Those who delve into the history of crime are quick to admit that theirs is no exact science. Numerous variables distort the picture. These include changing definitions of particular crimes and varying methods of calculation; wavering enthusiasm for strict law enforcement on the part of police, prosecutors, judges, government, and the public; numerous crimes that go unreported; and a plethora of general and particular causes of fluctuations in the rates of criminal violence. Even the definition of what constitutes a firearm is not as straight-forward as it seems. Add to this still other elements that bedevil an analysis spanning several centuries—inconsistent recordkeeping, social and economic change, demographic swings, the impact of war and of drastically different legal codes, changing norms of behaviour, improved medical skills—and any historical study seems foolhardy in the ex-treme. Yet, as V. A. C. Gatrell, one of the most distinguished historians of crime, responds to skeptics:

> it is not really necessary to know about the size of
> the gap between recorded crime and the dark figure,
> very large though it may be. In the nineteenth cen-
> tury, public, police and judicial responses to many
> offences could in the short term be highly erratic.
> But in the long term the dominant influence on the
> records of the serious crimes we shall be attending
> to was such that on the national scale at least, when
> large numbers of recorded cases were involved, it
> rendered the influence of these fickle short-term
> variables on trend highly incidental.[18]

Indeed, even modern crime statistics are unreliable. To a great extent the police control what is reported. For a start, they determine how crimes are classified. At one point the British Home Office insisted that every firearm stolen be listed as a firearm "involved in crime."[19] As a result the statisti-cal impact of the theft of a collection of ten antique weapons would be an additional ten firearms cited in the annual report as involved in crime. Police treatment of victims also has an important effect on their willingness to come forward. Some observers contend that crime figures tell us more about police policies and priorities than they do about crime.[20] Political motivations also seem to intrude on and may even dominate police calculations. In periods when no additional money was available to fight violence and it was in their interest to suggest that everything was calm and under control, the English police seem to have underreported crime. Indeed, Howard Taylor has made a credible argument that government crime statistics for the nineteenth and twentieth centuries, including those for murder, largely reflected "supply-side policies."[21] This underreporting is said to have changed abruptly in the mid-1960s, when a crime wave coincided with an increase in funds for crime-ridden areas. In those circumstances the police began to exaggerate their statistics.[22] The distortion became so flagrant that the government attempted to poll people directly. The Home Office conducted its own crime surveys in 1982, 1984, 1988, 1992, and 1998. The authors of a study that compared police crime reports with Home Office victim surveys were persuaded that police statistics "are an unreliable guide both to the extent of crime and to crime trends," noting that "the rises in crimes of violence and vandalism have been amplified by police statistics and this is the main source of the higher *overall* increase in police figures since 1981.[23] A decade later the police crime statistics were still so unreliable that the London *Times* twice suggested they be dispensed with.[24]

Despite all these problems, the issue of the relationship between weapons and violence is far too important to ignore. Historians, including this one, have found that even flawed evidence can yield key insights, especially when used in conjunction with a wide variety of materials and put into historical context. And that context is exceedingly rich and complex.

Understanding the actual relationship between firearms and violence is essential to developing policies that can provide law-abiding citizens with that personal security Blackstone dubbed first among the great and primary rights of mankind. It is my hope that the following history may contribute to that effort.

1

The Middle Ages: Laws, Outlaws, and Crimes of Violence

> Every era from the fifteenth century to our own day has produced witnesses eager to testify to the unprecedented violence and criminality of their own generation.
>
> —J. S. COCKBURN, "Patterns of Violence in English Society"

DO GUNS CAUSE CRIMES? If so, then a world without private firearms ought to have had a lower level of violent crime than one in which they were available. And the spread of guns ought to have announced itself through increased rates of murder, robbery, and other violent acts. Private firearms first came into common use in England during the sixteenth century. And so it is with the late Middle Ages, the fourteenth and fifteenth centuries, that our investigation must begin.

Two competing versions of violence in pre-industrial England have come down to us. The first sees the era as bucolic and quiet until the Industrial Revolution destroyed the traditional order, community, and family; the other paints the period as violent, lawless, unpoliced, and uncivilized. The first concept comes from great social theorists of the nineteenth and early twentieth centuries. The notion that modernization led to social breakdown, which in turn led to increased crime, developed from the theories of Marx, Tonnies, Durkheim, Weber, and others.[1] England, as the first nation to experience the full thrust of the Industrial Revolution, seemed to be the paradigm of a community that experienced the transformation from a placid society to a modern, lawless one. While some thinkers also posited a change in the type of deviance—from violent crimes to crimes against property—their underlying assumption has spawned the now commonplace view that drastic changes in living and working patterns create a seedbed for crime.[2]

The second scenario, projected by the people of pre-industrial England themselves, portrays medieval and early modern England as a boisterous and violent society obliged to maintain order with harsh legal codes and punishments inflicted with cruel and very intentional publicity. England may have shunned the judicial torture in use on the Continent and boasted a long tradition of jury trials, but the commission of minor theft brought men and women to the gallows. Traitors were publicly hanged, drawn, and quartered, and their heads left to rot on spikes at the ends of London Bridge as an object lesson to all and sundry. Individuals convicted of lesser crimes were sometimes branded or had their ears clipped.

Contemporaries bemoaned the dangers and depravity of their age, and often recounted with fascination and horror the details of particularly lurid crimes.[3] Printers fed the public appetite for tales of villainy with scores of pamphlets recounting the latest murders, robberies, and trials. The authors and publishers of the genre justified their subject matter on the grounds that it offered valuable cautionary lessons. Consider the titles of two typical pamphlets:

"A Discovery Of many, great, and Bloudy Robberies: Committed of Late by Dissolvte and Evill affected Troopers . . . since the late disbanding of the Army in the North . . . Wherein Is inserted the Description of a bloudy combate, fought betweene 9 Troopers and 6 Butchers, meeting on the High-way, and what ensued. With divers other Out-rages and Abuses, acted by them within this City" (1641)

"Inquest after Blood. Being a Relation Of the several Inquisitions of all That have Died by any violent Death in the City of London, and Borough of Southwark, Commencing from Jan. 1, 1669 . . . Also a brief account of those that were there found Guilty, with mention of their Crimes and Punishments. Published for the Satisfaction of some, and to prevent the Mistakes of others" (1670)

Alexander Smith's 1711 work, *The History of the Lives of the Most Noted Highwaymen, Footpads, Shop-lifts and Cheats of Both Sexes, in and about London and Other Places,* proved so popular that it went into five editions. Clearly, the era was no different from our own in its fascination with violence. Indeed, since there were no professional police until the nineteenth century and the responsibility for maintaining local order fell to local people, their preoccupation with criminal activity is even more understandable.

Skirmishes between the law-abiding public and criminals made hair-raising, if entertaining, reading. Yet if we listen exclusively to contemporary critics or depend upon our own notions of an unruly past, we run the risk of forgetting the tendency of every age to complain about prevailing conditions. As James Cockburn observed: "Most nineteenth-century Englishmen were convinced that crime was increasing as never before; eighteenth-century commentators were thoroughly alarmed by what they saw as a rising tide of violent criminality; and complaints of the imminent breakdown of law and order punctuated the Middle Ages."[4] J. A. Sharpe contended that although Englishmen frequently discussed lawlessness, they did not see it as "a problem."[5] However, Barbara Hanawalt's investigation of fourteenth-century England convinced her that "concern about the prevalence of disorder and felony was expressed in every quarter and by every class."

> The king promulgated statutes against lawlessness, undertook administrative reforms, and tried to rid himself of corrupt officials, while Commons pleaded for better law enforcement and punishment of corrupt officials. Lords kept household retainers to protect themselves against felons, but rural people complained that the lords' household troops were chiefly responsible for the violence. Justices pointed out that criminals brutalized and bullied them so that they could not do their work, while everyone accused the justices of selling justice like cows and punishing innocent men who could not pay them for acquittals. Peasant jurors would acquit their neighbors even after repeated criminal

> acts so that when the jurors themselves were
> caught, their neighbors would do the same for
> them.

Hanawalt conceded that such complaints are "part of the Western tradition of social griping."[6] But Cockburn in his study of the early modern period also found times when the community and Parliament were deeply disturbed about crime and attempted to stem it.[7] An act of 1692, for example, complained that "the highways and roads . . . have been of late time more infested with thieves and robbers than formerly" and that the murders and robberies they committed caused "the great dishonour of the laws of this realm and the government thereof." To encourage the public to inform against robbers a reward of forty pounds was offered for information leading to the apprehension and conviction of a highwayman. The informer was also promised the robber's horse, arms, and any property taken with him, provided these actually belonged to the robber.[8]

If preconceptions and anecdotal evidence can distort our perspective, so can documents. Scholars steeped in court records easily come to assume that the minority who were charged with crimes are typical. The records, the complaints, and the gossip need to be put into context. The chief problem, however, has been less skewed records than sketchy and idiosyncratic ones, especially before 1805, when national crime statistics began to be compiled. For the five and a half centuries from 1250 to 1800 only twenty sets of English criminal records survive, and these are from regions of varying sizes and characteristics and for different periods.[9] And even these sets of records are incomplete. A complete series of indictments for serious crimes does survive for the eighteenth century. Fortunately, homicide, the crime most pertinent to our investigation, is also the most likely category of crime to be recorded; but even some homicides escaped legal notice or were dismissed as accidents, self-defence, or the result of natural causes or "divine visitation."[10] Moreover, both the definition of homicide and attitudes toward it changed over time. A survey of the law and its evolution, as well as of the numbers of firearms and their role in crime, is therefore essential to our mission. But first we must consider what has been discovered about long-term trends in crime. On the key issue of the impact of firearms, it is noteworthy that neither those who believe in the existence of a peaceful pre-industrial England nor those who hold that it was a violent society see the proliferation of guns as precipitating any change in crime rates.

Disorder or Civility: The Long View

English historical records reveal a constant pattern, with property crimes far more common than crimes against persons.[11] And virtually all historians agree that crimes against persons, especially homicide, declined in England from the Middle Ages to our own century.[12] Thomas Green's research into English medieval juries disclosed that although homicides were common and made up "a very large proportion of the court agenda," the number decreased from the thirteenth through the nineteenth centuries.[13] Lawrence Stone estimated that "the homicide rates in thirteenth-century England were about twice as high as those in the sixteenth and seventeenth centuries and that those of the sixteenth and seventeenth centuries were some five to ten times higher than those today."[14] Others, less prepared to posit specific percentages, nevertheless agree with the general conclusion. Cockburn found "strong support for the thesis that the four centuries after 1560 saw a decisive decline in the incidence of homicide in England."[15] In 1984 James Sharpe cautiously agreed that although there was not a smooth decline, the evidence "gives the impression of a shift from a more to a less brutal society."[16] By 1996 he was more positive. A cluster of his samples suggested a "typical" thirteenth-century homicide rate of 18 to 23 per 100,000, which dropped to approximately 15 per 100,000 in 1600 and then fell "dramatically" over the middle of the seventeenth century.[17] This decline in violent crime, according to T. R. Gurr, "has a *prima facie* plausibility because it runs counter to increased public sensitization and official attention."[18] Sharpe muses that the reason for this decline "remains inexplicable."[19] The long decline in crime rates as well as its recent reversal in most Western countries also remains inexplicable.[20]

Firearms—muskets, birding guns, and pistols—began to come into common use in the sixteenth century, when homicides were already on the decline. From then until 1920 there were no effective restrictions on their possession. The two trends cross: violent crime continued to decline markedly at the very time that guns were becoming increasingly available.

That is the big picture, painted with broad brush strokes. We need to examine each era more closely to be surer of our ground, for beneath the general trends are important variables, among them changes in the availability of firearms, in legal practice, and in community attitudes toward homicide and robbery, those crimes that William Blackstone saw as "of a deeper and more atrocious dye."[21] It is these violent acts in which guns were most likely to play a role.

Homicide, Robbery, and the Law

The historical record is clear. Medieval England, without benefit of firearms, was in fact, as well as in theory, violent and rowdy. The homicide rate was extraordinarily high, approximately 18 to 23 per 100,000 in the thirteenth and first half of the fourteenth centuries; and these figures, as we shall see, are almost certainly an underestimate.[22] During the first half of the fourteenth century violent deaths accounted for 18.2 percent of all indictments for serious crime.[23] By comparison, in America in 1965 only 0.4 percent of all crimes were homicides. In the first half of the fourteenth century London had an average of eighteen homicides a year, compared to two homicides a year in an American city with a comparable population in 1965.[24] The far poorer state of medical care in the Middle Ages, of course, would have resulted in more wounds leading to death and swollen the murder rate to some degree.

Medieval criminal law was rudimentary but evolving. Its idiosyncrasies and development had a major impact on the labelling and treatment, and therefore on the recorded numbers, of murders. The Crown assumed jurisdiction over all homicides in the twelfth century on the rationale that murder harmed not only the victim but the king, whose peace was broken. There was a crasser motive, too, since the common law required forfeiture of objects associated with a man's death. If the accused was found to have acted in self-defence he was pardoned.[25] Bringing the most serious crimes under the jurisdiction of the royal courts strengthened the authority of those courts. Royal involvement resulted in better preservation of records and more uniform legal development. Yet jurisdiction, even for the most serious crimes, was still muddied by the tradition of "benefit of clergy," which exempted clergy from the authority of the secular courts. This privilege came to be extended to all those connected with the church and later to all "clerks," defined as persons who could read. The greatest punishment a member of the clergy could receive even for shooting dead an assailant who punched him was one year's imprisonment and branding on the "brawn of the thumb."[26] This overbroad privilege was rightly resented and gradually narrowed until after 1512 there were no longer exemptions from the full penalty for premeditated murder. But in the Middle Ages benefit of clergy meant that some persons accused of serious crimes up to and including homicide did not fall into the control of the secular courts.

Legal definitions, even of homicide, altered over time and had some impact on the crime rate. Writing in the seventeenth century, Sir Edward Coke explained that common law divided violent deaths into three sorts: murder, "homicide" or manslaughter, and "chance-medley." He defined murder as "unlawfully killing a reasonable creature, who is in being and under the King's Peace, with malice aforethought express or implied, death following within a year and a day."[27] But this was not always the understanding. Before 1400 the term *murder* seems to have been used only for secret or stealthy killings in which the killers were unknown. Not until later did murder come to mean "a malicious, premeditated or deliberate" killing.[28] Coke's "homicide"—manslaughter—was intentional slaying but without malice aforethought. The crucial distinction between murder and manslaughter troubled medieval courts and was gradually clarified by various statutes. "Chance medley," Coke's third category involved someone "slaine casually, and by misadventure, without the will of him that doth the act." It included both accidental death and killing in self-defence during a scuffle, affray, or sudden quarrel.[29] In cases of accidental death the court considered whether the act by which death occurred was itself lawful and proper. Killings committed by someone perpetrating a felony, even if unintentional, were regarded as deserving the severest treatment and were treated as premeditated. In his text on English legal history, George Crabb used the following example of such a killing: a man meaning to steal a deer shot at it and killed a person. Since the act was unlawful, the killing was held to be murder, or voluntary homicide.[30]

Those killings that caused the greatest disagreement during the Middle Ages, and produced common-law standards badly misunderstood today, were killings in self-defence. Self-defence was long recognized as not only *a*, but *the*, "primary law of nature." In this instance, Blackstone explained: "the law respects the passions of the human mind; and . . . makes it lawful in him to do himself that immediate justice, to which he is prompted by nature, and which no prudential motives are strong enough to restrain. It considers that the future process of law is by no means an adequate remedy for injuries accompanied with force."[31]

It was sensible public policy to permit such defence. Blackstone found it "impossible to say, to what wanton lengths of rapine or cruelty outrages of this sort might be carried, unless it were permitted a man immediately to oppose one violence with another." Accordingly, he insisted, the right to self-defence could not be taken away by the law of society. Even so the law had to be sure the killer really had been obliged to protect himself from grievous harm, harm that no future legal action could possibly make good. Therefore, rules hedged round killing in self-defence to assure, as Blackstone hastened to add, that "resistance does not exceed the bounds of mere defence and prevention; for then the defender would himself become an aggressor."[32]

Different standards of behaviour were required for different circumstances. In a claim of self-defence when a homicide had occurred during a brawl, "in hot blood," the defendant had to prove that he had retreated as far as he was able, or "until his back was to the wall," before resorting to deadly force.[33] This rule was clearly intended to reduce the chance that a brawl might turn into a deadly confrontation. In a 1369 case at Newgate a chaplain argued that he had slain in self-defence. The jurors explained that the man who was killed had pursued the chaplain with a stick and struck him, and that the chaplain had struck back and killed his attacker. The jury were careful to add that the slayer, "had he so willed," might have fled. They clearly felt this was not a valid instance of self-defence. The justices therefore found the chaplain guilty, since "he was bound to flee as far as he could with safety of life."[34]

Today some believe this insistence on the need for retreat in such cases was the *only* behaviour common law permitted. But common law recognized many instances in which an individual might legitimately use deadly force without the need to retreat, and these circumstances were expanded over time. For example, killings that occurred when a man was acting as peacekeeper or defending himself, his family, and property were classified as justifiable or excusable.[35] Justifiable homicide, the first of these, covered a variety of circumstances in which homicide was judged a blameless, or even a worthy, act. Killing anyone who was committing a felony was regarded as justifiable.[36] This leniency was imperative since the Crown expected an ordinary subject to shoulder a wide variety of peace-keeping tasks.[37] These included taking turns standing watch in his town or village at night, or ward during the day; raising a "hue and cry" when a serious crime had been committed; and, if necessary, accompanying the local constable or sheriff in pursuit of the culprit "from town to town, and from county to county" on "pain of grievous fine."[38] Men were also obliged to join the sheriff's posse to put down riots. At times these dangerous duties threatened the life of the peacekeeper or obliged him to use deadly force to capture a suspect. In taking a life under these conditions, the individual was helping to thwart crime. Indeed, it could be argued that in defending himself against a felony, he was not only saving himself from grievous harm but also preventing a crime. A case from 1221 combines both elements. Howel "the Markman," described in the report as a wandering robber, and his men assaulted a carter. The carter resisted and slew Howel, then defended himself against the rest of the gang and fled. The Worcester-shire court decided that because Howel was a robber the carter, whose flight had by the time of the decision taken him to Jerusalem, should "go quit thereof," and invited him to "come back safely, quit of that death."[39] A similar case the same year, *Rex v. Leonin and Jacob,* involved the killing of a poacher. Leonin and his servant Jacob killed John of Middle-ton in the royal forest of Kinfare. The jurors found that "in the time of the war" John came with many others to the king's forest "to offend in the forest, as was his wont." He was discovered by the king's servants and foresters with the whole body of a doe, but defended himself. In the process he "cut off a forester's finger and thus it was that he was slain." Leonin and Jacob were adjudged "quit thereof."[40] The fact such cases arose illustrates how careful the courts were even in cases of homicide committed in the course of stopping felons. Green explains that some two centuries after these cases, justifiable homicide was extended to remove any doubt that it was meant to shelter slayers of felons caught in the act of burglary, arson, or robbery.[41]

The expectation that ordinary citizens must help keep the peace, and the law's largesse in allowing them to use lethal force, if necessary, to do so became ever clearer as time went by. So too was the opinion that someone attacked by a felon had no need to retreat before he or she resorted to lethal force. Both concepts were joined by the duty of the individual to prevent a crime. Looking back from the vantage of the late eighteenth century Blackstone found that "one uniform principle" ran through English law "and all other laws": "where a crime, in itself capital [a felony], is endeavoured to be committed by force, it is lawful to repel that force by the death of the party attempting."[42] A century later A. V. Dicey wrote that for the advancement of public justice:

> every man is legally justified in using, and is often
> bound to use, force. Hence a loyal citizen may law-
> fully interfere to put an end to a breach of the
> peace, which takes place in his presence, and use
> such force as is reasonably necessary for the pur-
> pose. Hence, too, any private person who is present
> when any felony is committed, is bound by law to
> arrest the felon, on pain of fine and imprisonment
> if he negligently permit him to escape.[43]

Further, Dicey argued that the theory of the right to inflict grievous bodily harm or death upon a wrongdoer originated not in the need to keep the king's peace, but in self-defence, in "the right of every loyal subject to use the means necessary for averting serious danger to life or limb, and serious interference with his personal liberty."[44] Sir Michael Foster's explanation also links an assertive self-defence with the duty to keep the peace: "Where a known felony is attempted upon the person, be it to rob or murder, here the party assaulted may repel force with force, and even his servant then attendant on him, or any other person present, may interpose for preventing mischief; and if death ensueth, the party so interposing will be justified."[45] Although lethal self-defence was not permitted during a brawl if the slayer could safely retreat, the intended victim of a felony was not obliged to retreat. Indeed, if the felon fled or had wounded someone seriously, it was the duty "of every man to use his best endeavours for preventing an escape." And if during the pursuit the culprit was killed, *where he cannot otherwise be overtaken,* this will be deemed justifiable homicide. For the pursuit was not barely warrantable; it is what the law requireth, and will punish the *wilful* neglect of."[46] This principle was especially critical for prevention of crime in an era before professional police.[47]

Peacekeeping obligations extended beyond the village and even beyond the county. Men aged sixteen to sixty owed their sovereign service in the citizen militia. The militia was a defensive force charged to protect the realm against invasion and to suppress local riots and disorders. With the exception of the first years of Norman rule, English kings had chosen to trust their subjects with arms so they could participate in and equip the militia. By 1252 not only freemen but the richer villeins were ordered to be armed, and even unfree peasants were soon included. "The state in its exactions," F. W. Maitland wrote, "pays little heed to the line between free and bond, it expects all men, not merely all freemen, to have arms."[48] This medieval militia obligation persisted through the early modern era, although in the latter period select groups of men, special trained bands, were those most often called up in emergencies.

Despite these dangerous duties, anyone who killed a felon in defence of himself, his family, and his property would have to go to court to seek a royal pardon. Accidental or justifiable killings may never have been meant to attract the death penalty, but the remedy lay in the king's grace. The grant of a royal pardon in such cases already had become *pro forma* by 1278, but uncertainty remained regarding slaying in defence of one's family, and not until 1532 did Parliament make pardons unnecessary in cases in which persons were killed attempting to commit robbery or murder in or near the highway or in "mansion" houses.[49]

While justifiable homicide involved helping to maintain public order, excusable homicide included accidental homicide, killings committed by the insane, and those committed in self-defence during a brawl, or chance medley. This last category, those murders committed "in hot blood," was the most contentious not only because of the debatable circumstances but because of differences over what constituted legitimate self-defence. Legal opinion was often at odds with community values and, to some extent, has remained so.

Thomas Green's fascinating study of medieval juries revealed the jurors' tendency to refuse to convict indigents for theft and law-abiding individuals for an unpremeditated act of violence. Jurors had the power to show mercy by deft use of their duty to determine the facts. According to Green, "Jury discretion was most common in cases of sudden, unplanned homicides and in thefts that did not involve physical violence or housebreaking. In these cases . . . juries frequently manipulated the fact-finding process to prevent the imposition of capital punishment."[50] The law's insistence upon the death penalty for theft, the most common category of medieval crime, seemed too harsh to the community, and jurors simply refused to convict. As a result, two-thirds to three-quarters of those accused of theft were eventually acquitted.[51]

In cases of sudden, unplanned homicides, jury discretion "reflected opposition not merely to the level of sanction, the death penalty, but also to the rules of the substantive law itself." Their fact-finding role made their power to determine the fate of defendants absolute. As noted above, the law insisted that a man attacked in a brawl had to retreat until retreat was no longer possible, until his back was to the wall, before resorting to force. "At the trial," Green found, "the jurors always alleged such a predicament, and though it was sometimes true, a comparison of the coroners' rolls and the trial rolls reveal that it often was not and that a petty jury had so altered the facts as to make pardonable what the law considered nonpardonable." In short, the community felt that a man who was attacked ought to be able to stand his ground and use force to defend himself, even if he was in no danger of losing his life. Further, the harsh penalty prescribed—the death sentence—sometimes induced juries to find defendants innocent, or guilty of a lesser charge. Take the case of a 1363 homicide from Norfolk. The coroner's report explained: "William put his hand to his knife in order to draw it and strike Robert. Robert, fearing that William wanted to kill him, in self-defence struck William on the head."[52] Despite the fact that William does not seem to have actually drawn his knife, the jury found that Robert had killed him in self-defence. Green found that both before and after 1390 juries convicted only about 20 percent of all homicide defendants.[53] After 1390 convictions were obtained mainly in cases of premeditated murder.[54] Green's findings convinced him that during the later Middle Ages "jury convictions were largely limited to the most culpable homicides. Defendants who had committed simple homicides, loosely corresponding to the modern categories of unpremeditated murder and manslaughter, received acquittals or were found to have killed in the course of excusable self-defence."[55] The result, of course, was to understate the number of murders that actually occurred.

Historians have discovered not only how homicides were dealt with but how and where they were committed. A study of homicide in the thirteenth century found that most murderers, some 67.9 percent, seem to have had an accomplice and that most murderers were men. Only 8.6 percent of accused killers were women, although they accounted for some 19.5 percent of victims. As for the social rank of the murderers, few thirteenth-century records report direct violence between nobles. This may be because nobles hired someone to commit a murder or were seldom brought to trial. Nevertheless, J. B. Given, the author of this study, was persuaded that English nobles were a "generally non-violent ruling class," at least in contrast to nobles on the Continent.[56] As for the weapon of choice, Barbara Hanawalt found that the bow and arrow, a weapon men were required to own, was "surprisingly unpopular" in medieval homicides.[57] The bow would seem to have been a tempting weapon, as it could kill at a distance, and, unlike its successor the firearm, it was silent. But both

Hanawalt and Given found that most homicides took place during an argument or brawl and that the bow, a weapon of ambush, seldom figured in homicide. Evidence of the kinds of weapons used in thirteenth-century homicides is scanty, but Given reports that for 455 of the 2,434 murders for which a weapon was listed, 29.9 percent involved knives, closely followed by sticks and axes, with stones and pitchforks far behind.[58] Hanawalt's survey found that the most common murder weapons during the Middle Ages, responsible for some 73 percent of deaths, were cutting weapons.[59] Of these, knives caused 42 percent of deaths. This was followed at 27 percent by another frequently carried article, the staff. Weapons used in killings in hot blood tended to be items near at hand—tools, stones and sticks, or simply hands and feet.

We now know not only how medieval men were killed but where. Given found a higher rate of homicide in rural than in urban areas.[60] Hanawalt found that about one-third of rural homicides occurred in a house, whereas only one-quarter of urban homicides were indoors.[61] Most murders took place on Sunday.[62] Contrary to the assumption that alcohol consumption played an important role, tavern fights figured in only 7 percent of medieval murders. Robbery accounted for nearly all slayings in woods and some on highways, although a very large proportion of people killed by robbers were killed in a house, with women and children forming a disproportionate number of the victims. Most such victims were peasants.[63] Even so, Given found that less than 10 percent of homicides were committed in the course of a robbery. In fact the actual proportion may be lower if, as he suggested, this statistic masked some suicides.[64] In these cases jurors may have wanted to protect the deceased's family, since the law at that time punished a suicide by insisting his chattels were forfeit to the king.

High as the recorded homicide rate was in the Middle Ages, clearly the actual homicide rate was far higher, with popular lenience toward self-defence and the expansive legal definition of justifiable homicide minimizing convictions.

War, Dearth, and the Murder Rate

Impulsive men and *ad hoc* policing played a major part in the high rate of violent crime during the Middle Ages, but factors such as war and the food supply may have effected the crime rate as well. There are differing views on the influence of wars. Many fourteenth-century observers believed that wars, even foreign wars, caused an increase in crime, with more violence in the countryside. War on home ground certainly had that effect. When a royal army was in Yorkshire fighting against the Scots there was an increase in violent crime, although in this instance Scots raids may well have disrupted the judicial system.[65] But soldiers are frequently accused of crimes against civilians, and the disorder caused by war probably encouraged lawless individuals to act more boldly. Modern historians generally find that foreign wars lower the domestic crime rate because many troublemakers are out of the realm. Returning soldiers, on the other hand, often raised the level of violence. Oddly, during the Hundred Years' War the reverse seems to have been the fact. Crime was actually higher during 1342–1347, while the royal army was in France.[66] There was no increase in crime during truces, when veterans would be returning to England. Contemporaries blamed the greater number of English homicides on the king's readiness to pardon felons who agreed to join his army. In addition to war there was political turmoil during the same half-century but Hanawalt found little evidence that crime figures were affected by it.[67]

Another possible cause of violence from that day to this is economic hardship. Economists and historians have tested this hypothesis by comparing the pattern of crime with that of harvest failure and years of dearth. For the first half of the fourteenth century, when a large population put heavy pressure on food supplies, there does seem to have been a correlation between times of shortage and higher crime rates.[68] Both war and economic decline, especially food shortages, had an impact on violent crime in the pre-gun era, though not as straightforward an effect as might be expected.

Medieval England was boisterous and violent, more so than court records reveal. Many crimes that we would regard as homicides were excused as instances of self-defence or justifiable homicide, and many thefts went unreported or their perpetrators were acquitted. Most homicide was impulsive, "in hot blood" or in self-defence as it was defined by jurors. This high level of homicide and violent crime existed when few firearms were in circulation.

2

The Tudor-Stuart Centuries: Revolution in Church, State, and Armaments

Arms . . . [are] not only for the Defence against Foreigners, but in Watching and Warding, upon Hue and Cry, and otherwise to keep the Peace within the Realm, and for the Execution of Justice, by assisting the Sheriff when he shall have occasion to use the *Posse Comitatus,* and otherwise . . . And as the use of Arms is more general, so are they for the more immediate Defence.

—"Proceedings in the Case of Ship-Money" (1637)

ENGLAND IN THE ERA of the Tudors and Stuarts was singular in many respects. It was a turbulent time. During the sixteenth century dramatic religious switches—from Roman Catholic to Protestant under Henry VIII, to more radically Protestant under Edward VI, back to Catholic under Mary Tudor, to Protestant yet again under Elizabeth I—agitated the consciences of the body politic and added a new dimension that complicated and endangered the kingdom's internal stability and international position. In 1588 Spain, the greatest European power of the age, dispatched the Glorious Armada to conquer Elizabeth's island kingdom, but thanks, so men said, to a miraculous "Protestant wind," England emerged triumphant. Forty years later, however, in the mid-seventeenth century, the realm was torn by the peculiar agony of civil war and revolution; in 1660 it experienced a counterrevolution; and in 1688-89 it was disrupted yet again, if nonviolently, by the Glorious Revolution. Despite all this it was, for the most part, a prosperous and brilliant age. London grew from 60,000 souls in 1520 to double that by 1582, and nearly double again by 1605.[1] In the quieter sphere of the courts, the law of homicide became more sophisticated, and the definition of murder was both broadened and tightened.

Firearms now first came into popular use. By the middle of the sixteenth century they were commonplace, along with laws meant to govern how, and by whom, they were used. Before the end of Henry VIII's reign they were part of the ordinary militia equipment. During the latter part of the seventeenth century a concerted effort was made to restrict access to these weapons along class and political lines. This, along with James II's other threats to religious and political liberties, produced a backlash that swept James out in the Glorious Revolution and swept in a new king and queen, William of Orange and Mary Stuart, sworn to abide by a new Bill of Rights. Embedded in that document was the right of subjects to have firearms for their defence. A betting man would wager that this combination of events would produce a higher level of homicide and violent crime. He would be wrong. During the early modern era, in particular toward its end, both homicide and violent crime began a long, precipitous decline into the twentieth century.

In a period of so much change, there was striking continuity in the English pattern of crime. The general medieval model continued, with property crimes far outnumbering crimes against the person. In Cheshire property crimes accounted for between two-thirds and three-quarters of prosecuted felony.[2] In Essex from 1559 to 1602 no less than 84 percent of crimes were crimes against property; in Sussex and Hertfordshire in 1559–1625 property crimes accounted for 74 and 86 percent respectively of violent crime.[3] The pattern in London was even more pronounced. Despite its boisterous and crowded population, 92.5 percent of some 7,736 persons indicted for felony in Middlesex between 1550 and 1625 were charged with property offences, compared with just over 4 percent accused of murder and manslaughter.[4] Although the border areas tended to be more violent than the rest of the country, an initial study of felony indictments in late seventeenth-century Northumberland found a pattern similar to the one prevailing elsewhere.[5] As J. A. Sharpe pointed out, "Those attempting to relate changing patterns of serious crime with some preconceived notion of economic change must . . . confront the problem that the patterns of serious crime do not seem to have changed much between the fourteenth century and 1800."[6]

Homicides as a whole fluctuated more than murders, and, as in the past, most homicides were still committed "in hot blood." Of 364 killings investigated by the Kent assizes be-

tween 1559 and 1625, for instance, the vast majority were spontaneous, often the result of heavy drinking.[7] Not only were
few homicides premeditated, but few were committed in the
course of another crime. Apparently, "even habitual criminals
in this period were neither very brutal nor very violent."[8] A
study of Somerset homicides a century later found the same
true of that county.[9]

Not all old patterns continued. The most striking change
was in the number of homicides. These actually declined
markedly, especially toward the end of the seventeenth century. Lawrence Stone estimated that the homicide rates in
thirteenth-century England were about twice as high as those
in the sixteenth and seventeenth centuries.[10] In the thirteenth
century there had been an estimated 18 to 23 homicides per
100,000, but for the sixteenth century the rate for Nottinghamshire was less than 14.8 per 100,000, while the Middlesex
rate was approximately 6.3.[11] Although there were short-term
variations, sixteenth- and seventeenth-century homicide indictments in the counties of Essex, Hertfordshire, and Sussex
reveal a pattern at odds with contemporary complaints of
growing violence and brutality.[12] The last part of the early
modern era experienced an even greater decline in violence.
Between 1660 and 1800 there was a drop of two-thirds in the
homicide rate.[13]

Legal developments may have had little impact on this
happy trend. One the one hand, new statutes and interpretations broadened and tightened the rules against murder; on
the other they expanded the types of killings that fell into
the category of permissible self-help or justifiable homicide.
Among the additional felonies classified as homicide were two
relating to spontaneous fights, that prime cause of violent

death. The stabbing statute of 1604 was designed to curb the vicious scuffles between Scots and Englishmen that had become all too common as the two peoples jostled for favors at James I's court.[14] Now if one man stabbed another who had no weapon drawn, or had not first struck at the stabber, and the person stabbed died within six months, the stabber was guilty of murder. Another act made the killing of an officer of the law or a magistrate in the regular execution of his duty murder, even if the killing was not premeditated.[15] Yet judges did pay considerable attention to premeditation, that is, malice aforethought, the legal distinction between murder and manslaughter. In Sir Edward Coke's definition, murder involved "unlawfully killing a reasonable creature, who is in being and under the King's Peace, with malice aforethought express or implied, death following within a year and a day." Malice aforethought meant to Coke "intent to cause the death, or to inflict grievous bodily harm likely to cause the death, of the person killed *or of any other person;* or intent to commit *any felony,* at least if it involves an act, such as arson, known to be dangerous to human life."[16] However, judges felt free to twist the definition of malice aforethought to fit crimes they particularly wished to punish, such as the killing of a judge or a peace officer, even if these were unintentional. Through judicial interpretation the legal definition of that term became so artificial that it has been described as "an arbitrary symbol" that departed from "the natural meaning of words," for "the malice may have in it nothing really malicious, and need never be really aforethought." Another tightening of homicide law occurred in 1536 when a majority of judges agreed that if a person were killed, even accidentally, by one member of a gang engaged in a felonious act, all the members of the gang could be held guilty of murder.[17] In both these instances, the killing of a peace officer and a crime in the course of which a killing occurred, the intent of the law was to deter use of unnecessary force in the commission of a crime.

Murder was further extended during the seventeenth century by broadening the law on infanticide, the killing of a child up to a year of age by its mother. An examination of the attitudes and treatment of infanticide demonstrates the difficulties of relying too uncritically upon the records. A veritable "rise of infanticide" seems to have begun in the second half of the sixteenth century, continued during the seventeenth century, and declined in the eighteenth. This pattern persuaded Sharpe that infanticide was as much a distinctive crime of the period as witchcraft.[18] It is difficult to be certain whether this cycle actually indicated a real increase in infanticide or just greater determination to ferret it out and punish it.[19] What is certain is that most of those tried for the crime were young, unmarried, and poor. The shame and the financial penalty attached to giving birth to an illegitimate child were enormous. The mother would almost certainly lose her job and would find it difficult to get decent work again. With so much at stake it is perhaps not surprising that the crime seems to have been rather common. By the late seventeenth century there were as many infanticide indictments as those for all other kinds of homicide put together.[20] The community's horror at the crime is plain in the unusually high conviction and execution rate. Even so, attitudes toward infanticide varied over the years. The harsh law passed in 1624 made it a capital offence to conceal the stillbirth of an illegitimate child. This statute reversed the traditional presumption of innocence and presumed guilt unless the mother could produce a witness to testify that her baby had been born dead.[21] As the century wore on the 1624 act seems to have been less rigorously enforced. By the late eighteenth century Blackstone found it leniently applied. This was not, apparently, because of pity for the women involved, but from dislike of the statute's presumption of guilt, which was felt to be un-English.[22] In *Commentaries on the Laws of England* Blackstone wrote of the 1624 act:

> this law, which savours pretty strongly of severity, in making the concealment of the death almost conclusive evidence of the child's being murdered by the mother, is nevertheless to be also met with in the criminal codes of many other nations of Europe ... but I apprehend it has of late years been usual with us in England, upon trials for this offence, to require some sort of presumptive evidence that the child was born alive, before the other constrained presumption (that the child, whose death is concealed, was therefore killed by its parent) is admitted to convict the prisoner.[23]

When, after two centuries, the 1624 statute was repealed, the preamble of the new act admitted that the statute had been unenforceable for some time.[24]

Once government statistics began to be published, infanticide was included with other homicides, where it often equalled or surpassed the total of all the rest. This may have been the reason that in 1879 it was removed from the general category of homicides and made a distinct category.[25] Clearly the way in which this commonplace homicide was calculated, together with the underreporting of it, had a marked effect on the tabulation of total homicides.

Homicide was, and still is, the most accurately reported of violent crimes. The readiness with which all classes resorted to lethal force to assert their rights or to avenge any insult, real or fancied, gave early modern courts abundant opportunity to refine the legal distinctions between the various kinds of homicide, in particular that between murder and manslaughter. For example, in 1553 a court ruled that if A set on B intending to kill him and C intervened in the combat and also attacked B and B was killed, it was murder in A, but only manslaughter in C. Yet if ill words provoked two parties to fight, and one killed the other, this was to be treated as manslaughter, "for it is a combat between two upon sudden heat."[26] But the situation was complex. A case in 1600 in which a customer taunted a shopkeeper who then struck him, accidentally killing him, was first determined to be manslaughter. On appeal it was changed to murder because there was "insufficient cause to start a quarrel." J. H. Baker found that, as a result, the doctrine of chance medley vanished and the test of manslaughter came to be "not hotbloodedness, but the presence or absence of 'provocation.'"[27]

Provocation was the wellspring of the duel, which, as opposed to mere spontaneous brawls, became more common in the sixteenth and seventeenth centuries. Here the firearm often played a role, if only incidentally, as one of a variety of instruments the duelists might have selected. The duel is a form of revenge, if only for a perceived slight, and for this the law had a clear response. As Coke argued, the essence of legal order meant that revenge "belongeth unto the magistrate."[28] Coke's reminder notwithstanding, the penchant for dueling turned out to be very difficult to suppress. The so-called governing classes were especially prone to use this method and in the matter of an affair of honour were unwilling or unable to take their quarrels to the courts. The law, however, simply slotted the duel into its existing view of homicide. Unless the duel was fought "in hot blood," according to William Holdsworth, the man who killed his opponent was guilty of murder. All those who assisted in the duel, the seconds, were accessories. If a third person tried to stop the fight and was killed, both duelists were guilty of his murder. Should either or both duelists be wounded, both were guilty of assault or an affray. If neither was hurt both were guilty of an affray. The trickier problem was how to intervene to stop a duel before it took place. Royal proclamations and Star Chamber tried to do so by making the preparations for a duel a crime in themselves, punishable by a fine and imprisonment.

In ordinary homicide cases, the law dealt more harshly when more deadly weapons were involved. In 1612 judges ruled that if a man, provoked in hot blood, beat another with a weapon *unlikely to cause death* and it did cause death, he was guilty only of manslaughter. On the other hand, in 1666 the courts decided that if the accused had used a weapon *likely to cause death,* the homicide, though committed under similar circumstances, would be murder.[29] According to these rules any crime committed with a gun would be treated more harshly.

One crime seriously underreported that involved guns was highway robbery. The failure to report robberies was probably due to the fact that few violent assaults or murders were committed during the course of a robbery. The severe penalty prescribed for robbery—hanging—coupled with the fact that victims were reimbursed by the local community for much of their loss must have soothed the initial outrage. It was probably to discourage reporting that highwaymen were often ostentatiously polite to their victims and left them with their hearty good wishes and a few shillings to pay for their journey home. To the people of their time highwaymen possessed a veneer of glamour that other criminals lacked. Contemporary letters and journals abound with their exploits.[30] Even so "sensible and prosaic" a seventeenth-century Englishman as John Verney, in recounting the exploits of a pair of highwaymen, remarked at their capture, "'Tis great pity such men should be hanged."[31] When a robber was hanged he was usually accompanied to the place of execution by thousands of people cheering him and offering encouragement. In 1664 John Evelyn paid a shilling for a good spot from which to view such a hanging, although he complained that the crowd, which he reckoned at between twelve and fourteen thousand, made it difficult for him to see.[32]

The ranks of highwaymen were swelled by unemployed soldiers, younger sons down on their luck, and pickpockets ready for grander gains—all prepared to risk death for easy wealth preying upon travellers. Sensible men journeyed in armed groups. Robbers were so numerous that a Buckinghamshire proverb of the time claimed, "Here if you beat a bush, it's odds you'd start a Thief."[33] Although watchmen were posted along the roads, particularly where a crime had taken place, thieves easily spotted and eluded them. Many men obliged to stand watch were as unwilling to discover the robbers as the latter were to be spotted. But highwaymen lost much public sympathy when the number of thefts reached epidemic proportions during the 1650s and 1660s. By 1677 robbers became so brazen that a thief snatched the chancellor's mace from his bedroom while he slept, and would have stolen the Great Seal of England "had it not been under the chancellor's pillow."[34] In 1683, so the story goes, Judge Holt went to visit a friend in prison whom he had just sentenced. When the judge asked after their old college friends the prisoner replied: "Ah my lord they are all hanged now but myself and your Lordship."[35]

Where there was sympathy and little incentive to report the crime, many armed robberies went unreported. The fact that a prosecution and its expense were left largely to the individuals affected must also have deterred many victims. As was almost certainly the case with infanticides, the total figures for highway robbery may have been markedly understated. Nevertheless, a robbery that resulted in injury or death would normally have come to public notice.

As a rule acts of violence that did not result in death were rather inadequately punished during this period. But an outrage to one of its own members prompted Parliament to act. In late December 1670 the Commons were holding a hearing on the possibility of taxing patrons of playhouses. The king, Charles II, was fond of the theater, and his courtiers appeared before the committee to argue against the tax on the ground that "the Players were the King's servants, and a part of his pleasure."[36] Sir John Coventry, a member of the committee, asked if "the King's pleasure lay among the men or women Players." This quip reached the Court, and on Coventry's way home that night twenty-five royal guards ambushed him and slit his nose. His outraged colleagues took the first opportunity to pass an act that made certain forms of intentional disfigurement a felony.[37] This 1671 law was the only one of the period that dealt with aggravated assault.

      The rules governing criminal activity and its suppression in the sixteenth and seventeenth centuries closely concerned the common man, who, as in the Middle Ages, continued to play a major role in local peacekeeping. He was justified in taking all reasonable means to stop a crime committed in his presence and in fact was obliged to do so.[38] Looking the other way was not tolerated. A man was liable if he failed to intervene or to respond to a summons by a law officer to help suppress a riot or disperse an unlawful assembly, while the law officer could also be liable if he neglected his duty.[39] If no felony had been committed only "reasonable" force could be used, but if there had been a felony—and all rioters were guilty of a felony—every subject had a duty to apprehend them. According to Holdsworth, if a rioter was killed resisting arrest the homicide was justifiable. Clearly, it was vital for ordinary men to understand these distinctions and to be handy with their weapons.

  Both this civic duty and the need for personal defence made the cloudy legal formalities that still accompanied a charge of self-defence burdensome and costly. In the sixteenth century this situation led to a pivotal legal clarification of homicide law in the statute of Henry VIII, "That a Man killing a Thief in his Defence, shall not forfeit his Goods."[40] This act extended the category of justifiable homicide, that is, homicide that merited acquittal. Since English kings had first involved themselves in the murder cases of their realm, those guilty of killing, even in self-defence, were liable to have their property confiscated until the case was settled, and those found to have killed in self-defence received what had become a routine pardon. It is unclear how often such forfeiture still occurred by 1532, but its specific elimination was a boon to Henry's subjects. Public opinion was traceable in the decisions of trial juries ever since the twelfth century, when the imposition of the death penalty for all felonious homicides came up against very different community attitudes. Although no major study has been done to explain the timing of this largesse on Henry's part, the date, 1532, when the so-called Reformation Parliament was deeply involved in the series of moves that ultimately led to the separation of the English church from the church of Rome, is suggestive. The statute may well have been a sort of *quid pro quo,* a move on the king's part at little cost to himself to please those members of Parliament and the people of his kingdom from whom he was demanding and expecting so much. The preamble of the statute referred to the "Question and Ambiguity" that existed when any "evil disposed" person or persons were slain in an attempt to feloniously rob or murder any person or persons "in or nigh any common Highway, Cartway, Horse-way, or Foot-way, or in their Mansions, Messuages, or Dwelling-places, or that feloniously do attempt to break any Dwelling-house in the Nighttime." Hereafter any person or persons indicted or appealed of or for the death of any person or persons attempting to murder, rob, "or burglarily to break Mansion-houses" would not "forfeit or lose any Lands, Tenements, Goods, or Chattels, for the Death of any such evil disposed Person in such Manner slain, but shall be . . . fully acquitted and discharged, in like manner as the same Person or Persons should be if he or they were lawfully acquitted of the Death of the said evil dis-posed Person or Persons."

This act thus extended the category of justifiable, or blame-less, homicide to include those defending themselves from anyone who attempted to rob or murder them on or near a public highway or path or in their home at night. Although the existing uncertainty and pro forma pardon may not have constituted a great problem, major legal commentators from Edward Coke and William Blackstone to William Holdsworth and T. A. Green have singled out this statute as of crucial im-portance. Blackstone saw it as bringing English law into con-formity with the law of nature and prevailing legal practice, while Green pointed to it as "the final stage of a long process by which the common law adapted to social views on capital felony."[41] The upshot was that killings of would-be robbers, burglars, or other assailants by their intended victims were now justifiable, not just excusable. The issue of whether the slayer might have made his escape and hence avoided shed-ding blood was irrelevant.

Yet despite this broader inclusion of justifiable homicide on the one hand, and additional categories of murder on the other, despite alterations in sensibilities and legal distinc-tions, despite the major upheavals of these two centuries, vio-lent crime was on the decline.

Firearms in Early Modern England

Even as the numbers of homicides declined, guns first came into common use. Ordinary Englishmen were obliged to keep weapons for their various peacekeeping duties and to contrib-ute to, and be trained in, those needed for the militia. Guns became popular for these tasks during the sixteenth century. However expensive, inaccurate, and cumbersome they were, the new technology was increasingly popular. In vain did Sir John Smythe and other experts warn "misguided young men who thought that fire-arms were the weapon of the future" of the new invention's many flaws, especially compared with the proven sureness and efficiency of the longbow.[42] The English public began to buy muskets and pistols for self-defence, peacekeeping, and hunting as well as highway robbery. A variety of lighter firearms came into use along with the first pistols. English kings had been slow to introduce muskets into the militia. There was an attachment to the longbow, to which Henry VIII and his countrymen rightly attributed many glorious victories. Parliament tried to keep Englishmen interested in archery. Acts were passed to make every man under the age of sixty keep a bow and practice shooting, and every village was to ordered to maintain archery butts so villagers could practice on holidays "and at other times convenient."[43] Bowyers were ordered to manufacture cheap bows so families could afford to equip their sons from the age of seven. But progress would not be stopped, and it proved impossible to keep up use of the bow through acts of Parliament. As Cruickshank reported, "men bought their bows to give some appearance of obeying the law, but never loosed an arrow from them."[44] With Henry's fellow monarchs equipping their own troops with firearms, the king grudgingly gave in, although he still insisted that boys be supplied with a bow and two arrows by the age of seven and taught to shoot under pain of fine.[45] Once the musket became standard militia equipment thousands of Englishmen had to be trained in its use and when called upon were required to produce a serviceable weapon for the citizen army.[46]

Could Englishmen afford firearms? We know the cost of new weapons in the seventeenth century, for in 1631 Charles I required the gunmakers, in return for a monopoly, to fix their rates. A new musket with accompanying equipment, for example, sold for 15 shillings 6 pence and a pair of pistols for 2 shillings. By 1658, during the Commonwealth, the price had decreased to 11 shillings a musket, and in 1664 the government considered offering 10 shillings per musket to citizens who turned in serviceable weapons. Would an average individual have been able to afford 10 shillings? In 1664 a footsoldier was paid 18 pence a day while on duty, which would have permitted him to amass funds for a new musket in a little more than a week. Although he was unlikely to devote his entire wage to the purchase, the sum was affordable. The wage for standing watch was 8 pence a night, which would require a fortnight to raise the price for a new weapon. Used guns were, of course, less expensive. In 1628, when a new pair of pistols cost two pounds, a stolen handgun was valued at only 3 shillings. But the clearest evidence of the widespread ownership of weapons comes from court records. Indictments for misuse of firearms reveal an amazing array of persons of humble occupation—labourers, wheelwrights, bricklayers, carpenters, weavers, blacksmiths, farmers, and servants of both sexes—who appeared before the courts charged with misusing firearms.[47]

Just as with other weapons, however, there were restrictions on the use of firearms to ensure public safety. Among these was a statute of 1541 to restrict ownership of two concealable weapons popular with highway robbers, the handgun (described as any firearm with a barrel less than a yard long) and the crossbow, to persons with incomes of over 100 pounds a year.[48] This law is often misunderstood as restricting owner-

ship of all firearms to the upper classes. In fact it merely restricted the use of those bows and guns most common in
crime. Indeed, the statute was at pains to explain that gentlemen, yeomen, servingmen, the inhabitants of cities, boroughs, market towns, and those living outside towns could
"have and keep in every of their houses any such hand-gun or
hand-guns, of the length of one whole yard."[49] In the reign of
Henry's son Edward the use of gunshot, a dangerous type of
ammunition, required a special licence.[50] Other laws governed
proper use of firearms. They must not be brandished so as to
terrify peaceable citizens, and along with snares, bows, and
dogs their use for hunting was forbidden to the great majority of persons barred from that aristocratic pastime.[51] The
courts were anxious to preserve the distinction between legal
and illegal use and types of weapons and whenever crossbows
and handguns were confiscated because of improper use, the
courts were at pains to specify that the weapon in question
was "noe muskett or such as is used for defence of the
realm."[52] Such cases were unusual though, for court records
reveal a reluctance to bring cases that involved use only of
prohibited weapons, although there is ample evidence that
their use was widespread. Indeed, if we are to judge by court
records and other evidence from the seventeenth century, the
restrictions on ownership of handguns and use of gunshot
seem to have been generally evaded, and the evasion seems to
have been tolerated.[53] Judges either found little harm in their
use or found the laws impossible to enforce. When Sir Peter
Leicester, a Cheshire judge, was on circuit during the years
1660–1677, he reminded county grand juries of the crimes
they were to take cognizance of, such as illegal hunting and
riding armed so as to terrorize the populace, but he never

once mentioned the illegal possession of a firearm.[54] And in Nottinghamshire there were so many complaints about "the great number of persons . . . that keepe and shoote in Gunns contrary to the forme of divers Laws and Statutes" that the constables were charged with neglecting their duties.[55] As for the act of 1549 banning gunshot, when that statute was repealed 150 years later it was explained that "however useful" the act may have been "in those days," it "hath not for many years last past been put in execution, but became useless and unnecessary."[56]

After Henry separated the Church of England from the Catholic church, there were religious limitations on guns as well. Catholics no longer served in the militia, and although their need to defend their lives was conceded, the pope's insistence that they attempt to overthrow the Protestant monarchy made any Catholic's possession of a cache of firearms seem the prelude to an uprising. Further, at times of war or religious tension, Catholic subjects were often disarmed. With these caveats, guns were available and, as court records and cost analyses show, were popular among both men and women of all but the poorest class.[57]

When war between Charles I and Parliament broke out in 1642 both sides scrambled to increase production of muskets, pistols, and ammunition. Individuals and municipalities stockpiled caches of weapons. Yet with the return to peace in 1650 serious crime did not rise, nor did it increase with the political upheaval that led to the restoration of the monarchy in 1660.[58] On his return to England Charles II found his subjects "armed to the teeth," and many public stashes came to light over the months that followed.[59] While he and his new government considered it essential to keep firearms out of the

hands of all former and potential opponents, they did so because of the possibility of riot and revolution, not because of
fear of crime. The new regime used the prerogative powers of
the Crown for this work and urged the Cavalier Parliament to
approve a variety of measures to achieve this end.[60] The repub-
lican army that had welcomed Charles was cautiously paid off
and disbanded. A series of royal proclamations then made it
illegal for all those who had ever fought against the Stuarts to
"weare, use, or carry or ryde with any sword, pistoll or other
armes or weapons."[61] A new militia act authorized any two
deputy lieutenants to initiate a search for, and seizure of,
arms in the possession of any person they judged "dangerous
to the Peace of the Kingdom."[62]

To control firearms at the source, gunsmiths were ordered
to produce a record of all weapons they had manufactured
over the past six months together with a list of their customers. Thereafter the gunsmiths were to report to the ordnance
office every Saturday night the number of guns made and
sold that week.[63] Carriers throughout the kingdom needed a
licence to transport guns, and all importation of firearms was
banned.[64]

These attempts to clamp down on firearms that might be
used by enemies of the Crown had little impact on the mass
of ordinary people. Then, in 1671, Parliament passed an act,
ostensibly to prevent poaching, that for the first time prohibited the possession and use of a firearm for all persons unqualified to hunt. The last act that had addressed the issue,
the Game Act of 1609, set the income to hunt at 40 pounds a
year from land. The 1671 act, however, raised the qualification
to an annual income of at least 100 pounds from land, or 150
pounds in leases, but included anyone who was the heir of an

esquire "or other person of higher degree."[65] This new standard meant that the great majority of the population would
no longer be able to have a firearm. William Blackstone would
later point out with amazement that the property qualification to hunt was fifty times the amount needed to permit a
man to vote.[66] The 1671 act differed from previous game acts
in several important respects. Earlier game acts had banned
the possession and use of snares or hunting dogs, whose sole
purpose was to kill game animals, and the use of guns for
hunting, but no previous game act had banned firearms per
se. Now guns led the list of prohibited devices. All those not
qualified to hunt were declared "to be persons by the Laws of
this Realm, not allowed to have or keep for themselves, or any
other person or persons, any Guns, Bowes, Greyhounds . . . or
other Engines" for killing game. The act also established a system of gamekeepers, a sort of private police, appointed by
landed aristocrats to enforce the Game Act on their own es-
tates. These gamekeepers "or any person or persons, authorized by a warrant from a justice of the peace," could search
the houses, outhouses, "or other places" of persons unqualified to keep the prohibited devices. Any weapons they found
could be seized and "cut in pieces." All those accused of vio-
lating the new law could be tried before a single justice of the
peace—often the landowner—on the evidence of a single witness, usually the gamekeeper.

There was so little debate during and after passage of this
legislation that it is difficult to determine what M.P.s really intended or what impact this prohibition would have on the
ordinary individual's peacekeeping obligations. Parliament
claimed to be interested in protecting game and preventing
the idle poor from hunting, but there were already laws on the

books that could do that, while the financial requirement to hunt could have been raised without prohibiting ownership of firearms. The act enabled the landed aristocracy to share in the king's game prerogative. Blackstone listed four chief grounds for passage of game laws:

1. encouragement of agriculture and improvement of fields
2. preservation of several species
3. prevention of idleness and dissipation in husbandmen
4. prevention of popular insurrections and resistance to the government by disarming the bulk of the people

The last, he believed, was "a reason oftener meant than avowed by the makers of forest or Game Laws."[67] The very first game act to set a property qualification on hunting was passed in 1389 in response to the Great Peasant Rebellion. Its preamble admitted that it was intended to hinder "divers artificers, labourers, and servants" from assembling under pretence of hunting to plot against their superiors. But these acts merely prohibited common people from hunting or keeping purpose-built hunting equipment. A gun had other, serious and legitimate uses.

The 1671 Game Act doesn't seem to have been enforced. Enforcement was left to individual gentlemen and their gamekeepers and, practically speaking, would have been extraordinarily difficult. We have no figures for the proportion of individuals qualified to hunt during the seventeenth century, but in eighteenth-century Wiltshire less than 0.5 percent of the population is estimated to have been qualified, and in all of Staffordshire only some 800 persons were qualified.[68] The very small number who benefitted from the act as opposed to the great numbers of armed persons hurt, made enforcement very difficult and perhaps unrealistic. And of course the act came into conflict with the public's peacekeeping duties. There is little evidence to go by, since cases were heard privately, and only cases that were appealed to the assizes had to be recorded. But guns feature in quarter session records at the same rate before and after the 1671 act and for the same offences. For example, between 1658 and 1700 there is not a single case in Hertfordshire's quarter session records of anyone charged with illegal possession of a full-length firearm. Nor during this period was there a single case for the mere possession of a gun in Lincolnshire, Middlesex, or Nottinghamshire.[69] Although Warwickshire, with a large number of poaching cases, did show a decline in the use of guns in poaching, only one case is recorded for simple possession of a firearm.[70] Several cases came before the Buckingham quarter sessions in which the accused was charged with wrongfully keeping guns along with other devices for hunting, but the only instance of a defendant's being charged solely with "keeping guns" cited the statute of Henry VIII against handguns for its authority.[71] This does not seem to have been an isolated instance.[72] It is clear there was no widespread effort to disarm Englishmen. Gamekeepers hesitated to alienate their neighbours. Indeed, some were accused of having connived at poaching and the subsequent sale of game. Why then was the act passed if there was little interest or will in enforcing it? A likely explanation is that it gave country squires the power to disarm their tenants if they wished, especially any Catholics who may have seemed a danger and whom the Crown was often reluctant to disarm.

If that was the purpose, the accession in 1685 of King Charles's brother James, an avowed Catholic, increased the religious and political stakes and had an impact on possession of firearms. Not only was James intent upon enhancing the position of his co-religionists, but, more than any other Stuart monarch, he had the real possibility of making himself absolute. The majority of his subjects accepted his accession quietly, preferring an orderly succession. They also looked, at least at first, on the bright side. After all, the new king had promised to "maintain the Government both in Church and State, as by Law establish'd."[73] Moreover, even if he meant to alter the religion or suppress ancient liberties, he was already in his fifties. He and his Catholic wife, Mary of Modena, had no children, and his two Protestant daughters from a previous marriage, Mary and Anne, stood to succeed him. But not everyone was so complaisant. Charles's death and James's succession provoked two rebellions, one by the Scottish Earl of Argyll, the second, more dangerous, by Charles II's illegitimate and popular Protestant son, James, Duke of Monmouth. Politically these worked to James's advantage. As the French ambassador reported to Louis XIV, "The king of England is very glad to have the pretence of raising troops and he believes that the Duke of Monmouth's enterprise will serve only to make him still more master of his country."[74] That proved to be the case, for although these rebellions were handily suppressed, the threat persuaded his Scottish and English Parliaments to boost the already ample revenue they had voted him. The result was a yearly income reckoned at more than 2 million pounds, a sum that afforded James an unusual degree of independence.[75] The revolts also enabled James to more than double the size of his army, from 9,215 to 18,984. This strength would more than double again, to 40,117, by October 1688.[76] Even as James increased the size of his army, the Monmouth rising gave him an excuse to denigrate the citizen militia. Many militia officers had been in London attending Parliament when the rebellion broke out, and in their absence the militia regiments of the west either refused to fight Monmouth or deserted to his side. Elsewhere the militia rallied to the king, but these defections were enough to damn the lot. Barely two weeks after the rebellion had ended, James ordered lords lieutenant to estimate the monies needed to support the militia regiments in their counties in order to divert these sums to his army.[77] This move, together with his blunt comment to Parliament that "there is nothing but a good force of well-disciplined troops in constant pay that can defend us," raised fears that he meant to govern by an army.[78] Worse, it looked as if he meant to govern by a Catholic army. James had commissioned nearly 100 Catholic officers, exempting them from the Test Act against their employment. He allowed the militia to lapse and refused to order any musters or to allow lords lieutenant to order them. James's firearms policies in Ireland seemed a forecast of what lay in store for England. There, within two months of his accession he had begun disarming Protestants and discharging them from the militia only to replace them with Catholics.[79]

Shifting control of weapons from the citizen militia to a professional army was just one aspect of James's agenda. He also wanted to reduce the number of weapons in the hands of his English Protestant subjects. He began by strictly enforcing existing firearms regulations. He also ordered the disarming of "suspicious persons," his political opponents. These efforts included use of the game acts, and even the resurrection of an archaic emergency measure from 1328, that forbade men to ride armed "in affray of the peace" or to go armed "by Night nor by Day, in Fairs, Markets, nor in the Presence of Justice or other Ministers, nor in no Part elsewhere." When a key case that invoked this act was rejected by the court, James hit upon the notion of imposing the 1671 Game Act on his own initiative.[80] If successful he could have disarmed the great majority of his subjects. Given the dimensions of the task, James's unpopularity, and the few lords lieutenant who might have been willing to carry out this campaign, it is not surprising that it was stillborn. But James's measures achieved one significant result. They enraged the "political nation," those upstanding English squires whose families served the Crown for generations as justices of the peace and whom James was purging from their posts and disarming. They came to feel that if the Englishman's liberties were to survive, his ability to have weapons must be not merely a duty, but a right.[81] The Glorious Revolution soon gave them the opportunity to make that constitutional switch.

When the Convention Parliament assembled in January 1689 after James's precipitate flight from the realm, its members were anxious to shore up their rights, especially those rights James had imperilled. Despite the emergency nature of their proceedings—with no monarch on the throne—before recognizing William of Orange and Mary Stuart they decided to "not only change hands, but things."[82] The Bill of Rights they drew up listed James's trespasses on his subjects' liberties and religion and balanced these with a list of purported "ancient" rights. The sixth complaint referred to James's "causing several good Subjects, being Protestants, to be disarmed."[83] As the document developed, the corresponding claim of a right of subjects to be armed went through three different drafts. The first stated: "It is necessary for the publick Safety, that the Subjects, which are Protestants, should provide and keep Arms for their common Defence; And that the Arms which have been seized, and taken from them, be re-stored." This was changed in a second draft: "That the Subjects, which are Protestants, may provide and keep Arms, for their common Defence." The insistence that public safety required subjects to have arms had been dropped and the assertion that Protestants "should provide and keep arms" had been modified to "may provide and keep arms." The original version implied that there was a duty to acquire arms for the public good, whereas the amended version made having arms a legal right. The article still referred to the use of private arms for "their common Defence," but the rephrasing shifted the emphasis away from the public duty to be armed and toward keeping arms solely as an individual right. A last-minute meeting with the Lords altered the article for the third and final time. It now read: "That the Subjects which are Protestants may have Arms for their Defence suitable to their Conditions and as allowed by Law." The phrase "may provide and keep arms for their common defence" had been altered to read "may have arms for their defence," and two new restrictions had been added at the end. The bill passed the Commons without recorded dissent and was presented to William and Mary the next day. The final language had shifted the article still further away from a right to private ownership of arms as a political duty and toward a right to have arms for individual defence. To J. R. Western's mind these changes "emasculated" the article, since "The original wording implied that everyone had a duty to be ready to appear in arms whenever the state was threatened. The revised wording suggested only that it was lawful to keep a blunderbuss to repel Burglars."[84] But J. H.

Plumb pointed out that since the "sanctions clauses" of the Bill of Rights specified that "there was to be no standing Army and Protestant gentlemen were to be allowed arms, the right of rebellion is implicit."[85]

Whatever the potential right of rebellion, the first question is whether the new claim actually guaranteed the right for English Protestants to have firearms. The two final clauses of the arms article had the potential for limitations based on class as well as permitting existing and future legal restrictions. These clauses might, as some modern commentators believe, have made the right to be armed "more nominal than real."[86] A careful search of subsequent court cases, legislation, and firearms use, however, makes it clear that ordinary Englishmen did have a right to be armed. At the time of the passage of the English Bill of Rights some of the rights proclaimed were not yet established in existing law. The right to be armed was one of these. The Game Act of 1671, still on the books, specifically forbade those without the legal qualifications to hunt—the great majority of the community—from owning or keeping a firearm. Three years after passage of the Bill of Rights Parliament braced itself to reconsider the entire array of game legislation. The result was a new act "for the more easie Discovery and Conviction of such as shall Destroy the Game of this Kingdom." This first revision of game law since 1671 provided the opportunity to bring game law into line with the right of Protestants to be armed. The statute began with the usual complaint that existing game acts were not being enforced and ordered the strict execution of "every article and thing in them contained, and not herein and hereby altered or repealed."[87] Did the act alter or repeal the prohibition against firearms? In the 1671 act guns led the list of prohibited devices; the new act did not list them at all. Guns might arguably have been included under the final catch-all prohibition against "other Instruments for destruction of Fish, fowl, or other Game," but if this was intended it is hard to see why guns were removed from the list of devices expressly named. According to the seventeenth-century rule of law for such omissions, "a later statute, contrary to a former statute, takes away the force of the first statute, without express negative words."[88] In fact a later case followed this rule in deciding whether a person was qualified to hunt under the new law. The court found that "the qualifications being distinctly and severally mentioned, the omission of one is fatal."[89] And as we shall see in the next chapter, within a century after its passage legal experts were prepared to testify that such a right not only existed, but that it had always existed.[90] Moreover, they were also prepared to endorse the Whig view that the right was meant not only for personal defence but to enable the people to protect their liberties if these were endangered.

The Impact of Guns on Crime

Firearms first entered general circulation and then became commonplace during the sixteenth and seventeenth centuries. This was the same time that homicides and other violent crimes decreased dramatically. Still, it is possible that many homicides were committed with guns. Was that the case?

Guns were certainly the regular equipment of highway robbers, but most English homicides were committed in hot blood, not during the course of a felony. Many violent deaths in the second half of the sixteenth century were due to the growing popularity of dueling.[91] Unfortunately there is insufficient evidence for a thorough statistical analysis. A few studies for particular counties are helpful, albeit not conclusive. Cockburn's study of Kent revealed that from 1560 to 1660 there were only fourteen fatal shootings in the county. Six of these were with handguns, one—a shooting by an eleven-year-old boy—seems to have been an accident, while another apparently occurred during a duel.[92] Only one of the fourteen, a shooting in which a labourer was attacked by two men on Shooter's Hill, was associated with the commission of a crime. The eight remaining gun homicides were committed with long-barrelled firearms. Of these one was accidental. Not one was associated with the commission of a crime. J. A. Sharpe's examination of seventeenth-century Essex found that in about half the homicides that occurred between 1620 and 1680 the weapons used were hands and feet. The second leading category of murder weapon was sticks or staffs. This is a change from evidence from the Middle Ages that edged weapons caused the majority of homicides. Of the eleven sorts of weapons Sharpe lists as used in homicide, guns were fourth.[93] He also found that those accused of killing with knives were unusually likely to be executed. This is not surprising, since attacks with a weapon likely to cause death were treated far more harshly. More surprisingly, despite that rule, a disproportionate number of shootings resulted in acquittal on grounds of accidental death.[94] Sharpe attributes this accident rate to carelessness and failure to observe safety rules. It should be added, though, that guns in that era were often dangerous and unreliable devices.

To conclude, this era in which firearms first came into common use in everyday life as well as for the citizen militia, the century in which an Englishman's right to have "arms for his defence" was proclaimed, also witnessed a sharp decline in violent homicide. This is the more extraordinary because of the political turbulence of the period.

3

The Eighteenth Century: "Fruitful in the Inventions of Wickedness"

There is hardly a criminal act which did not come within the provisions of the Black Act; offences against public order, against the administration of criminal justice, against property, against the person, malicious injuries to property of varying degree—all came under this statute and all were punishable by death.

—Leon Radzinowicz, *A History of English Criminal Law*

Judged by its criminal law the eighteenth century was the most violent and vicious era in English history. Never before or since were so many new capital crimes created. In 1715 the Riot Act was passed, followed in 1723 by the notorious Waltham Black Act, which alone added a record 200 to 350 new felonies; and in 1752 Parliament felt obliged to devise a punishment literally worse than death to deter murderers.[1] Such legislation, Lord Hardwick insisted, was absolutely necessary given "the degeneracy of the present times, fruitful in the inventions of wickedness."[2] Some modern scholars agree that the times were indeed violent. Yet despite the repressive legal code J. M. Beattie found eighteenth-century society guilty of a "high tolerance of violent behavior" in homes, schools, taverns, and the courts, and although murder was reported many other forms of violence went unreported and unindicted.[3] French theorists argued that with the rise of capitalism in the seventeenth and especially the eighteenth centuries, property crimes exceeded violent crimes.[4] Yet the prevalence and treatment of firearms seem at odds with these reports. Guns and edged weapons were freely available, but not one of the many laws meant to curb criminal behavior or to criminalize all sorts of petty disturbances restricted the ownership of firearms.

Of course laws and the passions that create them can mislead, and the eighteenth century deserves, and has had, a mixed press. On the positive side the Jacobite rebellion, continuing religious dissension, and periodic riots never equalled in extent and bitterness the rebellions and upheavals of the sixteenth and seventeenth centuries. Instead eighteenth-century England was preoccupied with almost continuous foreign wars and with colonial expansion. Middle-class industrialists and traders prospered from Britain's new imperial power and from the first fruits of the Industrial Revolution, albeit the landed aristocracy still topped the social pyramid. The ordinary Englishman had his share of troubles but also prospered. Thanks to a rising birthrate and the end of three centuries of visitations of the black plague the population nearly doubled.[5] And despite contemporary opinion and the mixed effect of the new, uniformly harsh legal code, despite the availability of firearms and other weapons, the homicide rate between 1660 and 1800 dropped by two-thirds.[6] What impact, if any, guns or the draconian criminal laws had on this happy and unexpected trend deserves a closer look. We shall begin by examining these newly enacted crimes, then consider the effect of war, the economy, and the transportation of criminals on the rate of violent crime. Finally, with all this in mind, we will consider the role of firearms on violent crime.

The Riot Act

The first of the new felonies came in with the new dynasty. When Queen Anne died in 1714 she was succeeded by George, Elector of Hanover, whose right to the throne was challenged by a rebellion on behalf of James II's son, James Edward. The Jacobite rebellion proved to be short-lived, the fighting limited to Scotland, but the alarmed regime was prepared for the worst. Among its first steps was the promulgation of "An Act for preventing Tumults and riotous Assemblies, and for the more speedy and effectual punishing the Rioters," a statute better known as the Riot Act.[7] According to the new legislation any group of twelve persons or more "unlawfully, riotously, and tumultuously assembled together, to the Disturbance of the Publick Peace" could be ordered to disperse by the local sheriff, undersheriff, mayor, or other official who read them the text of the Riot Act. If twelve or more of the group continued to linger for more than an hour after such reading, each was guilty of a felony punishable by death "without Benefit of Clergy."[8] Government officials whose duty it was to read the Riot Act and round up resisters were authorized to commandeer the services of "all his Majesty's

Subjects of Age and Ability to be assisting to them therein." If, in the course of arresting them, any of the rioters were killed, maimed, or hurt, the officer and his assistants were considered blameless. As is often the case with emergency measures, the Riot Act outlasted the threat posed by the 1715 and 1745 Jacobite risings and remained on the statute books for 250 years. It was read for the last time in 1919 and not finally repealed until 1967.[9] Some members of these "tumultuous" eighteenth-century crowds may have been carrying weapons, but Parliament made no move to limit their access to firearms. Quite the opposite.

The Black Act

A far more significant act, one unique in the history of English criminal law, was the Waltham Black Act.[10] It was passed with little debate in May 1723, purportedly to stop men in disguise and with their faces blacked from destroying the game, fish, and trees in Epping forest, near Waltham in Hampshire.[11] Blackstone believed the so-called Waltham blacks had patterned themselves after the followers of Robin Hood, but E. P. Thompson, in his excellent study of the Black Act, argues that the blacks were leaders of community resistance to a rigorous enforcement of the ancient forest law.[12] If Parliament's aim was merely to quash the Waltham blacks, the solution went far beyond the problem. The loosely drafted act created a large number of new capital offences, broadened some existing ones, then listed seven distinct groups of potential offenders, magnifying the impact in such a way that the exact number of new felonies is uncertain. Categories of offenders were those:

1. armed with swords, firearms, or other offensive weapons and having his or their faces blacked
2. armed and otherwise disguised
3. having their faces blacked
4. otherwise disguised
5. any other person or persons involved
6. principals in the second degree (aiding and abetting)
7. accessories after the fact in certain cases

It is striking that although being armed and disguised with a face blackened, or simply appearing disguised was now a felony, simply appearing armed was not. Most of the new felonies were rural crimes against game and farm property, crimes already illegal but, at least in regard to game and its protection, subject to relatively modest penalties.[13] First and foremost, however, was appearing armed and disguised on high roads, open heaths, commons, downs, forests, parks, paddocks, enclosed grounds where deer "have been or shall be usually kept," or in warrens or any other places "where hares or rabbits have been or shall be usually kept." Soon after the act was passed it was extended to make the simple appearance with face blacked or disguised in any of these places without any other crime's being committed or even attempted, a capital offence. Unlawfully hunting a red or fallow deer armed and in disguise, or in the king's forest merely hunting a deer with or without disguise and arms, was made capital, although in these instances judicial rulings eventually reduced the penalty. Among other new capital crimes were stealing hares, rabbits, fish "out of any river or pond"; destroying the mound of any fishpond "whereby the fish shall be lost or destroyed"; cutting down or otherwise destroying any trees in any avenue, garden, orchard, or plantation; maliciously killing, maiming, or wounding any cattle; sending an anonymous letter to extort money; rescuing anyone in custody of any officer or other person for any offence under the act; and "wilfully and maliciously shooting at a person" even if "neither death nor maim should ensue." This last had the dangerous consequence of creating the same penalty for the attempt to commit the crime as for the crime itself. However neither an accidental shooting nor a shooting in hot blood without malice aforethought—both reducible in common law to manslaughter—came within the provisions of the Black Act. In fact an assault "in any other manner"—that is, neither willful nor malicious—was considered only a misdemeanour.[14]

To improve the chances of conviction, and doubtless as a precaution against a jury of sympathetic neighbors, the act stipulated that an offence did not have to be tried in the county in which it had occurred. The prosecutor had the option of initiating the prosecution in that county of England that seemed to him appropriate "for the better and more impartial trial of any indictment or information."[15] The statute of limitations for a crime was also extended from the 1692 Game Act limitation of one year to three years.[16]

The Black Act, like the Riot Act, was introduced as a temporary, three-year measure but renewed in 1725, 1733, 1737, 1744, 1751, and made permanent in 1758. It remained in force for another half-century despite the grave doubts of the most distinguished legal experts and numerous attempts to repeal it.[17] Indeed, the act was expanded repeatedly to cover new crimes until there was scarcely a criminal deed that did not come within the compass of the Black Act. Scores of additions were made to protect property.[18] And for all offences the governing classes had only one remedy, death.

Before assessing the impact of this draconian legislation on the use of firearms and violent crime, it is helpful to try to understand how the political community justified enacting this harsh code, which, as Leon Radzinowicz pointed out, punished with death a great many different offences against order, "without taking into account either the personality of the offender or the particular circumstances of each offence" or even the gravity of each offence.[19] Members of Parliament probably agreed with Sir Matthew Hale's view that the purpose of punishment was to deter potential offenders

> so that they may not offend, and so not suffer at all, and the inflicting of punishments in most cases is more for example and to prevent evils, than to punish. When offences grow enormous, frequent, or dangerous to a kingdom or state, destructive or highly pernicious to civil societies, and to the great insecurity and danger of the kingdom and its inhabitants, severe punishments, even death itself, is necessary to be annexed to laws in many cases by the prudence of law-givers, tho' possibly beyond the single demerit of the offence itself simply considered.[20]

E. P. Thompson saw in the act a decline in the old methods of class control and discipline "and their replacement by one standard recourse of authority; the example of terror. In place of the whipping-post and the stocks, manorial and corporate controls and the physical harrying of vagabonds, economists advocated the discipline of low wages and starvation, and lawyers the sanction of death."[21] It is the supreme impoverishment of the law when its only solution for all offences is the most extreme remedy.

The Black Act and the many other newly created felonies are important for the effect they may have had on violent crime. Over the century armed crime, particularly homicide, sharply declined. Was this a benefit of the Black Act and other repressive measures? There seems little reason to support that view. In fact the uniformly repressive criminal code was likely to have had the reverse effect. Since the commission of a petty crime carried the same penalty as murder, the offender had little incentive to spare the life of a victim. As Dr. Johnson pointed out, "to equal robbery with murder, is to reduce murder to robbery; to confound in common minds the gradations of iniquity, and incite the commission of a great crime to prevent the detection of a less."[22] Furthermore, although numerous offences now carried the death penalty, the manner in which killings were dealt with by the courts did not change. Murder was not covered by the Black Act, and those killings that were in self-defence, accidental, in hot blood, or excusable remained subject to traditional common-law rules. The one act that directly attempted to make the punishment for murder more terrible sped up the time of execution for a convicted murderer and ordered that after execution his body be delivered to the surgeons' company for dissection.[23]

Second, the extreme harshness of the Black Act led to a variety of strategies to mitigate its impact. Crimes against the person and other offences may have been underreported for this reason, leading to Beattie's finding of a high tolerance of violence, much of which went unreported and unindicted. Indeed, in 1811 Lord Holland argued as much in seeking repeal of capital punishment for some offences. He complained that many people "were deterred from the prosecution of offenders lest they should endanger the life of a fellow-creature, for the value of the paltry sum of five shillings, or even of forty shillings."[24] By 1819 members of London's middle class frankly admitted that they were unwilling to bring charges against shoplifters and pilfering servants lest those accused be hanged as a result.[25] In the county of Essex less than 10 percent of offenders were indicted, even for serious crimes such as robbery and burglary.[26] For cattle stealing the proportion was even lower, with only about one in twenty offenders indicted between 1768 and 1790.[27] When crimes *were* reported and indicted, eighteenth-century jurors, and even judges, committed what Blackstone termed "a kind of pious perjury," distorting the facts in order to avoid extreme penalties. Since the theft of a chattel over the value of 12 pence was grand larceny punishable by death, Blackstone explained that a jury might "bring in larceny to be under the value of twelve pence, when it is really of much greater value."[28] Lord Holland told of a case in which the charge was stealing a 10-pound note. The jury, "in the warmth of their humane feelings," committed perjury and reduced it in their verdict to a nominal value below 40 shillings.[29] Even in a case of "malicious shooting at someone in a dwelling house," a jury seized upon a technicality—the fact that the indictment confused the first names of the plaintiff and defendant—to find a verdict of not guilty.[30]

Judicial interpretations and decisions also often softened or even thwarted the punishment for crimes that had been punished more leniently before the Black Act. For instance, judges reduced the penalty for killing red deer. As for the destruction of trees, the courts tended to resort to "considerable subtleties" to avoid imposing the penalty.[31] For example, the expression "cut down or destroy" was often interpreted to mean that if the tree could be engrafted after being cut down it had not really been destroyed. To come within the meaning of the act, therefore, a tree had to have been actually up-rooted. Thus, a man who out of resentment had cut down five hundred trees in his master's nursery was not found to be within the jurisdiction of the Black Act, because the trees could be engrafted.[32] Finally, should an offender be convicted there was still the possibility of escaping hanging if he could obtain a pardon on condition of transportation. The heavy reliance upon transportation may have had a substantial impact on the rate of violent crime in England.

Transporting or deporting convicted criminals and other undesirables was first employed in 1597, when justices in county quarter sessions, accustomed to banishing vagrants to other counties, were also authorized to banish rogues, vaga-bonds, and sturdy beggars from "this realm and all other the dominions thereof" or to send them to the galleys forever. The evicted individuals were conveyed at the expense of the county. If they returned they were to be executed. The idea that individuals sentenced to death might instead be trans-ported to English colonies was suggested as early as 1611, and there were instances in 1622 and in 1638 when reprieved pris-oners asked to be transported to Virginia. In the 1650s, in the aftermath of the English Civil War, it was prisoners of war, Irish Catholics, and pirates who were transported. But it was after the restoration of the monarchy in 1660 that the system was fully legitimized. Now a pardon might be granted to a convicted felon immediately after conviction on condition that he or she agree to be transported to the colonies for a term of years. Formerly, imprisoning someone overseas had been illegal, but the landmark Habeas Corpus Act of 1679 spe-cifically excepted "any person or persons lawfully convicted of any felony, [who] shall in open court pray to be transported beyond the seas, and the court shall think fit to leave him or them in prison [rather than executing them] for that purpose."[33] After Monmouth's rising in 1685 and the Jacobite rebellion of 1715 large numbers of rebels were transported on conditional pardons. Problems arose toward the end of the seventeenth century, however. The management of the transportation system by English merchants as a business had led to abuses, and colonies slated to receive convicts grew unwilling to accept any more. Maryland and Virginia passed laws against it.[34] But a concept that gave the legal system an alternative to either dire punishment or release of criminals was too good to abandon. Therefore, with the advent of the Hanoverian regime came the Transportation Act of 1718. This act made transportation a punishment rather than a choice for certain crimes.[35] Those guilty of less serious offences—crimes normally punished by whipping, burning the hand, or hard labour—could be sent to America for seven years where, according to the preamble of the Transportation Act, there was "great want of servants." Persons convicted of more serious offences might also be pardoned on condition that they were transported, but in these instances the term was more likely to be fourteen years. Until the American Revolution the American colonies were the government's destination of choice, although Beattie argued that by midcentury transportation to America was "losing its sting" as a form of punishment.[36] Younger criminals, those between the ages of fifteen and twenty, could contract to be transported for eight years.[37] With the outbreak of the American Revolution an alternative destination was needed. As an emergency measure criminals were sent to hulks on the Thames and employed to clean the river. In 1779 the system of transportation resumed, with some convicts dispatched to Africa. But from 1788 until 1853 Australia replaced America as the place of banishment and, hopefully, of rehabilitation. Banishment to a wilderness may have seemed harsh, but it was certainly preferable to hanging, the only alternative for many.

Did the Transportation Act alter the rate of homicide and armed crime in England by removing large numbers of potential murderers? Before we can address that question, two others must be answered. First, how many people were actually transported during the eighteenth century, and second, were these people likely to have committed murder if left in England? Although exact figures are unavailable, one study sets the number transported by 1776 at 50,000, while V. A. C. Gatrell found that between 1787 and 1830 another 41,000 people were transported from England and Wales.[38] About one-third of these were Irish. In the 1830s about 45,500 men and 7,700 women, one-quarter of the felons convicted at English and Welsh assizes, were transported. Transportation would remain an important factor in English crime control well into the nineteenth century. A study of English hangings during the eighteenth century found an average of sixty-seven executions a year, a number far higher than that of other European countries.[39] Yet of a staggering total of 35,000 persons condemned to death in England and Wales between 1770 and 1830, only about 7,000 actually were hanged. It is a tribute to the strategies employed to evade the rigors of the Black Act that of these 7,000 very few were executed for crimes under that statute. Most were charged with offences that had been capital crimes for centuries.[40] Of the 80 percent convicted but not hanged, most were reprieved and sent to the prison hulks or transported to Australia.[41]

Were these thousands of convicts murderers or likely to

have become so had they not been transported? The type of offence that resulted in these forced deportations altered with each new version of the transportation program. The first deportees, the vagabonds and beggars of the sixteenth century, made way in the seventeenth for prisoners of war, Irish Catholics, and pirates. With the Restoration Middlesex magistrates, for example, were again transporting vagabonds and idle and disorderly persons. In 1685 these were joined by the Monmouth rebels. Along with these Beattie found an assortment of highway robbers, horse thieves, and those charged with offences for which, because of the archaic "benefit of clergy" rule, they might have got off with a branded thumb.[42] On the whole transported felons were "incorrigible minor offenders," not murderers.[43] According to an official list from 1795, the great majority of crimes punishable by transportation were crimes against property—-buying and receiving stolen goods, grand larceny, stealing lead, setting fire to wood, embezzling naval stores, thefts of under one shilling, assault with intent to rob, stealing fish, roots, trees, plants, or "children with their apparel," and bigamy.[44] There was a tendency to transport the youngest and least dangerous offenders. In any event, since the transportation of felons involved a pardon and murderers could not be pardoned by either the king or the courts, they could not be transported.

What impact, then, did the new felonies created by the Black Act and other statutes have on violent crime? The evidence seems to indicate that these acts meant to terrorize the populace instead induced the community to evade the spirit of the laws and vitiate their impact. As Lord Holland summed it up, "from the extreme rigour of the existing laws, the actual punishment of offenders became very uncertain; and thus, instead of restraining the commission of offences, they were in effect multiplied."[45] On the other hand, that old felony, murder, was dealt with as before. The possibility that equalizing the penalties of all types of crime would increase the numbers of murders does not seem to have been the case, since homicides declined dramatically. As for the impact the transportation of thousands of petty criminals may have had, few deportees were likely to have graduated to murder had they remained in England. The great majority were guilty of crimes against property, not against persons. All in all these acts don't seem to have had any decisive effect on homicide or armed crime. There are two other aspects of eighteenth-century life, however, that may well have influenced the homicide rate, war and economic privation.

The Impact of War and the Economy on Crime

The eighteenth century was an era of almost continuous foreign war. Since foreign war has an impact on domestic crime, this seems an appropriate point to consider what that impact was, for it would influence both the crime rate and government attitudes toward private firearms in the late nineteenth and the twentieth centuries. Both national and local studies have come to the same conclusion: crime declined during wartime and rose with the return of peace.[46] War removed tens of thousands of young men from the kingdom, particularly those from the laboring poor.[47] Local troublemakers were especially recruited. In his study of Essex, Peter King found that most communities had one or two rambunctious young men who were among the first to be impressed or recruited. Indeed, some criminals were pardoned on condition they enlist.[48] The offences these prisoners were most likely to have committed before enlistment were property crimes.[49]

Contemporaries seemed fully aware that crime declined during a war and rose with peace. Clive Emsley, in his sweeping study of crime in England, cited a report in the *Gentleman's Magazine* of November 1772 that in the final two years of the last war (1759 and 1760) "the number of criminals condemned at the Old Bailey amounted to 29 only, and the days of the Judges' attendance to 46; but that during the two last years of peace, viz. 1770, 1771, the number of criminals condemned have amounted to 252, and the days of the Judges' attendance to 99."[50] Essex indictment rates were one-third higher in peacetime than in wartime. "So great a number of felons," the *Chelmsford Chronicle* reported, "is not remembered to have been in our gaol at any one time for upwards of fifty years past." Once the wars against France began however, that journal announced "the smallest number [of felons] ever remembered upon the calendar."[51] Indeed, during the Napoleonic wars the *Leicester Journal* found "but one prisoner for trial" at the Lincoln assizes, "at Cambridge not any; and at Norwich during the last year, there have been but six persons." "This at least," they concluded, "is one benefit arising from the war."[52] In 1763 a letter from London printed in the *Maryland Gazette* complained that since the end of the French and Indian War "not a day or night passes without robberies, such swarms of rogues has the peace let loose upon us, which are daily increasing as the ships are paid off."[53] In 1783 even George III expressed fears that the corps of highway robbers during the war "now will naturally increase from the number of idle persons that this peace will occasion."[54] Englishmen had ample opportunity to observe these fluctuations, since between 1740 and 1820 there were no less than four major demobilizations, the largest of which involved more than a third of a million men. The impact of these demobilizations was exacerbated by the fact that they were carried out as rapidly as possible to minimize public expense.

There are many reasons for the increase in crime that came with peace. Many newly demobilized soldiers were unemployed and footloose, many criminals who had enlisted were home again, and of course war tended to brutalize combatants. Furthermore men who had faced the hardship and drama of war abroad were sometimes unwilling to return to the deferential, narrow world they had left behind, or sought to better their conditions within it. Social unrest often appeared in the aftermath of war. As Rudyard Kipling, speaking in the voice of a demobilized soldier, put it:

> Me that 'ave been what I've been—
>> Me that 'ave gone where I've gone—
> Me that 'ave seen what I've seen—
>> 'Ow can I ever take on
> With awful old England again,
> An 'ouses both sides of the street,
> An 'edges two sides of the land,
> And the parson an' gentry between,
> An' touchin' my 'at when we meet—
>> Me that 'ave been what I've been?[55]

But it is economic downturns and harvest failures rather than war that historians and criminologists have long suspected—or assumed—caused an increase in crime. "Want, horrid want," William Cobbett wrote in 1821, "is the great parent of crime."[56] It was property crime rather than violent crime, however, that tended to fluctuate with the English economy.[57] In his research of Essex, King found indictments for property offences affected by the "exceptionally bad" harvests of 1800–01 and saw a correlation between wheat prices and property crime indictments.[58] All this is no surprise, but the relationship between even property crime and economic hardship is less striking than Cobbett assumed. Douglas Hay pointed out that in peacetime the relationship between the price of wheat—the staple of the poorer folk—and recorded crime was negligible.[59] In wartime the state of military operations appears to have had a much more decisive influence on the crime rate than the size of the harvest.[60] Major peaks of crime followed or accompanied the demobilization of troops rather than periods of harvest failure. With all the rising and falling, and despite all the new legislative protection, indictments for property crimes fell between the late sixteenth and the early eighteenth centuries.[61] More important for our investigation, violent crimes continued their steady, indeed dramatic, decline in the same period.[62] Lawrence Stone found that by the third quarter of the eighteenth century the convicted murder rate (admittedly not the same as the homicide rate) for London and Middlesex was on average only four a year. And as the eighteenth century drew to a close, foreign visitors travelling through England commented on its very low level of violent crime.[63] If want was the parent of crime, it was not the parent of violent crime. Those attempting to relate changing patterns of serious crime "with some preconceived notion of economic change," Sharpe warned, must confront the problem that the patterns of serious crime do not seem to have changed much between the fourteenth century and 1800.[64]

Firearms, the Law, and Armed Crime

It is difficult to keep twentieth-century notions from intruding into historical studies, especially on as controversial a topic as the relationship between guns and violence. Just as scholars with preconceived ideas of the impact of economic change on crime must reckon with the awkward fact that English patterns of personal and property crime changed little over four centuries, those with preconceptions about the impact of guns on rates of violent crime are often tempted to leap to conclusions. J. S. Cockburn's examination of violent deaths in the county of Kent between 1720 and 1850 is a case in point. According to Cockburn, the Kent figures substantiate the thesis that "homicide is most often committed in societies where weapons are readily available. In early modern England both prudence and fashion dictated the bearing of arms." Just what led Cockburn to this conclusion? First he discovered that until 1750 about half the homicides in Kent involved the use of "side-arms, cudgels or staffs."[65] Unfortunately he doesn't—presumably can't—report what proportion of these deaths were from firearms. Even Cockburn's rather sparse evidence from Kent assumes that it was a typical county, but in the eighteenth century this was far from the case. In that era smugglers infested the Kent coast protected by their own armed "fighting men." Gun battles occasionally broke out between smugglers and government agents. Therefore even Kent's unspectacular level of firearm homicides may well have been above average. As for who used and misused guns, Cockburn finds that the "overwhelming majority of gun-related homicides" after 1660 were committed by men described as labourers in circumstances that imply that firearms were readily available to all but the poorest Englishmen after as well as before 1660. He reports that by the second half of the eighteenth century "more traditional weapons" had been "largely replaced by firearms," and these caused 21 percent of the homicides between 1720 and 1810.[66] This result is in line with the findings of Thomas Birch that 19 percent of London murders during the eighteenth century were caused by fire-arms.[67] John Marshall's figures for London homicides with guns were somewhat higher. His study, published in 1832, reported that between 1690 and 1730 twenty people were shot, thirty-six were stabbed, and twenty-two died by the sword.[68] Eric Monkkonen assumes that not all of the deaths by shooting were murders, although most of the stabbings probably were. If these figures are typical he concludes there were "at least three times as many sharp-instrument murders as shooting murders during the period."[69] By the first half of the nineteenth century, however, Cockburn found guns and bladed weapons together caused only 13 percent of violent deaths while 41 percent of killings were the result of hitting and/or kicking. On the evidence merely of a sharp decline in firearms homicides, he presumes that sidearms of all types "apparently became less prevalent during the first half of the nineteenth century." This logic leads him to the conclusion that "bearing arms" causes more violence.

As we have seen, rather than escalating, violent crime and homicide declined dramatically over the eighteenth century, just when Cockburn finds that firearms had largely replaced traditional weapons. Still, preconceived notions are preconceived for a reason: they seem logical, and the carrying of side-arms might have increased homicide. It is important to tap other evidence to find out whether that was the case.

Given the anxiety of eighteenth-century Parliaments about maintenance of order and their penchant for proclaiming new felonies, it seems likely that the right of Protestants to be armed would have been restricted to the privileged few, that a commoner bearing a firearm would be committing a criminal offence, very likely a felony. But history is full of surprises. The drafters of the 1689 Bill of Rights and their successors apparently meant what they proclaimed, that Protestants could have "arms for their defence." Ironically it was in the eighteenth century, so harsh in its approach to order, that the right of Protestants to be armed became fully established. Indeed, by that century's end the view that these private weapons were a bulwark of the constitution and could, *in extremis,* protect, or if necessary restore, the people's liberties was embraced by orthodox legal scholarship.

At first, however, the practical effect of the proclaimed right was unclear. This was true for many of the articles in the Bill of Rights, for when the document was enacted there were still laws on the books that contradicted or infringed some of the rights it asserted. In the case of private ownership of firearms, the Game Act of 1671 still explicitly forbade all those unqualified to hunt from owning or using these weapons. Parliament's next revision of game law, the 1692 Game Act, omitted guns from the list of devices prohibited to those not qualified to hunt, but left the rest of the 1671 Game Act in place. This move was suggestive but not necessarily conclusive, and I have been unable to find any information about the intention of Parliament in omitting guns. Early in the eighteenth century, however, Parliament passed yet another game act, again omitting guns from the list of devices forbidden to the unqualified, although the list did include a catchall prohibition against "other Instruments for destruction of Fish, Fowl, or other Game."[70] This time we have the testimony of a member of Parliament who argued for the continued omission of guns from the list of prohibited devices, and a series of court cases explicitly removing all doubt about the meaning of that change. Evidence that the omission was intentional comes from Lord Macclesfield, who was present in the House of Commons when the 1706 act was drafted and told the solicitor-general that he had himself objected to the insertion of the word *gun* in it "because it might be attended with great inconvenience."[71] As Joseph Chitty, an expert on game law, explained in 1826: "We find that guns which were expressly mentioned in the former acts were purposely omitted in this [the 1706 act] because it might be attended with great inconvenience to render the mere possession of a gun *prima facie* evidence of its being kept for an unlawful purpose."[72]

The new act was passed before the accession of the first Hanoverian king and the rash of new felonies that followed. The anxieties accompanying that change of dynasty may have altered the government's willingness to protect a dangerous public right. Again the facts prove otherwise. Two key court cases later in the century make it clear that guns were not prohibited per se by the 1706 act. In 1739, more than a decade after passage of the Black Act, the Court of King's Bench heard the case of *Rex v. Gardner.* The defendant had been convicted by a justice of the peace of keeping a gun contrary to the 1706 act.[73] There was no evidence that his gun had been wrongfully used, but it was argued that a gun was mentioned in the Game Act of 1671 and considered there an engine for the destruction of game, and the act of 1706, having the general words "other engines," should be taken to include a gun. The defence objected "that a gun is not mentioned in the statute [of 1706], and though there may be many things for the bare keeping of which a man may be convicted, yet they are only such as can only be used for destruction of the game, whereas a gun is necessary for defence of a house, or for a farmer to shoot crows." The court agreed with the defence and concluded: "We are of the opinion, that a gun differs from nets and dogs, which can only be kept for an ill purpose, and therefore this conviction must be quashed." When a similar case came before King's Bench in 1752, a year after yet another renewal of the Black Act, this decision was reaffirmed. In *Wingfield v. Stratford and Osman* the plaintiff had appealed his conviction and the confiscation of a gun and dog, the dog being a "setting dog," the gun "an engine" for killing game.[74] By this time the court was not only adamant that guns were not illegal per se, but amazed that anyone should think they were. The conviction was overturned because it amounted to a general issue, but the court made a point of explaining that it would have been bad in any case because it was not alleged that the gun had been used for killing game:

> It is not to be imagined, that it was the Intention of
> the Legislature, in making the 5 Ann. c. 14 to disarm
> all the People of England . . . as guns are not ex-
> pressly mentioned in that Statute, and as a gun may
> be kept for the Defence of a Man's House, and for
> divers other lawful Purposes, it was necessary to
> alledge, in order to its being comprehended within
> the Meaning of the Words "any other Engines to
> kill the Game," that the Gun had been used for kill-
> ing the Game.

During the eighteenth century the view that Protestant subjects had a right to have weapons became increasingly explicit. Even more surprising in that era of fears and new felonies, the Whig view that armed subjects were a necessary check on tyranny also came to be accepted. It was William Blackstone who set the stamp of orthodoxy on the need for an armed citizenry to protect English freedom. In 1765 in the first chapter of *Commentaries on the Laws of England* Blackstone listed the rights of Englishmen and then acknowledged that "in vain would these rights be declared, ascertained, and protected by the dead letter of the laws, if the constitution had provided no other method to secure their actual enjoyment. It has therefore established certain other auxiliary rights of the subject, which serve principally as outworks or barriers, to protect and maintain inviolate the three great and primary rights, of personal security, personal liberty, and private property." Blackstone identified five such rights, the last being the right of the people to have arms:

> The fifth and last auxiliary right of the subject, that
> I shall at present mention, is that of having arms
> for their defence, suitable to their condition and de-
> gree, and such as are allowed by law . . . and is, in-
> deed, a publick allowance under due restrictions, of
> the natural right of resistance and self preservation,
> when the sanctions of society and laws are found
> insufficient to restrain the violence of oppression.[75]

The so-called Gordon riots, which shook London in June 1780, severely tested the national commitment to the right of an Englishman to be armed. The actions taken and statements made during and after the riots provide a piercing light into constitutional attitudes at the time. Briefly, Parliament's passage of an act to relieve Catholics of the civil liabilities imposed upon them was the immediate provocation for a petition of protest signed by nearly 120,000 Protestants.[76] A deeper cause of discontent was the hardships faced by working-class Englishmen. Led by Lord George Gordon, some 60,000 persons marched to Parliament to deliver the petition.[77] What started as a peaceful protest became violent, and for several days Londoners were at the mercy of the mob. By the time order was restored some 450 people had been killed, Catholic chapels and homes ransacked, prisons opened, and the Bank of England and other public buildings attacked. Members of Parliament were furious at the government's inability to maintain order. Among other complaints was the charge that some measures that had been taken were unwarranted and illegal. Lord Jeffrey Amherst, the senior army officer in London, was accused of thwarting the lord mayor's plan "to arm all the inhabitants or housekeepers of every ward," instead ordering the lieutenant colonel on duty in London to disarm city residents. Amherst's disarmament order excepted only members of the city militia or those specially authorized by the king to be armed. His letters to this effect, the lord mayor's plan, and the English Declaration of Rights were read to the House of Lords and a formal inquiry demanded. The Duke of Richmond, who led the protest in the Lords, pointed out that Amherst's instructions were "a direct violation of one of the leading articles in the sacred and inviolable statute." He moved that Amherst's letters be branded "an unwarrantable command to deprive the Protestant subjects of their legal property, and a dangerous attempt to violate their sacred right, 'to have arms for their defence, suitable to their conditions, and as allowed by law.'" Amherst's defenders excused his conduct by citing the circumstances of the crisis. They insisted that no "sober" citizen had been disarmed and that the letter had been misconstrued. Richmond's resolution was defeated, but not before all sides had acknowledged the right of all Protestants, even poor ones, to be armed. Outside Parliament questions arose about the use of voluntary military associations in the crisis, and whether the right to be armed included a right to form armed groups. The recorder of London, the city's legal advisor, was called upon to give his opinion of the legitimacy of these organizations and did so in July 1780. His response is the clearest summation of the extent of the individual's right to be armed at the time of the American Revolution and just after the Gordon riots and is worth quoting at length:

> The right of his majesty's Protestant subjects, to
> have arms for their own defence, and to use them
> for lawful purposes, is most clear and undeniable. It
> seems, indeed, to be considered, by the ancient laws
> of this kingdom, not only as a *right,* but as a *duty;*
> for all the subjects of the realm, who are able to
> bear arms, are bound to be ready, at all times, to as-
> sist the sheriff, and other civil magistrates, in the
> execution of the laws and the preservation of the
> public peace. and that right, which every Protestant
> most unquestionable possesses, *individually,* may,
> and in many cases *must,* be exercised collectively, is
> likewise a point which I conceive to be most clearly
> established by the authority of judicial decisions
> and ancient acts of parliament, as well as by reason
> and common sense.[78]

In conclusion, at the very time that the individual right to be armed was becoming well established and guns were replacing earlier weapons, the homicide rate continued its precipitous decline. Individual studies for particular counties bear witness to this trend. The 302 homicides recorded in Hanoverian Somerset between 1720 and 1820 showed a steady drop in homicide indictments, from an average of 2.5 per 100,000 population for the first nine years of that period to 0.7 per 100,000 for the last nine years. This low rate accords with the experience of other counties. A similar decrease has been found for the Home and Western Circuits.[79] A study of Surrey and Sussex showed a "straightforward decline over the period." Surrey went from some 6.2 homicides per 100,000 in 1660–1679 to 0.9 in 1780–1802. The Sussex homicide rate declined from 2.6 per 100,000 in 1660–1679 to 0.6 in 1780–1802.[80] At the national level the homicide rate between 1660 and 1800 dropped by two-thirds.[81] The great majority of these recorded homicides, as in the past, were impulsive and did not involve firearms. As S. C. Pole concluded from the Somerset records, "The unpremeditated character of most homicides is also implied by the instruments used." In instances in which a weapon was noted, it was "normally a stone, working tool, or some other implement likely to have been lying readily at hand."[82] There is no sign in any of the evidence, in the homicide figures, the reported use of firearms in crime, or Parliament's treatment of armed Englishmen, that use of guns increased either homicide or crime generally. An era quick to point the figure at danger and to draft repressive legislation saw no reason to restrict ownership and use of firearms. Rather, private ownership of guns for personal defence and constitutional purposes was lauded and protected.

4

The Nineteenth Century: "An Era of Rare Success"

Certainly, the rhetoric of liberty, justice and impartiality
has always been usefully turned against the pretensions of
the great; but those values have been more frequently com-
promised before the more expediential, discretionary and
prejudicial devices of law as they were wielded in practice by
policemen, judges and politicians. Historians might profit-
ably remind themselves that the history of crime is a grim
subject, not because it is about crime, but because it is
about power.

—V. A. C. GATRELL, "Crime, Authority
and the Policeman-state"

AGAINST PRODIGIOUS ODDS violent crime
plummeted during the nineteenth century.
From midcentury up to the First World War reported assaults fell by 71 percent, woundings by 20 percent,
and homicides by 42 percent.[1] As for the use of guns in violent

crime, in 1890 only three people in all of England and Wales were sentenced to death for murder committed with a revolver, in 1891 the number rose to four, and in 1892 it dropped to three again.[2] Some thing, or combination of things, went marvelously right. Success, it is said, has many fathers, but which "father" or set of fathers can claim the credit is unclear. True, the governing classes were, for good reasons, preoccupied with order—or, more precisely, with disorder. The kingdom's arsenal for preserving the peace as it entered the new century included the brutal Black Act, a self-sufficient armed population charged with helping keep order but potentially a menace to it, an often ineffective citizen militia, and a professional but distrusted army.[3] The challenges to order were formidable. As the century dawned the turmoil and violence of the French Revolution were still spreading war and revolution across Europe. England was fully engaged abroad and feared uprisings at home. But with the defeat of Napoleon came domestic threats beyond those created by the return of unemployed soldiers. A politically self-conscious, industrial working class had become well organized and was demanding reforms. At times England's leaders felt the country "teetering on the brink of revolution."[4]

On a more prosaic level, ordinary crime ought to have been rampant, and contemporaries were often under the impression that it was.[5] Englishmen were beginning to speak of "the criminal classes." The age was cursed with every ill modern society pegs as a cause of crime—wrenching poverty alongside growing prosperity, teeming slums, rapid population growth and dislocation, urbanization, the breakdown of the working family, problematic policing, and, of course, wide ownership of firearms. Governments were anxious to keep guns out of the hands of potential revolutionaries, but they were also dependent upon the public to help preserve the peace and well aware of the passionate attachment to the right to be armed. It is indicative of how fine a line the government walked that while possession of private weapons remained a jealously guarded individual right, Englishmen were not prepared to extend it to the newly created professional police. The truncheon would do for the constable. There is a clear disconnect between the availability of firearms and the sharp decline of violent crime, but that is only part of the story, for notwithstanding all the century's troubles and impressions to the contrary, violent crime reached a record low. Just how Englishmen were able to achieve an unprecedented state of interpersonal civility in such unpromising conditions is a puzzle. The role of privately owned guns in this enviable situation is the subject of this chapter. First, we will examine what impact firearms had on the century's domestic upheavals. Next we will explore how guns figured in the reform of the criminal law, the creation of professional police, and the crime rate. Woven into all these developments were the approach taken by different ministries and the attitudes of members of Parliament toward an armed public.

Fears of Disorder as the Century Begins

Fears of mob violence and control of ordinary criminal violence competed for government and popular attention and took legislative policy along very different trajectories. Indeed, the move to reform the criminal law was stymied for a time by fear of mob actions. It is difficult now to appreciate the fright the French Revolution put into the English governing classes. Charles Kingsley, reminiscing in midcentury, recalled the terror of mob violence: "young lads believed (and not so wrongly) that the masses were their natural enemies, and that they might have to fight, any year or any day, for the safety of their property and the honour of their sisters."[6] To protect the status quo Crown and Parliament set to work to pass new, short-term legislation. Even as cherished a right as habeas corpus was suspended in 1794 and again in 1798 for anyone suspected of plotting to subvert the English constitution in order to introduce "the System of Anarchy and Confusion which has so fatally prevailed in *France*."[7] As it clamped down on habeas corpus, Parliament took care to stipulate that all its own "ancient Rights and Privileges" and those of its members would remain inviolate. The suspension must have seemed inadequate, for the next year two additional measures were approved. The Treasonable and Seditious Practices Act gave the king and Parliament a weapon against "the continued Attempts of wicked and evil disposed Persons" determined "to disturb the Tranquillity" of king and kingdom through publications, speeches, intimidation, plots, or assistance to enemies of the kingdom.[8] The Seditious Meetings and Assemblies Act made it a crime to hold an unauthorized meeting of fifty people to consider "Petitions, Complaints, Remonstrances, Declarations, or other Addresses." So comprehensive was its scope that special exceptions had to be made to enable the universities and schoolmasters to continue to teach "those confided to their care."[9] Unlike the Riot Act, which enabled the authorities to break up a meeting, this act was preemptive.

Although some rights were sacrificed in the name of security, until 1819 the right of individuals to be armed was not among them. In fact the authorities seemed to encourage it. As the government clamped down hard on the rights of dissidents, it called upon respectable people to help with peace-keeping and defence. In 1794 it created the yeomanry corps to assist against a French invasion or trouble at home.[10] The yeomanry were armed volunteers, mostly tenant farmers and landowners, led by the landed gentry and organized into mobile mounted units that could be called up by local officials. Whatever the likelihood of a French invasion, the yeomanry were well placed to take action against English rioters. In 1802 Parliament also passed another militia act to consolidate earlier acts and make the citizen militia more effective.[11] In 1803 *The Times* reported that to defend the kingdom against a possible French invasion the militia had been called up, a supplementary militia embodied, an army reserve of some 50,000 added, a measure adopted "for calling out and arming the whole mass of the people" in case of emergency, and, at the time of writing, nearly 300,000 men enrolled in volunteer, yeomanry, and cavalry corps.[12]

The French revolutionary wars were followed by the return of thousands of unemployed soldiers to England. Their presence only exacerbated the decline in real wages, a decline made far worse by the artificially high bread prices produced by the Corn Laws. English workers gathered to protest their terrible working conditions, their meager wages, and the Corn Laws and to push for reform of Parliament. Meetings led to riots in Yorkshire and other industrial districts and aroused fears for public safety. The hammer of the law descended upon the rioters, and further protest meetings were restricted. But the workers' grievances had not been dealt with, and tensions remained high. In August 1819 the festering sore burst. A large, peaceful crowd of working men and women had assembled at St. Peter's Fields in Manchester to protest the Corn Laws and to demand reform of Parliament. The local magistrates arrived accompanied by a force of armed yeomanry and demanded that the crowd disperse.[13] They refused. The magistrates panicked and ordered the yeomanry to fire. When the shooting stopped a dozen people had been killed and hundreds more hurt. This event, which promptly became known as the Peterloo Massacre, caused widespread public dismay and outrage. An angry debate in Parliament culminated in six statutes that imposed further restrictions on individual liberty. The Six Acts were described by John Lord Campbell, then a barrister, as "the most obnoxious bills," "the latest violation of our free Constitution."[14] They included a ban on public meetings without licence, a high duty on newspapers intended to limit circulation, a prohibition against groups practicing military drills without permission or carrying arms "under suspicious Circumstances," and the Seizure of Arms Act. The last two impinge directly upon our topic.

The first of the Six Acts, indeed the first act that session of Parliament, was a measure to prevent unlawful "Training of Persons to the Use of Arms, and to the Practice of Military Evolutions and Exercise."[15] The penalty for those present for training and their instructors was transportation for up to seven years, or imprisonment for up to two years. Any justice of the peace or constable could break up a group and arrest everyone present. Still, Parliament seemed unsure of its ground, or hoped the measure would be regarded as temporary, for the final paragraph noted that it might be repealed in whole or in part, or even amended during the current session of Parliament. As it turned out this hastily drafted statute has survived into our own century and was last amended in the 1980s.

While the Unlawful Drilling Act did not intrude upon any man's personal right to keep and carry firearms, the Seizure of Arms Act did.[16] Justices of the peace in "certain disturbed Counties" were authorized to seize guns and other weapons they believed were kept for purposes dangerous to the public peace. The mere keeping of weapons was not supposed to be sufficient to initiate the search and seizure: there had to be some evidence, or at least some assertion, that an ill purpose was intended. The seriousness of the act was underlined by the power granted justices of the peace, on the testimony of a single witness, to issue warrants "to enter any place day or night," by force if necessary, to search for and confiscate weapons kept "for a purpose dangerous to the public peace." In addition to keeping weapons, any person found carrying them in a way that a justice of the peace found suspicious was liable to arrest for a misdemeanor. The act was limited to those areas that had been affected by riots, but could be extended by proclamation. The act was to expire in two years.

Despite the alarm about riots and the temporary and geographically limited nature of the Seizure of Arms bill, it was hotly contested in Parliament. The authorization for search and disarmament was itself disturbing. Lord Rancliffe noted that similar statutes for Ireland had served "but to open the door to the greatest oppression, and to rouse the most fiery passions of hatred and revenge. The atrocities perpetrated in that country under such an act as this," he argued, "were such as no man could contemplate without horror."[17] T. W. Anson accused the government of exaggerating popular disorders and dangers "for the purpose of obtaining the concurrence of Parliament in measures hostile to the freedom, and repugnant to the feelings of Englishmen." He took particular exception to the Seizure of Arms bill:

> the principles upon which it was founded, and the temper in which it was framed appeared to him to be so much at variance with the free spirit of their venerated constitution, and so contrary to that undoubted right which the subjects of this country had ever possessed—the right of retaining arms for the defence of themselves, their families, and property—that he could not look upon it without expressing his disapprobation and regret.

George Bennet opposed the bill "because he held that the distinctive difference between a freeman and a slave was a right to possess arms; not so much, as had been stated, for the purpose of defending his property as his liberty." "Neither could he do," Bennet protested, "if deprived of those arms, in the hour of danger. It was a violation of the principles of a free government, and utterly repugnant to our constitution." Lord Castlereagh, the government spokesman, conceded "that the principle of the bill was not congenial with the constitution, that it was an infringement upon the rights and duties of the people, and that it could only be defended upon the necessity of the case" which he felt "now existed; the security and general interests of the subject demanded the sacrifice."[18] The bill passed, but when its two-year term had elapsed it was permitted to expire. The right to be armed for personal self-defence had proved resilient. The ability of Englishmen to organize and train as an independent armed force was permanently suppressed.

Were government fears legitimate? Were the protesting workers armed and dangerous? There is no mention that the peaceful crowd gathered at St. Peter's Fields was armed. But those who gathered near Burnley afterward to protest Peterloo and consider "the best means of bringing the instigators and perpetrators of the late Manchester massacre to justice, and to embrace . . . Parliamentary Reform" clearly were.[19] The several thousand people who assembled that November 15 of 1819 had come in defiance of warnings from local magistrates. Many carried sticks. When a cry was raised during the meeting that soldiers were approaching they produced pikeheads they had concealed about them and began screwing them onto the sticks. Others produced pistols. When a second alarm convinced the organizers to cancel the meeting, some of those with pistols fired into the air.[20] Several of the organizers were later arrested. At first they were charged with treason, but this charge was reduced to conspiring to assemble an unlawful meeting, attending an unlawful meeting, and causing people to go armed to a public meeting. Six of those arrested were convicted. Their trial, *Rex v. George Dewhurst and Others,* dealt with the status of the subject's right to carry arms and the separate, and thornier, issue of armed gatherings. There was general agreement about the individual's right to be armed for self-defence, but the Crown's attorney insisted that although "people have a right to meet to discuss public grievances . . . by the law they cannot meet armed for the purpose of redressing or deliberating on any question."[21] The defence attorney cited Blackstone who, "speaking loudly and largely of the rights of the people of England" had designated this the fifth auxiliary right of the subject. The attorney then launched into a stirring defence of the right to assemble.[22] In his summation to the jury Justice Bailey referred to the arms article from the Bill of Rights and its vague final clauses and asked: "But are arms suitable to the condition of people in the ordinary class of life, and are they allowed by law?" He answered: "a man has a clear right to arms to protect himself in his house. A man has a clear right to protect himself when he is going singly or in a small party upon the road where he is travelling or going for the ordinary purposes of business." He even agreed that arms could carried to a public meeting, with one exception: "You have no right to carry arms to a public meeting, if the number of arms which are so carried are calculated to produce terror and alarm."[23]

For the next decade there were no more Peterloos, but tensions remained. Between 1802 and 1840 Parliament passed measures to encourage prosecutors to act, and the number of trials in the kingdom's higher courts increased sevenfold.[24] This does not mean that crime increased to that degree, but the rise in prosecutions fueled public anxiety.[25] In 1830 Sir Francis Burdett, M.P. for Westminster, advocated declaring the counties "out of the King's peace," reenacting the Alien Act against foreigners, and, above all, arming the householders.[26] And the same year John Hobhouse, Lord Broughton, a radical M.P., complained that he had been imprisoned in Newgate for eleven weeks "for saying that if the soldiers did not protect the House of Commons the members of that House would be pulled out of it by the ears." He added: "I was imprisoned by the offended party without a trial, without being heard, without being even seen; and this monstrous injustice has been committed with the approval, or at least without the opposition, of many of those who call themselves, and are called, the friends of popular rights, but who think that some such power should reside in the House of Commons."[27]

Then in 1837 the Chartist movement, described as the dominant working-class movement of the century, erupted.[28] The Chartists' basic grievances, like those of workers earlier in the century, were set against a background of poor harvests, high food prices, decline and depression in many handicraft industries, and a serious decline in real wages.[29] They sought political reforms, lower prices, better working conditions, and repeal of the Poor Law of 1834, which sent people to the workhouse. Were the Chartists armed? There is contradictory evidence about this, made still less clear by the disagreement among Chartist leaders whether to resort to physical force or rely upon moral force. Many, if not most, Chartists were impoverished, and probably could not have afforded guns. Yet reports from many widely separated districts claimed that Chartists had obtained firearms as well as other weapons.[30] Mather notes that in April 1839 young Chartists of Llanidloes had "borrowed" muskets from local farmers. In 1848 the Metropolitan Police, however, found that only 122 guns and 162 pistols had been purchased by poorer Londoners from local gunsmiths in the first half of that year.[31] This list does not include secondhand weapons bought from individuals, weapons more likely to be within the means of Chartists. There is evidence that they came to some protest meetings with weapons. Certainly some Chartist orators urged them to arm and seemed to assume they had access to firearms. Raymer Stephens, accurately labelled a "firebrand," urged Chartists to arm in any way they could. "If the musket and the pistol, the sword and the pike were of no avail," he urged that "the woman take the scissors, the child the pin or needle. If all failed, then the firebrand—aye the firebrand—the firebrand, I repeat. The palace shall be in flames."[32] In 1839 and 1848 Chartists prepared for military action, drilling and even forming a National Guard.[33] Armed meetings were held in Bethnal Green in January 1848, and in August seventy armed Chartists were said to have set off to shoot Manchester magistrates. In Ashton-under-Lyne several groups of men paraded in the dead of night armed with pikes and guns, while London police burst into taverns to swoop up groups of armed Chartists.[34]

Clearly, on occasion at least some Chartists were armed. In his study of the movement F. C. Mather had little doubt that "a considerable quantity of pikes and second-hand muskets and pistols found its way into the hands of the working classes."[35] Parliament held heated debates on the issue. Alarmists pushed for ever more extreme measures. In 1839 householders, or at least the London shopkeepers, were considering arming, as they fretted about a working-class uprising.[36] The government did not want to be seen setting class against class and took a cautious attitude. In 1839 Lord John Russell, the home secretary, tried to calm fears. He assured Lord Harewood that the Chartist rabble-rousers' call for the people to arm "is not likely to induce them to lay out their money on muskets and pistols. So long as a mere violence of language is imployed without effect, it is better . . . not to add to the importance of these mob leaders by prosecutions."[37] Russell announced that he had canvassed the gun trade and found that no very considerable quantity of arms had been made by the regular manufacturers for domestic sale.[38] But weapons of a dangerous nature had been made by others, and while he did not want any exaggerated notion of there being large bodies of men regularly armed, "he believed there were a considerable number of persons in possession of very dangerous and offensive weapons."[39] As for new measures, he reminded members, "As soon as Parliament is approached for new powers there was aroused in that body a certain sympathy and jealousy with regard to the constitution."[40] Anyhow, sufficient restrictive legislation was already in place against armed drilling, sedition, and dangerous gatherings. Other M.P.s agreed that fears were unjustified. Mr. Thomas Attwood was convinced there had not been fifty muskets or fifty pikes bought in England and did not believe "that the people of England had gone mad enough for that, or that they had ever thought of arming themselves. He was convinced they knew too well where their strength lay to take up arms."[41] Toward the end of the debate the Home Secretary summed up the government's view of the private carrying of firearms:

> it might be necessary to take some measures for the restriction of that which was an abuse of the rights secured by the Bill of Rights. It was, undoubtedly, true that every person had a right to have arms in his own defence; but the arming of a portion of the population, exhibiting and brandishing those arms to the terror and alarm of her Majesty's subjects, was an abuse of the right, and one which it might be necessary to meet by legislative enactment.[42]

In 1819 after the Peterloo Massacre Parliament had come down hard on protesters, but in the 1830s the government did not want to give the impression it was arming the middle and upper classes against the workers. However, other measures had been taken. In 1839 Lord Francis Egerton, a Lancashire magistrate, complained: "I passed yesterday with the Grand Jury, shovelling in bills against the rioters and orators by dozens: I am happy to think we have been suddenly transformed to an absolute despotism as to speaking and arming. A copper cap or a piece of wadding [is] sufficient evidence against anybody."[43] Indeed, there were sufficient laws to enable magistrates to arrest all sorts of potential troublemakers. In 1842 a series of riots led Manchester officials to pick up a record number of people in short order for a variety of offences from assault to begging.[44] "They have trapped us into violence," Ernest Jones, a Chartist leader, fumed, "and then punished the outbreak they were glad to see." By the spring of 1848 the government was prepared to risk giving an impression of arming one class against another. Chartists bitterly resented the curbs on weapons and drilling by their supporters, with orators such as Ernest Jones insisting that "if the middle class have a right to arm, so have the working class."[45] The Chartists had drafted a petition to present to Parliament and planned a massive meeting at Kennington Common to endorse the document and march to Westminster to deliver it. The government armed its friends to face down the threat. There was ample precedent when danger threatened for arming and organizing the "well-affected."

In the early part of the century rural peace was still maintained by a high constable appointed by Quarter Sessions and petty constables who were largely untrained and too few to cope with a serious uprising. Theirs was an unpopular, poorly paid office, and many petty constables were illiterate and of uncertain reliability. In times of crisis justices of the peace could swear in special constables—usually from the middle class—and compel them to serve. The specials were ordinarily equipped with staves, but in 1839 the government offered them cutlasses and pistols. To avoid the charge of arming class against class Sir Robert Peel's government recommended that magistrates call in army troops rather than arming special constables. The government could also call upon the yeomanry. It was they who were implicated in the attack upon the peaceful crowd at St. Peter's Fields. Their numbers had shrunk from 17,818 in 1817 to 14,000 in 1838 and they were concentrated in the Midlands and western counties.[46] Politically most were Tories, and Russell admitted that the Whig government "would rather that any force should be employed in case of local disturbance than the local corps of Yeomanry."[47] Tory governments also preferred to use regular troops. The yeomanry were expensive, were otherwise occupied during harvest, when the worst riots tended to occur, and as residents of the area seemed to be parties to the dispute. Worse, they were accused of being "over-zealous for cutting and slashing."[48] In 1839 the government felt that more armed help was needed and tried to encourage formation of other voluntary associations. In May a circular letter was sent to lords lieutenant of some counties pledging to provide firearms to those "principal inhabitants of the disturbed district" who were willing to form an association "for the protection of life and property."[49] At first the response was disappointing, as only two associations formed, although one, the association of tenant farmers in Monmouthshire, helped keep peace during the arrest of a Chartist orator.[50] In late May and June, however, many offers came in. Some were rejected by Russell—they were not from "principal inhabitants"—and when the government reneged on its promise to supply weapons the acceptable volunteers quickly became discouraged and withdrew. Clearly, the government was uneasy about seeming to be arming certain groups to oppose others, afraid it would give the Chartists an excuse to arm themselves more avidly. After all, on what basis could the government forbid working people from arming and drilling when it encouraged middle-class groups to do so? It seemed wiser to turn to the well-disciplined soldiers who were neutral but were quite ready, if ordered, to fire upon crowds. They fired "without demur" at Bolton and Newport in 1839 and at Preston, Burslem, and Halifax in August 1842.[51] After 1839 the government made no further attempt to develop armed formations of volunteers. But by then they had a growing police establishment to turn to.

Despite previous qualms about using force against the Chartists, in April 1848 the government was unwilling to take any chances. It swore in thousands of special constables—some 170,000 in the London area alone and a similar number in the provinces—and mobilized army troops under the Duke of Wellington.[52] For their part Chartist leaders were frightened by the government's move to create thousands of special armed constables and took care that a meeting scheduled for April 10 be unarmed. All forty-nine delegates to their national convention signed a statement that they did not intend a revolution but merely a demonstration of moral force. "It was authority," they pointed out, "not the Chartists, that was armed to the teeth on 10 April."[53] Every public building was provided with armed guards while they disarmed any of their followers found carrying weapons.[54] Confronted with the real risk of bloodshed, the Chartist leaders backed down and cancelled the planned procession.[55] In late spring and early summer the Chartist leaders were rounded up and charged with seditious speech. All received sentences of two years' imprisonment.

To sum up: during the tumultuous first half of the nineteenth century the right of individual Englishmen to be armed was unimpeded, with the sole and temporary exception of the Seizure of Arms Act. Many Englishmen were armed or able to get arms when necessary, and the kingdom was in danger of becoming an armed camp, with one class pitted against another. Parliament clamped down on unauthorized persons drilling with weapons or going to large gatherings armed, and the emergency act against armed drilling became permanent. When working-class rioting returned in the 1830s and 1840s the government switched from the repressive tactics it had used in 1819, both because there was already a battery of measures available and to avoid the incendiary impression that it was arming one class against another. Fortunately, better economic conditions, the 1832 Reform Act broadening the franchise, the Factory Acts, and the reform of the criminal law helped improve the lives of workers and reduce tensions. Britain avoided the revolutions that swept the Continent in 1848 with individual rights still largely intact.

Violent Crime and Reform of the Criminal Law

Within ten years of the Peterloo Massacre there was major reform of the criminal law. The Black Act's enormous roster of capital crimes was sharply reduced, and landmark political and social reforms quickly followed. The ground had been laid for the introduction of more-humane punishments in 1796 in the midst of the panic over the French Revolution.

Many parliamentarians were anxious to reform the statute book. A committee was appointed to examine expiring laws and make recommendations, although twenty years were to pass before substantial reform was enacted. The importance of a more humane and effective criminal code was frequently before the Commons.[56] In 1808, for example, Sir Samuel Romilly made a passionate speech in Parliament on what, he said, "had long been recognized as one of the greatest blots on the English criminal law . . . the frequency of capital punishment" and was able to get the death penalty removed for the crime of picking pockets.[57] In 1811 an attempt was made to repeal capital punishment for stealing from homes and shops, on canals, and in the bleaching grounds of Britain and Ireland. The arguments used in the debate over the bill were typical of those brought up time and again both for and against moderation. The bill's supporters pointed out that inflation had devalued the sum of one shilling set over a century before, which had moved theft into the capital category. Lord Holland, the main proponent in the Lords, was convinced that since the brutality of the existing code led to underreporting of crime and evasion of punishment, the criminal laws were having the opposite impact from that intended: "From the extreme rigour of the existing laws, the actual punishment of offenders became very uncertain; and thus, instead of restraining the commission of offences, they were in effect multiplied." Lord Erskine praised the British nation as "the most moral of any nation now known" but noted that "when out of a thousand prosecutions . . . only one conviction and execution followed . . . the legislature must see, that the pain of death was not applicable to such offences." Still, the lord chancellor praised "the principles and practice" of the

existing criminal code where judges were granted broad discretion, and concluded that "as long as human nature remained what it was, the apprehension of death would have
the most powerful co-operation in deterring from the commission of crimes: and he thought it unwise to withdraw the
salutary influence of that terror." The House divided with ten
lords in favour of repeal, twenty-seven against.[58] Parliament
did abolish capital punishment for the crime of stealing from
bleaching grounds.[59] Bit by bit proposals to make punishment more humane gained acceptance. In 1816 bills to stop
use of the pillory met with partial success. In 1817 the public
whipping of women and girls was stopped.[60] Still, the widespread use of capital punishment remained. In 1819 James
Mackintosh moved for a parliamentary committee to review
use of capital punishment for felony. Although more than
two hundred crimes carried the death penalty, he pointed out
that from 1749 until 1819 London and Middlesex had regularly
punished only twenty-five of these with death. Surely, Mackintosh argued, the "letter of the law should be brought nearer
to its spirit."[61] The current law and practice could not both be
right. His motion was carried, and a committee reported later
that year. Unfortunately, that summer the Peterloo Massacre
took place, and Parliament's immediate reaction was to pass
the restrictive legislation discussed above.

Seen from this distance, Peterloo was a turning point, but
that fact was not at all obvious at the time. Beginning in 1823
the sentiment in favour of reform became so strong that the
home secretary, then Sir Robert Peel, took up the cause himself. Reform was accomplished not through direct repeal, but
through a series of acts ostensibly to consolidate and ratio-
nalize the common law. The first move toward consolidation

of the criminal law, however, seemed more akin to the repressive Six Acts. The Vagrancy Act of 1824 permitted preemptive disarmament. It gave officials new power to restrain and disarm vagrants with techniques that set a useful precedent for twentieth-century Parliaments.[62] Any constable or police officer could arrest, without warrant, anyone he found "lying or loitering in any highway, yard or other place during the night, and whom he has good cause to suspect of having committed or being about to commit any felony against this Act." Anyone could apprehend someone offending against the act and deliver the accused to a justice of the peace. There had been vagrancy laws since the sixteenth century, when displaced peasants and other unemployed poor wandered the country in large numbers. The earlier approach had been to give the vagrants a beating and send them back home to be looked after there. This new act subjected vagrants to arrest on the grounds they were loitering "with intent to commit a felony." Part and parcel of such intent was the crime of carrying an offensive weapon. According to the 1824 act, offenders, defined as "rogues and vagabonds," included "every Person having in his or her Custody or Possession any Picklock Key, Crow, Jack, Bit or implement with Intent feloniously to break into any Dwelling House, Warehouse, Coach, House, Stable, Outbuilding, or being armed with any gun, Pistol, Hanger, Cutlass, Bludgeon or other offensive weapon, or having upon him or her any Instrument with Intent to commit any felonious Act." Any weapon found on someone "loitering with intent" was forfeit to the king, while its owner was liable to serve up to three months' hard labour.[63] There must have been some concern that constables would be unenthusiastic about enforcing the act, for they were threatened with a five-pound fine if they neglected to do so. This statute shored up the discretionary power to disarm and arrest before any reduction in Black Act penalties.

Reform did follow. In the name of consolidation and rationalization of the criminal law, almost by sleight of hand, the measures Peel introduced in 1827 moderated old penalties. For example, Peel argued that there was no logical reason to distinguish petty from grand larceny or why theft of property under a shilling should be punished at the option of a magistrate while death was mandated for theft of property over that value. His solution was to have a single crime of larceny for which the maximum punishment was transportation for seven years. As for the capital crime of stealing something worth forty shillings from a dwelling house, he proposed that the threshold sum be raised so high that capital convictions would be "considerably diminished." The law against malicious damage to property, he suggested, should "be beneficially altered, and confined within proper limits," and the law against cutting down hop-fences, stakes, and hedges was to be abrogated altogether.[64] The stiff law against infanticide, which presumed that concealment of a stillborn birth was murder, was no longer an automatic indictment for that murder.[65]

Peel insisted that these consolidation bills "had not, after all, proposed any very important alterations in the criminal statutes."[66] Yet by 1841 the more than two hundred capital crimes on the books when the century began had been reduced to eleven.[67] One aspect of the new legislation that seemed out of keeping with the rest strengthened the right of self-defence and self-help. It was proposed that all cases "in which a person should be killed by another in order to prevent a commission of a felony, should be held by law to be justifiable homicide."[68] There was great enthusiasm for the changes, which brought the law into greater harmony with practice. But just as the right to be armed had proved resilient, even in 1819, so the great consolidation of the laws on crimes against the person, which lessened the punishment for all sorts of offences, strengthened the hand of the armed individual. To protect his life and to prevent any felony, an Englishman was free to inflict even a mortal wound on a would-be felon.

The Forces of Order: The New Police

The very idea of a professional police force was abhorrent to eighteenth- and nineteenth-century Englishmen. Since "the natural impulse of the English people is to resist authority," Walter Bagehot wrote, he was not surprised that the introduction of policemen was not liked:

> I know people, old people I admit, who to this day consider them an infringement of freedom, and an imitation of the *gendarmes* of France. If the original policemen had been started with the present helmets, the result might have been dubious; there might have been a cry of military tyranny, and the inbred insubordination of the English people might have prevailed over the very modern love of perfect peace and order.[69]

But by the mid-eighteenth century reliance upon the public to keep the peace was failing. In his 1755 book, *A Plan for Preventing Robberies within Twenty Miles of London,* John Fielding told the story of a captain of the guards who had been robbed on Hounslow Heath while in a postchaise. The captain took one of his horses and set off in pursuit of the robbers. Although he rode through a town at noon crying out "highwayman" in full view of the public, not one person joined the pursuit.[70] The customary system that relied upon a haphazard congeries of peacekeeping officials assisted by a public obliged to follow the "hue and cry" was not working. The great growth of London also made the old system inadequate. In 1792 the ideas of John Fielding and his half-brother Henry for specially designated peacekeepers set in motion a plan for "real thieftakers" that would become the first step toward the creation of professional police forces.[71] Sir Robert Peel's Bow Street runners to help keep the peace were a great success and led in 1829 to Peel's Act, which established a system of paid, professional constables for Westminster. The system was expanded through the 1835 Municipal Corporations Act, which organized police in chartered boroughs. In 1839 another act permitted justices to apply to the secretary of state for permission to create constabularies for a county or division of a county. Finally, in 1856 all counties and cities were required to establish a police force and to appoint a chief constable to head it.[72] With professional police came increasing control over these forces by the central government through the Home Office.

Both the police bill and the prospect of increased central control encountered popular and parliamentary resistance.[73] Both Whig and Tory governments found ratepayers outraged at the possibility that more monies would be demanded for police purposes. Westminster was already paying part of the cost, but any increase in the subsidy would have met with staunch opposition in the Commons.[74] An extreme instance of public resentment occurred when police attempted to break up a protest meeting of workers at Coldbath Fields, Clerkenfield, in May 1833.[75] The crowd had been urged to come armed, and it apparently obliged, bearing a motley collection of knives, brickbats, cudgels, and lances. Some six hundred police, outnumbered ten to one, were ordered to break up the meeting. In the ensuing scuffle the police suffered heavy casualties, and one constable, Robert Culley, was stabbed in the chest and killed. The jury found this a case of "justifiable homicide" because the Riot Act had not been read to disperse the crowd, and the police were accused of having behaved in a brutal manner. The jurymen were hailed as local heroes. Each was presented with a silver loving cup and treated to a boat trip on the Medway River. Other communities protested more quietly if no less insistently against the police. In Manchester the borough council, ratepayers' meeting, and police commission were united in their opposition to the new establishment. The Birmingham town clerk had canvassed council members and reported to the home secretary: "I find amongst them one strong feeling of indignation at the 1839 measure as insulting and despotic, insulting to themselves personally as members of the Town Council, and despotic as tending to that system of centralization which every good Englishman must utterly abhor and abjure." In 1840 a Todmorden magistrate wrote: "The County Police will shortly be established here, and the very circumstances of their introduction being odious to the greater portion of our inhabitants, renders it more than probable some serious disturbance will be attempted."[76] Riots erupted against the police at Colne in 1840 and when sixty-five constables attempted to disarm an electioneering crowd at Ashton-under-Lyne in 1841 the police were forced to take refuge in the police station.[77] In areas where Chartism was strong, hostility was even greater. This near-general dislike came despite the fact that, with rare exceptions, the police were armed only with truncheons and were restrained when coping with crowds.

Peel pressed ahead, eager to impose central control on policing. For those anxious about the threat to individual liberty, government commissions considered the issue. A 1839 Royal Commission on the Criminal Law concluded that rights could be pruned for the greater good without undue harm. Another report the following year judged "that all specific laws for the security of persons or property would be unavailing, unless the due operation of such laws were protected by imposing efficient restraints upon forcible violations of public order." The 1839 Royal Commission on the County Constabulary admitted that police might intrude upon individual liberty but explained: "the [criminal] evils we have found in existence in some districts, and the abject subjection of the population to fears [of crime] which might be termed a state of slavery . . . form a condition much worse in all respects than any condition that could be imposed by any government that could exist in the present state of society in this country." His study of the development of this "policeman-state" convinced V. A. C. Gatrell that with it "the protection not of natural rights but of social and political order—equated with the state itself—was elevated into law's primary objective."[78]

The numbers of police grew rapidly. In 1861 there was one policeman for every 937 people in England and Wales; by 1891 there was one for every 731. The cost of policing rose dramatically as well, from 1.5 million pounds in 1861 to two and a half times that amount by 1891 and almost another four and a half times that by 1911.[79] Their activities are frequently regarded as one of the reasons for the dramatic decline in serious crime. A series of acts gave them great discretionary power, or what Gatrell labels "anticipatory prohibition," a kind of preventive justice.[80]

Guns and Violent Crime

Firearms had been necessary for the public to help keep the peace but also liable to misuse by rioters and criminals. With the establishment of the national police the government may have felt that armed individuals were no longer needed to protect one another and therefore the state had less need to assume the risks an armed public entailed. Were guns a factor in violent crime in this era? One of the benefits of the national police force was the inception of national crime statistics. Although these represent only crimes recorded by the police, they offer real figures to work with, if only to map trends. Despite all the usual caveats about their unreliability, most historians have endorsed the official picture.

The homicide rate for England and Wales was as high as 2 per 100,000 only once during the century, in 1865; otherwise it was about 1.5 per 100,000 and occasionally as low as 1 per 100,000, a record low.[81] Between 1857 and 1890 there were rarely more than 400 homicides reported each year, and in the 1890s the average was below 350.[82] In 1835–1837 9 percent of all English crimes were violent crimes, and from 1837 through 1845 the share declined to 8 percent.[83] Even that 8 percent is inflated by the fact that of the crimes against the person some

25–33 percent were cases of infanticide, which would not have involved firearms. Crimes committed with guns were rare. Between 1878 and 1886 the average number of burglaries in London in which firearms were used was two per year; from 1887 to 1891 this rose to 3.6 cases a year.[84] "It was a rough society," David Philips concluded after examining Victorian crime, "but it was not a notably homicidal society. The manslaughter cases do not show a free use of lethal weapons."[85] On the other hand, ordinary citizens were free to use lethal weapons to defend themselves. And as the difficulties of imposing restrictions on private firearms indicate, members of Parliament and their constituents were vigorously opposed to such attempts.

The amount of violent crime had remained relatively steady despite the sharp rise in population. By 1751 there were between 6 and 6.5 million people in England.[86] A century later there were 16.8 million and by 1871 some 21.4 million.[87] Between 1850 and 1914 the population doubled, and the urban population trebled.[88] Yet in 1900 police recorded fewer than 3 crimes of all sorts for every 1,000 people. By contrast, in 1974 almost 4 crimes were reported for every 100 people, or 13 times as many indictable offences.[89] This great decline in violent crime came about despite the greater sensitivity of the public and the close scrutiny of the police. As Gatrell marvelled,

> other things being equal, many pressures should
> have pushed recorded rates upwards in these dec-
> ades. Policing was expanding, more people were ac-
> quiescing in and co-operating with it, prosecution
> was becoming easier, sentences shorter and impris-
> oned offenders were released into society more rap-

idly. That theft and violence rates in all these circumstances *declined* in the half-century or so before 1914 suggests . . . the policeman-state really was enjoying an era of rare success.[90]

Despite the plummeting crime rate, English governments hoped to bring firearms under greater control and were not above resorting to subterfuge to accomplish this. In 1870, for instance, a gun licensing bill was introduced by the chancellor of the Exchequer as a simple revenue measure that would also help preserve game. Indeed the preamble of the resulting statute stated only that it was for "raising the necessary supplies to defray your Majesty's public expenses, and making an addition to the public revenue."[91] However, the parliamentary debates on the bill tell a very different story. As proposed, any gun—defined as a firearm of any description—other then one kept in a dwelling or the yard around it—would have to be licenced at an annual fee of one pound, a significant sum for working-class people. Many M.P.s immediately suspected that the government's agenda was not increased revenue, and branded the proposal unnecessary and repressive. Indeed, in his introductory remarks the chancellor had expressed hope that the measure "would put an end to the carrying of revolvers."[92] Clearly, he was taking a page from Henry VIII's book, but whereas Henry had limited handguns to the wealthy, the chancellor hoped to make all firearms too expensive for the poor to carry.[93] The bill would also create a national registry of firearms. Mr. Taylor, M.P. for Leicester, condemned it as having "every conceivable vice that a tax could possibly possess." Not only would it "operate most unequally and unjustly. It was an attempt to bring our laws and customs into harmony with those of the most despotic of Continental Governments—it was an attempt to disarm the people." He moved for a three-month postponement. Mr. Newdegate agreed that the chancellor's aim "was to pass an Arms Act for this country; but he did not know what the people of England had done to deserve a penal measure." He also saw the bill as "a most arbitrary police measure for interfering with the freedom of Englishmen without excuse."[94] Tellingly, when one member proposed that the licence fee be reduced from one pound to the more affordable 10 shillings the chancellor readily accepted.[95] The debate at the third reading was just as acerbic. An M.P. for Norfolk had numerous objections: the bill was useless, since its purpose was only to make up for revenues lost through a reduction in the price of game certificates; it would be an imperfect register of firearms, since a man could keep any number of guns in his house, which would not be searched; it was not needed to reduce shooting on the highway, since there was already an act that fined anyone who fired a gun on or within twenty-five yards of a highway; further, it would impose restrictions upon "the honest livelihood and innocent pleasures of the lower middle class," and he was sure a farmer "would look twice before he paid 10s. each for his sons to carry a gun." Indeed, a gun was "absolutely essential" to a farmer. "Government might as well impose a tax upon a plough." Mr. Taylor found the bill "unconstitutional," since it would disarm the country to a great extent. In the present state of European affairs he "thought it well that every ploughboy in the land should know how to aim a gun and pull a trigger." Mr. Macfie agreed that in "these times that man was the best friend of his country who encouraged every honest man, young and old, to accustom himself to the use of arms. He had no fear of the people, and he must deprecate the taking away from them of a privilege which from time immemorial they had enjoyed in this free and happy land." Mr. White added, "it had always been a distinguishing mark of this country that the people might possess arms, and this Bill was a very grave invasion of what was always meant to be a common right . . . Though not an alarmist, he should be glad if every adult in this country at the present moment possessed a rifle, and knew how to use it."[96] On the other side Sir Henry Selwin-Ibbetson supported the measure "on the sole ground that it would prove useful in securing a registration of arms in this country."[97] Oddly, supporters never mentioned the government's official support for the National Rifle Association, an organization launched in 1859 to promote training and target practice. At the time it was established the secretary of state for war had informed Queen Victoria that the intent was "to make the rifle what the bow was in the days of the Plantagenets."[98] Instead the chancellor, dropping the pretence that revenue was the primary aim of the bill, retorted:

> The object of the Bill is to check lawless habits. In answer to those who say it is a sign of freedom that the lower classes should go armed, I say it is the greatest proof of the absence of freedom when every man goes armed. What is the use of civilized institutions, of assemblies like this, of law and of Judges, and of all the paraphernalia of justice, if all it comes to is that every man is to be left to be the avenger of his own quarrel?

"I think it is a good object," he went on, "to discourage the lower classes from habitually carrying deadly weapons . . . I wish to keep the poor out of crime." He claimed that the habit of carrying firearms had "grown inveterate"; there were "100 complaints a day [in London] of persons shooting everything which comes in their way, such as pigeons, fowls, and cats."[99] The government may have been especially worried about "the lower classes" being armed because the falling price of firearms, in particular of handguns, made them more affordable for those of modest means.[100] A modified version of the bill was passed with important exemptions for guns used or carried in a dwelling or its immediate surroundings and another for those who had game licences.[101]

With the introduction of the 1870 licencing act we have government figures for the number of firearms licenced, although they are only a fraction of the guns actually owned, since there were various exemptions from the act, and many people were also probably unable or unwilling to pay the annual licence fee. But even statistics for guns carried outside home property can be valuable if they are complete.

On the question of the accuracy of gun licence statistics we have to thank the efforts of a civil servant, the Right Honourable C. B. Stuart Wortley, M.P. for Sheffield, Hallam. Wortley was busy behind the scenes over the next few years pressing the government to introduce firearms restrictions. Swept to office with the Conservative electoral victory in 1886, he was appointed parliamentary undersecretary of state for the Home Department when Henry Matthews became secretary of state. Wortley's interest in gun control bordered on obsession, and when he received two complaints about dangerous use of revolvers and suggestions for further restrictions he immediately began to make inquiries.[102] His researches provide a rare glimpse into the difficulties of licence enforcement. At his instructions the Inland Revenue, whose responsibility it was to collect the gun licence fee, was told that the home secretary had been receiving "all these letters about revolver carrying" and asked whether they had any reason to suppose that the licence to carry guns was being largely avoided.[103] The reply was not reassuring. The Inland Revenue Board had "every reason to believe the 'Gun Licence Act' of 1870 is largely evaded in respect to the carrying and using of revolvers."[104] This state of affairs was not new. Government records contain an 1884 order to the London Metropolitan Police calling for vigorous enforcement of the licencing act and referring to orders seven years before to the same effect.[105] Wortley's first thought was that it was "a question of costs," that the cost of prosecuting a case was greater than the penalty, and ordered an inquiry into the costs expended and penalties recovered since the passing of the 1870 act.[106] No returns existed, and the Inland Revenue was considerably annoyed at the suggestion that costs might deter it from carrying out its duty.[107] Wortley tried again, suggesting that if costs weren't the problem the secretary of state would "be glad to be informed of any cause to which the experience of the Board of Inland Revenue lead them to believe that difficulty is due." The formal reply was evasive, but he learned from a private conversation that the problem was spotting evaders. The act did not apply to guns inside a dwelling, and outside his house and grounds the owner of a revolver "is careful to keep his weapon in his pocket." Police had no powers to search that pocket, nor were they obliged to volunteer information that came to them when off duty. In fact it didn't seem advisable that they should act as informers, since "it would injure their position towards the public in the conduct of their general duties as Police." Further, the police "regarded themselves as the maintainers of public order and not as taxgatherers." Wortley was advised that further legislation to improve detection would merely excite popular indignation.[108] When asked to what extent the act was evaded, the Inland Revenue Board replied that "the instances are so extremely rare in which persons who carry or use such weapons without payment of the licence-duty are detected, that there are no grounds upon which the Board could base any opinion as to how far the Gun Licence Act, 1870 is evaded, whether in the Metropolis or elsewhere."[109] Wortley then ordered letters sent to every chief constable asking what was being done to enforce the act. When the replies made it clear that little was happening, he ordered a letter sent explaining the secretary of state's concern that "many accidents arise from the practice of carrying loaded pistols" and instructing the police to report all cases of evasion and what they were doing to enforce the act. At this point Wortley's assistant tactfully asked if this was "the sort of matter on which the Secretary of State's pleasure should be taken."[110]

The upshot is that any figures of guns licenced under the 1870 act represent only a portion of the firearms in the kingdom. Still, they provide a unique base number of privately owned firearms and illustrate fluctuations over the years. The graphs presented in the Appendix show how the number of licenced firearms rose and fell from 1875 until 1964. The key finding for our purposes is that the number of licenced firearms seems to have fluctuated with the level of prosperity along with other consumer goods. The number of weapons does not appear to have affected or been affected by changes in crime rates, either the long decline in the nineteenth and early twentieth centuries, or the sudden rise from the 1930s and especially from the 1950s.

The government now had a national register of firearms, however imperfect, and a licence fee that might discourage poorer people from carrying guns. But it was on notice that further efforts to clamp down on guns would be very difficult, all the more so as violent crime was declining.

Crime and violence were not declining in Ireland, however, and while Parliament carefully guarded the Englishman's right to keep guns, it had been persuaded to pass severe restrictions on Irishmen owning and carrying them without special licence. When the act came before the Commons for renewal in 1881 the Liberal government proposed a five-year extension. The debate on this measure affords a sampling of the attitude of M.P.s toward government restrictions on firearms, even in Ireland. Lord Randolph Churchill described the bill as "a Coercion Bill of the most unlimited character, perhaps, that had ever been introduced into Parliament—a Bill giving power to the Lord Lieutenant to make any regulations he pleased in respect of the carrying, or the possession, or the searching for arms." Sir Edward Watkin found "the necessity of supporting the Bill was one of the most painful incidents in his Parliamentary life, said, it was a very serious thing to refuse to any man the right to bear arms, and Parliament ought to have a record of all such refusals." Mr. T. D. Sullivan pointed out that "the English people would not like to be compelled to give up possession of their arms, for which they had a great affection. In this country there were instances of the abuse of the possession of firearms, yet the Legislature did not propose to take the right of bearing arms from the people."[111] Serjeant Simon asserted: "The persons who would be subjected to the operation of this Bill would be respectable men, not ordinary felons, criminals, village tyrants, or dissolute ruffians." As for the government's claim that it was more efficient to make this a five-year, rather than an annual, statute, Mr. O'Connor reminded the home secretary, Sir William Harcourt, of a speech Harcourt had made in 1875 opposing a long duration for this bill on the grounds that "it would be most objectionable that any Bill suspending important rights of Her Majesty's subjects should be allowed to continue for so long a period as suggested by Her Majesty's Government . . . The liberty of the subject had never been made dependent on the discretion of any Government."[112]

Both Conservative and Liberal governments realized that Parliament would not easily endorse restrictions on guns, but their determination to control private firearms never wavered despite extraordinarily low rates of armed crime. The Liberal government continued mulling over the issue and in 1883 introduced a bill to regulate the possession of revolvers and other firearms and to amend the 1870 Gun Licence Act. The measure would have made it a misdemeanour to carry a loaded firearm in any street or public place within a city, town, or village. If caught with a loaded weapon an individual could be discharged only if he "had reasonable grounds" for believing that carrying it was necessary for self-defence. The bill was dropped after the second reading.

Four years later a Conservative government tried again, with the tireless Wortley now installed at the Home Department. This time the bill was "for the better Prevention of the Felonious Use of Firearms and other Weapons."[113] The text noted a great increase in the use of firearms by burglars and stipulated that anyone convicted of having at the time of commission of a burglary any gun, rifle, revolver, pistol, or other firearms could, at the discretion of the court, be kept in penal servitude for life or for not less than ten years. There is no further notice of the bill, but Wortley and the government were not about to let the issue of controlling guns drop, especially under the leadership of the Marquis of Salisbury, an outspoken critic of the Reform Act and of broad-based democracy in general.

When the town clerk of Ramsgate wrote in January 1888 to complain about misuse of guns and urge control as to the "class of person" who could have them and, second, to urge that all firearms be licenced, his complaint was passed on to the police commissioner of the Metropolitan force.[114] The precedent hit upon for registration of guns was the act to regulate the sale of poisons, which required a careful record of the purchase.[115] The commissioner was asked whether it was possible or desirable to carry out these suggestions. A recorded response, possibly from the commissioner, argued that such a system "would lead to great public dissatisfaction" and asked, "Besides what would be gained by making such a register? The Burglar or thief who arms himself with a revolver—and there are not many such—would certainly not take out a licence, and Public security against thieves would not be increased by any such modification of Licencing Act. I do not see that the advantage to be gained would be commensurate with the irritation likely to be caused." An irritated Wortley failed "to see who will be irritated" and while admitting that stricter firearms registration would not deter burglars added: "I am obliged to press this question as I have reason to know that some members of the Cabinet are anxious that the undoubted public uneasiness on the subject, evidenced by these requisitions from Chief Constables, grand juries and judges, should if possible be . . . allayed."[116] In fact only four such complaints seem to have come into Wortley's hands. Whether it is true that Cabinet members were anxious to take action is problematic, but someone was anxious to do so, for the next year the Foreign Office, seemingly at the request of the Lords, sent a circular letter to Britain's representatives in Europe asking them to report on the laws in the country where they were based on private persons carrying firearms in public places.[117] Their responses were published. It makes interesting if ironic reading, since the English, who always prided themselves on being freer than citizens of arbitrary foreign governments, were polling those same governments on their methods of controlling private firearms. It is notable that the republics were far more permissive than the monarchies, with Russia, for example, having strict prohibition while Switzerland had "no Law of any kind" prohibiting carriage of private firearms. No action was taken. Wortley's Conservatives lost the 1892 election, but twice in the early 1890s Gladstone's Liberal government carried on the campaign to clamp down on firearms. In 1893, on the pretext that a rash of handgun violence and accidents constituted "a serious public evil," the government introduced a measure to restrict ownership of firearms less than fifteen inches long.[118] Herbert Gladstone, the prime minister's youngest son and now undersecretary at the Home Office, seems to have been the architect of the bill. He sketched out the goals in a letter to Asquith, the Home Office Secretary—that a purchaser must have a reasonable motive to purchase, that young persons be prevented from having revolvers, and that police powers be increased to enable them to enforce the law and supervise sales.

He advised Asquith that it was "quite possible that public opinion would accept the proposed restriction in toto" and that "it might run through Parliament pretty easily." He should have been warned by the comment of one of those shown the plan, who labelled it "A drastic scheme," and his own observation that the practice of carrying pistols was increasing; "even ladies are taking to it."[119] The final bill left out Gladstone's requirement that to purchase a pistol an individual must have a reasonable motive. Instead it limited ownership to those over eighteen who had a licence and restricted dealers to those having a licence.

Some members of the Commons were not only unpersuaded, but angry that the bill had been given a second reading. There was a move to reject the first clause, which empowered authorities to search for weapons. Mr. Conybeare proposed that the definition of firearm be amended to exclude toy pistols and "other such harmless weapons." But Gladstone insisted that the definition was satisfactory as it stood, and Asquith rejected the insertion of the words "capable of inflicting grievous bodily harm" as "most objectionable, because serious injury was often inflicted with toys." Charles Hopwood suggested exempting a householder who kept a pistol "for protection of person or property" and observed that the government's claim of numerous gun accidents was not supported by its own investigations.[120]

In fact these statistics record an astonishingly low rate of gun-related violence in the late nineteenth century. The Home Office reported the results of three separate inquiries: hospital figures throughout England for fatal and nonfatal wounds arising from handguns in 1890–92; coroners' inquests on such accidents; and the number of burglars found carrying firearms over five years ending with December 31, 1892.[121]

In the course of three years, according to hospital reports, there were only 59 fatalities from handguns in a population of nearly 30 million people. Of these, 19 were accidents, 35 were suicides, and only 3 were homicides—an average of one a year. The report noted that in the 1890 pistol homicide both the murderer and the victim had been foreigners.[122] The number of injuries treated in hospitals for revolver or pistol wounds over the three years was 226.[123] The coroners' inquests relative to the use of both pistols and other firearms for the same three years was 536, of which 443 were suicides, 49 were accidents, 32 were homicidal, and 12 not known. As for armed burglaries, no policeman had been shot dead, although several had been wounded by gunfire. Over the five-year period only 31 burglars had been found carrying arms, and only 18 had escaped by the use of guns.[124] On the basis of these modest figures the bill was objected to as "absolutely unnecessary . . . and that it attacked the natural right of everybody who desired to arm himself for his own protection and not to harm anybody else." Hopwood suggested that the government legislate with regard to knives and daggers, since the number of murders and suicides committed by them was "infinitely greater . . . than those committed by means of revolvers." As with the 1870 licence statute, this bill was attacked as class legislation. Mr. Conybeare thought it would be better to drop it "so that the efforts of the Government might be devoted to some more worthy measure."[125] The debate was adjourned until the next day, but in light of its reception it was prudently withdrawn. Behind the scenes, however, a House of Lords standing committee was at work during 1894 to produce a more acceptable bill.

The government became more cautious, and when the revised measure resurfaced in 1895 it was sponsored by a private member, the Marquess of Carmarthen, who admitted he would have preferred a bill "providing that nobody except a soldier, sailor, or policeman, should have a pistol at all." Again the justification was the "enormous" number of pistol injuries, which could be counted by the hundred. The bill called for identification marks on pistols; raised the licence fee for selling them to one pound to check the sale of cheap pistols; and gave anyone owning a pistol one month to obtain a licence, which would have to be renewed annually. Herbert Gladstone gave "the experiment" the government's blessing while conceding that "the evil with which the Bill sought to deal was not of such magnitude as to justify legislation by the Government" itself. He then fell back on the rationale that if they "could save one life or one human being's eyesight, then trouble would not be thrown away." He also informed the House that for the last twenty years—presumably since passage of the 1870 licence act—successive home secretaries "had pledged themselves to deal with this question if possible . . . The police were of opinion that a measure of this kind was very much needed, and there was nobody in the country in a better position than the police to know."[126] He also confessed that he didn't think the measure "could reach the majority of cases, but it might reach a considerable proportion of them, and if it saved the lives of eight or ten unhappy lads in the course of a year, and prevented many more cases of serious injury, it would be doing a good work. The question was, Would the Bill be likely to do any harm? He could not see what harm it would do by any possibility."[127] The wholesale restriction of firearms was plainly on the agendas of successive governments and the police, despite the fact that firearms violence was statistically insignificant.

Hopwood again led the attack, pointing to "the utter futility of such legislation, its grandmotherly character, and its disregard of individual liberty."[128] He pointed to the government's earlier figures on the very low rate of gun violence.[129] Hopwood and others branded the bill a piece of "class legislation," which the wealthy would get round while "only those who were sufficiently low in the social scale" would come within the cognizance of the police. "A poor man with a pistol would be haled up by the police, and the man with a good coat would not."[130] Mr. Cyril Dodd opposed the need to apply to the chief of police; "the police were the servants . . . and the people had no intention of making them their masters." While Mr. Pease supported the bill and argued that the licence duty of 10 shillings instituted in 1870 for carrying arms was "inoperative," Mr. Cross found the power to stop and search individuals "monstrous, and ought not to be embodied in a Bill applying generally to the whole country."[131] Others asserted that the restrictions on personal liberty "passed the bound"; it was a sample "not only of grandmotherly, but of great-grandmotherly legislation," "silly and babyish." "They should not be invited to pass Bills like this," Mr. Moulton concluded, "interfering with such a large number of people in the hope that they might reduce an accident list which amounted to something like eight or nine cases a year."[132] Despite vigorous objections the bill was sent to committee. It did not reappear until the twentieth century.

End of a More Civil Era

The nineteenth century ended with firearms plentifully available while rates of armed crime had been declining and were to reach a record low. Even those prone to magnify crime were struck throughout the century by the low level of violence. A

Select Committee on Police of 1816–1818 heard evidence from a police officer that "daring, desperate things seem to be worn out, except daring forgeries"; and John Nares, a police magistrate of twenty years' standing, confirmed this testimony: "The committee have had in evidence, and indeed the observation of every one must have given him the information without the evidence, that atrocious crimes have of late years considerably diminished."[133] In his study of crime in Victorian England J. J. Tobias found that people throughout the country "accepted that criminals were becoming less violent, each generation seeing an improvement over the previous one."[134] In 1831 the reformer Francis Place and the attorney and sanitation reformer Edwin Chadwick agreed that crimes had decreased "in atrocity" and that acts of violence had "diminished."[135] In 1839 a Royal Commission on a Constabulary Force concluded that in the towns "burglaries and depredations in the streets are now rarely accompanied by violence."[136] This satisfactory state of affairs was interrupted in 1862 and 1863, when London experienced the garotting panic. Woundings and assaults rose as violent street robbers pounced upon and choked their victims. Robert Sindall has argued that the media played a key role in creating panic about street crime even as crime was actually declining.[137] Whatever the case about the extent of garotting, Tobias concludes that "over the whole of the century there is evidence, much of it from sources entitled to our respect, that the use of violence in crime had decreased; and the conclusion that this is true seems irresistible."[138]

One caveat must be added. The law on self-defence and the protection of property still held that the householder whose property was invaded could take vigorous action to defend it. Thus, some killings considered self-defence at that time might not now seem justified. Nonetheless, while many homeowners were armed few burglars carried firearms. And although guns were freely available, gun accidents and impulsive shootings were rare, and armed crime was minimal. Undoubtedly contributing to the rarity of armed crime was the fact that statutes such as the 1824 act against vagabonds and rogues punished anyone found carrying a firearm or other weapon "with Intent to commit Felony."[139] Firearms clearly did not contribute to violent crime, but it is unclear whether gun ownership helped reduce it. There was a sturdy tradition of self-defence and legal encouragement to intervene to prevent a felony. The great Whig historian Thomas Macaulay maintained that the right to be armed was "the security without which every other is insufficient."[140] And in the 1870s James Paterson asserted that "in all countries where personal freedom is valued, however much each individual may rely on legal redress, the right of each to carry arms . . . and these the best and the sharpest . . . for his own protection in case of extremity, is a right of nature indelible and irrepressible, and the more it is sought to be repressed the more it will recur."[141] Although we have no way of knowing how many Englishmen actually owned firearms, it is clear that criminals could expect people to be armed and prepared to use force to protect themselves and their property. It is also clear that despite the zeal of successive governments to restrict private ownership of firearms as a source of potential danger to the state, guns did not increase violence and may even have played some role in its steep statistical descent.

5

1900–1953: The Government Takes Control

[It is] . . . a domestic tragedy of the war that the country which went out to defend liberty is losing its own liberties one by one.

—THE NATION, May 1916

The war has brought a transformation of the social and administrative structure of the state, much of which is bound to be permanent.

—REPORT OF THE WAR CABINET FOR 1918

IN 1901 THE CRIMINAL registrar announced triumphantly that "a great change in manners" had taken place: "the substitution of words without blows for blows with or without words; an approximation in the manners of different classes; a decline in the spirit of lawlessness."[1] Like much else in the strangely innocent prewar world, however, that happy state of affairs was to change. After nearly half a millennium both the extraordinary decline in violent crime and the ancient tradition of an armed population came to an end. But this reversal was preceded by the removal of the Englishman's right to be armed.

The era from 1902 until 1918 is characterized in a recent book as "The Emergence of the Interventionist State." Although the legislation that removed the right of Englishmen to be armed was enacted two years later, it was part and parcel of that trend, as was the Pistols Act of 1903, which laid the ground for things to come. Certainly, there was much that deserved intervention. England was still a country of great inequalities. Even as industrial profits rose the real wages of the working class sank.[2] Only 200,000 of the nation's 3 million children, for example, reached secondary school.[3] Reformers were anxious to ease some of the worst hardships of the poor through the introduction of unemployment insurance and old-age pensions. As these programs were being debated, workers began taking matters into their own hands. They flocked to trade unions, which by 1914 boasted 4.1 million members, fully prepared to assert their power. A series of major strikes broke out in 1910. In July a four-day railway strike took place in the northeast, in September a strike in the Lancashire cotton industry involved 120,000 workers while a fourteen-week lockout of boilermakers was under way. In November a mining dispute culminated in a three-day riot. In 1911 a national sailors' and firemen's union strike spread to all ports and was followed by a dock strike. In 1912 a record 41 million working days were lost as a result of strikes.[4] As in the nineteenth century, growing pressure for ameliorating the worst hardships endured by the working class was propelled by the threat of massive disruption.[5] Some government interference seemed necessary to institute public welfare measures. The government was also nervous about the potential for riot or, in the worst case, revolution. The trick was to decide where that government interference and control should stop.

The move toward greater government intrusion in everyday life was bitterly opposed by such luminaries as Hilaire Belloc and A. V. Dicey, who fought "in the last ditch to resuscitate the ideas of mid-Victorian individualism."[6] But the seeds of this switch, according to V. A. C. Gatrell, had been planted at the very beginning of the Victorian era in the campaign for professional police, where he detected a clear preference for security over rights. When the subject was crime, Gatrell discovered that "even in Whig discourse" the natural basis of individual rights was no longer regarded as self-evident. The protection "not of natural rights but of social and political order—equated with the state itself—was elevated into law's primary objective." Campaigners for a national police seemed to consider the principle of liberty "a mere derivative of the principle of order: liberty was what was left over when order was guaranteed." The 1839 Royal Commission on the County Constabulary conceded that centralized policing might reduce liberty, but argued that this measure was essential, since "the [criminal] evils we have found in existence in some districts, and the abject subjection of the population to fears [of crime] which might be termed a state of slavery . . . form a condition much worse in all respects than any condition that could be imposed by any government that could exist in the present state of society in this country."[7] This assessment was not revisited when crime dropped to record lows.

Restricting Firearms

The 1903 Pistols Act was the natural successor of the failed 1893 and 1895 pistol bills and in keeping with greater government regulation.[8] Both of the previous bills had been vigorously opposed and failed to get a third reading. In neither case had the government's real concern been to reduce the use of pistols in crime or in accidents, since the impact of firearms on these was minimal. That situation had not changed. Nevertheless, another bill was introduced in 1903 and this time met with little objection. The Pistols Bill was introduced in the Lords by Earl Donoughmore, who assured his colleagues that it was far less extreme than its predecessors. It restricted purchase of a pistol—defined as a gun with a barrel not exceeding nine inches—to persons over eighteen and not "drunken or insane." Purchasers had to obtain a 10 shilling excise licence, which would be given as a matter of course. Seventeen years later, during the debate on the far broader Firearms Bill, Major Barnes, undersecretary to the Home Office, claimed that the real fear in 1903 had been the callousness toward life engendered by the Boer War. If so, the 1903 act did little to keep pistols from the hands of the calloused. In his study of firearms in England, Colin Greenwood argued that there was little objection to the bill, precisely because it was "weak and ineffective, so full of loopholes that it was unlikely to have any effect in controlling pistols."[9] Indeed, it was soon criticized for that failure. It did have the almost immediate effect of ensuring that pistol barrels grew to a length exceeding nine inches.[10] Greenwood was undoubtedly correct that the Pistol Act's main achievement was reaching the statute book.[11] Perhaps that was the government's actual aim. There were few prosecutions under the act—in 1908 only 26 in all England and Wales, and in 1909 only 16.[12] Either the problem had been very small or the act was not being enforced. And after as before 1903, there was no serious problem of armed crime. From 1911 through 1913 the average number of armed crimes of all types in London—then the largest city in the world—was 45. From 1915 through 1917 this would fall to 15. For the entire country during the years 1908–1912 there were 47 cases in which policemen were fired upon, with 6 policemen killed, another 24 injured. Half of these fatalities occurred in a police battle with London anarchists in 1910. Yet people seem to have been well armed, as the 1909 incident known as the "Tottenham Outrage" illustrates. As London police dashed across the north of the city after a group that had attempted a wages robbery, they borrowed four pistols from passersby while other armed citizens fulfilled their legal obligation and joined the chase. Richard Munday, who recounts this incident, adds that modern Englishmen "might be shocked by such a thought; [but] Londoners then were apparently more shocked by the idea of an armed robbery."[13]

Although firearms were not a serious factor in crime, by 1911 the Liberal government was ready to build upon the 1903 base with a revised Pistols Bill and with extensive pistol controls embedded in a Prevention of Crime Bill.[14] The new Pistols Bill may merely have aimed to stop the evasions of the 1903 act by extending the length of a pistol barrel to fifteen inches, but the crime bill incorporated a host of new controls. The possession as well as the purchase of a pistol would require a certificate from the police. To obtain a certificate an applicant would now need a character reference from a reputable householder. Further, police would be able to stop anyone on the street who they believed might be carrying a pistol and demand to see his certificate. If they found a gun but the owner had no certificate, they could seize the weapon. Ammunition would also be regulated, and manufacturers, wholesalers, and dealers of pistols would have to be registered, keep records, and might lose their registration if convicted of a violation of the act.

In December 1910, while this bill was being prepared, fate intervened. A group of armed Russian anarchists broke into a London jewelry shop. When police arrived, a gun battle broke out. The unarmed policemen were at a grave disadvantage, and three of them were killed and two others injured. Two anarchists escaped and were later discovered and besieged in a house on Sidney Street. In desperation the authorities called upon the army for help. The siege ended when the house burned to the ground with the anarchists inside. Alarm at this incident led to the transformation of the 1911 Crime Prevention Bill into the Aliens Bill, which focused instead on preventing an alien from keeping or using a pistol without permission from his local chief of police. The Aliens Bill never got beyond the first reading. Very likely the government preferred to introduce the more extensive pistol controls it had planned. But it delayed bringing such a bill forward, and then fate intervened again in the shape of the First World War.[15]

During the war there was a further effort to discourage the use of firearms by suspect persons, in the form of a new Larceny Act. In addition to the standard definitions of crime, the act incorporated the crime of loitering with intent to commit a crime, an offence created by the Vagrancy Act of 1824, which permitted preemptive disarmament. Anyone found at night "armed with any dangerous or offensive weapon or instrument, with intent to break or enter into any building and to commit any felony therein," was guilty of a misdemeanour. While anyone found with housebreaking tools without excuse was guilty until proven innocent, the list of tools did not include a firearm. Still, the statute reaffirmed the precedent of criminalizing intent to commit a crime and placed the burden on the accused to prove his innocence. It was an approach Blackstone had found "un-English" when it was used in the 1624 Infanticide Act.[16]

The First World War jolted the British government into drastic measures of a far broader sort. To cope with the emergency it rushed the Defence of the Realm Act through Parliament. This granted the administration vague, enormously expanded economic and legal powers, some at the expense of basic rights.[17] The act gave the government authority over key industries and transport, over import and export, the power to restrict the production, sale, and disposal of firearms, and the right to impose strict censorship on speech and the press. Prominent critics of the war could be imprisoned even if their objections were based on ethical, rather than political, grounds. For example, in December 1915 a British court, using emergency legislation, sentenced two men to six months in prison for publishing a leaflet setting out the Christian doctrine on war "according to the Sermon on the Mount."[18] In one notorious case thirty-four conscientious objectors were dispatched to France, where they were court-martialed and sentenced to death. Thanks to the protests of Bertrand Russell and others, their sentences were commuted to hard labor. Through postal censorship the government compiled lists of 34,500 British citizens with supposed ties to the enemy, and another 38,000 who were under suspicion for some act or hostile association. The Defence of the Realm Act created a whole series of new and proliferating offences for all of which the accused was subject to a court-martial.[19]

While the Defence of the Realm Act might have led to the sort of firearms controls the government had been seeking, and the government later claimed the act had reduced the number of criminals using guns, it does not appear to have affected gun ownership in England.[20] War was not the time to reduce firearms. Millions of men were under arms. Moreover, the government required commissioned officers to purchase their own service pistols, which became their personal property. Furthermore, in case of a German invasion it might be necessary to make use of armed, "well-affected" subjects to defend the realm. Clearly, as in other times of danger the government was torn between curtailing the right to be armed and needing the assistance of armed civilians. *The Times* of January 8, 1915, reported a debate on this issue in the House of Lords, a continuation of a discussion in November 1914. The issue was what measures ought to be taken to protect the realm in case of invasion. There was great confusion in the counties about this, with even basic lines of administrative direction uncertain. The Duke of Rutland argued that the time had come "when it would be well if the instructions were somewhat consolidated." Lord Curzon reminded them of their earlier discussion, when "there was no general idea of what the duty would be in case of invasion of civilians who wanted to take up arms and fight or of civilians, who for various reasons were incapacitated from fighting." All sorts of questions had arisen, among them whether civilians should take up arms. Secret orders had since been sent to lords lieutenant of each county, but these varied considerably and had not been made public. Curzon noted that "we had an almost exact parallel to the present state of things 100 year ago, when everybody awaited an invasion by Napoleon." In the meantime, though, an association of armed volunteers, the Volunteer Training Corps, had been authorized and permitted to wear a sort of uniform. The members of the corps provided all their own equipment, arms, and ammunition or had it donated by subscribers. There were fears in the Lords that this group would be useless and even a danger unless it had proper military training and supervision. But the chief anxiety was that in an invasion these armed civilians might not be recognized as combatants by the enemy, who might make the corps's existence "an excuse for some of the excesses we have seen elsewhere." In time of peril the government turned readily to armed civilians for help. When danger passed and peace returned, it was determined to disarm those same civilians.

The Firearms Act of 1920

Less than a year after the Great War ended, Parliament passed a comprehensive firearms statute that eliminated the right of individuals to be armed. It was the culmination of fifty years of effort by British governments of every political stripe. The announced rationale by the ruling coalition government was, as usual, an increase in armed crime, yet statistics for London show no such increase. The truth was that before there was a British government, the English government had been uneasy about the widespread ownership of guns, especially by those it did not see as "well-affected." And while the public longed for the end of the war, the government approached that eventuality and the return to its normal powers with some trepidation. Regulation 40B of the Defence of the Realm Act, which gave the government the power to impose stringent restrictions upon the manufacture, sale, and possession of all firearms and ammunition, was due to expire on August 31, 1920, nearly two years after the armistice. Private Cabinet papers make clear that the government was afraid not of crime but of disorder and even revolution, the same fears that had fuelled government control measures in the past. According to the Cabinet secretary, Cabinet meetings in the first two months of 1920 had an almost hysterical tone. He left one of these meetings, he wrote, with his "head fairly reeling. I felt I had been in Bedlam. Red revolution and blood and war at home and abroad!"[21] There were real grounds for fear. The Bolshevik Revolution was in full swing. Later in 1920 the Communist party of Great Britain was founded and union membership would rise to 8 million, nearly double prewar numbers. There was every likelihood of renewed industrial unrest, since wages were still low and unions were calling for a general strike.[22] Ireland was descending into civil war. Demobilization was bringing hundreds of thousands of soldiers, many brutalized by a vicious war, streaming home. The prime minister warned the home secretary that the force of 10,000 men he hoped to raise would be "of little use," while other ministers considered distributing weapons to "friends of the Government."[23] Parliament became so alarmed later in 1920 that it passed the Emergency Powers Act, granting the king the power to declare a state of emergency and to give the government those "powers and duties as His Majesty may deem necessary for the preservation of the peace."[24] This statute would be used to combat major strikes.[25]

On February 27, 1918, more than two years before the Defence of the Realm Act was due to expire, the government had
assembled a committee to "consider the question of the control which it is desirable to exercise over the possession, manufacture, sale, import and export of firearms and ammunition
in the United Kingdom after the war." The committee was to
consider "internal policy" as well as arms trafficking and imperial defence.[26] It was chaired by Sir Ernely Blackwell, the
assistant undersecretary of state for the Home Office, and
included three other government officials, the solicitor general for Ireland, an inspector of constabulary, and three men
whose positions have not been identified. Theirs was one report that would not gather dust.

The Blackwell Committee's confidential report is important both for its candor and for its scheme for firearms controls, which the government adopted. There was "no question," the committee agreed, "that the public interest
demands that direct controls shall in future be exercised in
the United Kingdom—whatever may be the policy of other
powers—over the possession, manufacture, sale and import
and export of firearms and ammunition, and the only practical question for consideration appears to be—how this control
can be most efficiently established." It recommended that pistols, revolvers, and ammunition be placed under the most
stringent controls and even recommended curbs on sporting
rifles and air guns. It would give key authority to local police.
Whereas the 1911 bill had instructed police to grant a firearms
certificate to an applicant who had a statement from a reputable householder, the Blackwell Committee gave the local
chief of police full power to determine whether an applicant
was of good character and had a good reason for having the

gun. There was provision for a right of appeal. The certificate would have to be renewed annually. The police would also control ammunition by fixing the quantity purchasable by individuals and clubs and entering that amount directly on a firearm certificate. All manufacturers and sellers of firearms were to keep records. The committee report included the outline of a bill to carry out this scheme.[27] The report's first paragraph and its final summary of recommendations refer to the "right" to purchase, possess, use, or carry a firearm or ammunition, but, as the summary explains, this right would be limited "to persons, who, in the opinion of a Chief Officer of Police, may possess a firearm without danger to the public safety."[28] The secretary of state was to have "general power . . . to make rules for the carrying out of the Act." This clause was incorporated into the Firearms Act and became the means by which the original, more lenient version of the 1920 statute would be transformed into a very different sort of measure.

In the spring of 1920 the timing seemed favourable for passage of sweeping firearms regulation. Crime was not a problem, but the public was repulsed by the violence of "the war to end all wars" and ready to establish the longed-for peaceable kingdom. They had become accustomed to granting government broad powers. Labour turmoil loomed. The administration was apprehensive about the reception of its scheme, but time was of the essence if something was to be enacted before the Defence of the Realm Act expired.[29] The Firearms Bill was introduced to the House of Lords on March 31, 1920, on the customary pretext that there was a crime wave.[30] The Earl of Onslow told the Lords that in addition to helping prevent guns from getting into the hands of criminals and other undesirable persons it would enable Britain to carry out its obligations under the Arms Traffic Convention signed in Paris. Despite the government's contention, however, domestic arms restrictions were not required by any international commitments signed by the British government; the treaty signed at Versailles on June 28, 1919, did not include general arms limitation agreements.[31] The Covenant for the League of Nations that was made part of the treaty did set up a framework for reducing armaments though, and Article VIII of the Covenant provided that the League Council should formulate plans for reduction for the consideration of member governments. This seems to have chiefly been President Wilson's initiative. In his second inaugural address Wilson proposed that a nation's arms be "limited to the necessities of national order and domestic safety."[32] At the fourth meeting of League of Nations, however, when Article VIII was first discussed, the Japanese proposed that the words "national safety" be substituted for "domestic safety." Other delegations promptly agreed. Gerda Crosby, in her book on postwar disarmament and British politics, finds this a significant change, one that "cleared up any doubts remaining as to the general scope of postwar disarmament."[33] Still, when the Firearms Bill was introduced to the Lords no one present seemed to notice the discrepancy. The Lords made no protest about the bill, and even suggested changes to strengthen it. Two months later, on June 1, it had its first reading in the Commons. The scheduled second reading and full debate the following day were canceled. A week later, at 10:49 in the evening, without advance warning, the bill was brought before the House with two other bills scheduled for consideration in the few minutes remaining before adjournment. Only a handful of members were given copies of the bill. Shortt, the home secretary, introduced it as "quite a short Bill . . . which in all probability will commend itself to the House and be regarded as non-controversial." It would keep weapons from the hands of criminals and other dangerous persons but not, he assured members, hamper "legitimate sport." Shortt left the impression that other dangerous persons included soldiers "who had become used to violence in the War" and might become "a menace to the public."[34]

The government's obvious strategy to slip the bill through aroused anger. Members raised all the old objections to restrictions on the right to be armed. The act might be applied to "grant the use of firearms to one class of people and absolutely deny it to another." It would not reduce crime, since "so far as burglars are concerned it will really have no effect . . . there is nothing in this Bill which will adequately deal with them."[35] Only one member, Mr. Jameson, argued that ordinary people needed firearms for their personal protection.[36] Lieutenant-Commander Kenworthy raised a series of objections, describing the new legislation as redundant. He also thought shifting the power to determine fitness for a certificate from a civil magistrate to the police ran "contrary to English practice." Kenworthy then turned to the deeper issue:

> There is a much greater principle involved than the mere prevention of discharged convicts having weapons. In the past one of the most jealously guarded rights of the English was that of carrying arms. For long our people fought with great tenacity for the right of carrying the weapon of the day . . . and it was only in quite recent times that was given up.

"It has been a well-known object of the Central Government in this country," he went on, "to deprive people of their weapons. I do not know whether this Bill is aimed at any such goal as that." Kenworthy then expressed his view of what the people's chief protection against oppression seemed to be in 1920. If the honourable gentleman "deprives private citizens in this country of every sort of weapon they could possibly use," he informed the home secretary,

> he will not have deprived them of their power, because the great weapon of democracy to-day is not the halberd or the sword or firearms, but the power of withholding their labour. I am sure the power of withholding his labour is one of which certain Members of our Executive would very much like to deprive him. But it is our last line of defence against tyranny.[37]

The government's supporters leapt upon Kenworthy's constitutional argument. Major Earl Winterton charged him with holding "the most extraordinary theories of constitutional history and law," in particular that "it is desirable or legitimate or justifiable for private individuals to arm themselves, with . . . the ultimate intention of using their arms against the forces of the state." Dropping all pretence about crime waves, he blurted out, "it is because of the existence of people of that type that the Government has introduced this Bill." Kenworthy interrupted to point out that "the very foundation of the liberty of the subject in this country is that he can, if driven to do so, resist," adding, "I hope he will always be able to resist. You can only govern with the consent of the people." The Earl claimed that before the war the majority of Englishmen "had almost forgotten that there were such things as firearms and it was not necessary that the Home Secretary or the police should possess the powers which are necessary to-day." Those "who wish to overthrow the State by violent means" must not be allowed to obtain firearms.[38] Major Barnes, undersecretary to the Home Office, returned to the constitutional theme to add that the time for that method of redress "has gone." But, he added, "We have in our methods of election, in our access to Parliament, and in other ways, means of redress against the action of the State which in times past were not afforded." By giving the subject "opportunity through Parliament and through the Courts to find redress," he added, "we shall most effectively turn his attention away from using weapons."[39] When the question was put the House divided, with 254 voting in favour of the bill and only 6 against.[40]

The new act required a firearm certificate for anyone wishing to "purchase, have in his possession, use, or carry any firearm or ammunition."[41] The local chief of police was to decide who could obtain such a certificate and exclude anyone of intemperate habits, unsound mind, or anyone he considered "for any reason unfitted to be trusted with firearms." In addition to being certified as temperate and law-abiding, the applicant had to convince the police officer that he had a "good reason for requiring such a certificate." In the House of Lords the government conceded that "good reason" would be "determined by practice." Clearly, both criteria were highly subjective and flexible. The certificate specified not only the weapon but the quantity of ammunition an individual could buy and hold at any one time. Each certificate expired after three years. Renewal involved an additional fee and the need to be requalified.[42] The penalty for a violation of the act was a fine not exceeding fifty pounds—a substantial sum in 1920—or imprisonment with or without hard labour for a term not exceeding three months, or both.[43] The right of individuals to be armed had always been, in the words of the 1689 Bill of Rights, "as allowed by law." This new law, which made the right conditional upon the whim of the Home Office secretary and individual policemen, transformed the right into a privilege.

Between the Wars

In contrast to the Pistols Act, the 1920 Firearms Act seems to have been enforced with vigor. Before the year was out Parliament heard two complaints about overzealous enforcement, and the home secretary, in response to numerous other complaints, issued instructions to assist the police "in carrying out, on a fair and reasonable basis, the administration of the Act."[44] So began the series of classified Home Office directives to police chiefs that defined what constituted a good reason to grant a firearms certificate. The first directive gave these guidelines on the need of a weapon for self-defence: "It would . . . be a good reason for having a revolver if a person lives in a solitary house, where protection against thieves and burglars is essential, or has been exposed to definite threats to life on account of his performance of some public duty."[45] This guideline was far more restrictive than Parliament had been led to expect, but the directive was secret, and neither Parliament nor the public had an opportunity to debate the subject.[46] In 1920, with crime rates quite low, perhaps the actual need for self-defence seemed problematic to the home secretary. Yet over the years, even when the crime rate began to soar, the range of acceptable reasons to be armed continued to narrow. The second criterion, that of fitness, was also spelled out. The chief of police was to be satisfied that the grant of a certificate to the particular person was "without danger to the public safety or to the peace" and must judge this "chiefly by the person's character, antecedents and associates, so far as it can be ascertained."[47]

The number of prosecutions under the Firearms Act was much higher than those for the 1903 Pistols Act. In 1926 there were 618 prosecutions and 486 convictions, the majority for possessing a firearm without a certificate. In 1929 these had fallen slightly, to 386 prosecutions and 290 convictions.[48] If, on the other hand, when the 1920 controls were instituted only a fraction of the hundreds of thousands of guns were registered, those numbers are less impressive.[49] Given the large number of unregistered weapons handed in during special amnesties years later, a great many people may never have registered their guns, but simply kept a firearm at home, some perhaps war souvenirs, to defend themselves and their property.

Armed crime had been very low before the act and continued to decline during the 1920s although property crimes rose. According to official crime statistics the number of all crimes reported to the police went up from 1920 through 1923. Indeed, the 110,206 offences reported in 1923 was the highest figure in the sixty-seven years for which such statistics were available.[50] A dramatic increase in 1923 occurred in shopbreaking and obtaining by false pretences, which rose a startling 85 and 94 percent respectively. But a 1925 report on those homicides and attempted homicides known to the police found a decline from an annual average of 426 homicides in 1909–1913 to 369 in 1923, a drop of 13.4 percent, while burglaries fell from 1,739 to 1,522, a drop of 12.5 percent. No separate record of the use of firearms in these offences was given, but the authors of the report concluded: "Homicide and other crimes of violence against the person are steadily falling. The movement extends, though in a less degree, to assaults and other minor offences of violence which are within the ordinary jurisdiction of the summary courts."[51] The report concluded, "the opinion may be hazarded that crime in general has steadily diminished over a considerable term of years, and in addition the reduction is greatest in the more serious forms of law breaking."[52] The authors did not attribute this drop to the firearms restrictions, but to a decline in drunkenness.[53] No statistics seem to have been collected on the use of firearms in crime just before the Second World War. Figures presented to Parliament, however, do show that in the eighteen months from July 1936 through December 1937 just twenty people arrested in the entire London metropolitan district were in possession of guns, and twelve of these were air guns and one a toy pistol.[54] Only seven had firearms. On average there were about fourteen cases a year of people arrested with firearms. This was a reduction from 1911–1913 and 1915–1917, when the averages were 41 and 18 respectively, although, as Colin Greenwood pointed out, "the greater reduction—41 to 18—was achieved without any real firearms controls."[55] As for causes, a study of homicide on the eve of the Second World War convinced Leon Radzinowicz and Joan King that it was not firearms, but "social and cultural conditions that determine both the murder rate and the penal response."[56]

If the real aim of the Firearms Act was to prevent riot and

revolution, the government was quickly to put it to the test. The period from 1919 through 1922 was swept by major strikes, which provoked a drastic government response.[57] When railwaymen threatened to strike over a wage cut in September 1920, the government divided the country into twelve administrative divisions, declared a state of emergency, and called on citizens to join a citizen guard to combat "the menace by which we are confronted today." The following spring, when miners threatened to strike with the support of other unions—the Triple Alliance—the government ordered preparations to mobilize the territorials and to call up the army, navy, and air force reserves. It also made plans to take control of food, coal mines, and sale of firearms and to regulate public meetings. Prime Minister Lloyd George informed Parliament that the nation faced "a situation analogous to civil war." Some 70,000 men were eventually enrolled in the defence units.[58] The miners went back to work with wage cuts. Strikes diminished in 1922, to be replaced by surging numbers of unemployed and hunger marches. During the 1920s unemployment stood at between 1 million and 1.5 million. By 1932, in the midst of a worldwide depression, the number of unemployed hit 3 million. These miserable conditions led some moderate Englishmen to talk of revolution, but their actions were generally restrained. Martin Pugh finds that the classic form of protest during the 1930s was a small, dignified group of marchers who delivered a petition to Parliament and went home.[59]

From 1920 through 1933 no further legislation was approved dealing with firearms use. Thereafter, despite the low and declining rate of armed crime, the government continued to tinker with gun regulation. As the 1920 Firearms Act did not prevent criminals from obtaining weapons, the Firearms and Imitation Firearms (Criminal Use) Bill was submitted to Parliament in 1933, couched as a preventative measure. At its second reading in the Lords the Earl of Lucan admitted that "the profession of a gunman is, happily, a novel one in this country" but warned, "the combination of the revolver and the motor car has given the criminally minded a power against the community which might grow to serious proportions if it is not promptly and efficiently checked."[60] The Criminal Use Act increased the punishment for the use of a gun in a crime and made it an offence punishable by up to fourteen years' imprisonment for anyone to "attempt to make use" of any firearm or imitation firearm to resist arrest or to prevent the lawful apprehension or detention of himself or another person. Even if a suspect made no attempt to use the firearm or imitation firearm, if he had one, unless he could prove he had it for a lawful object he was liable to an additional seven years in prison. In 1934 a government committee chaired by Sir Archibald Bodkin examined the operation of the 1920 Firearms Act and recommended various modifications, including a clearer definition of firearms and the exemption of more groups from the law.[61] The resulting statute also raised from fourteen to seventeen the minimum age for purchasing a firearm or air gun, but "selling" and "purchasing" did not encompass giving, lending, transferring, parting with possession, accepting, or borrowing, all of which remained permissible.[62] Further amendment followed in 1936, when yet another Firearms Act incorporated more of the recommendations of the Bodkin Committee. These included extending controls to shotguns and other smoothbore firearms with barrels less than twenty inches, transferring machine-gun certificates to military oversight, imposing elaborate regulations on firearms dealers, and granting chief constables the power to add conditions to individual firearms certificates.[63] To incorporate all these amendments into a single statute, Parliament passed the Firearms Act of 1937.[64]

Despite the ever denser thicket of controls on privately owned guns, the government still wanted, and needed, at least some civilians to be experienced in their use. The British National Rifle Association, founded in the nineteenth century, was one of the groups exempt from the restrictions of the 1920 Firearms Act. The National Rifle Association had been launched to promote rifle training and target practice after the French war scare of 1859. Its intent, the secretary for war informed Queen Victoria, was "to make the rifle what the bow was in the days of the Plantagenets."[65] Military-style training was gradually separated from target shooting and finally split when the reserve forces of England were restructured in 1908 by Lord Haldane. In the years before the First World War Lord Roberts, taking his theme from the notion that civilian rifle practice was the modern equivalent of the Plantagenet bow, promoted a smallbore shooting movement that established rifle ranges in towns and larger villages throughout England. It was the Rifle Association that began target shooting as a sport. Yet it was regarded as more than a sport. A 1913 history of sport at Oxford and Cambridge questioned whether shooting should be included, since "target practice ought to form part of the early training of every Englishman."[66]

As the popularity of shooting waned between the world wars the association could count on government, and even royal, support to encourage target shooting in the interests of defence. The association's constitution stated its aim to "pro-

mote and encourage Marksmanship throughout the Queen's
Dominions in the interests of the Defence and the perma-
nence of the Volunteer and Auxiliary Forces, Naval, Military
and Air."[67] In 1920, the year the Firearms Act was passed,
Winston Churchill, then at the War Office, acknowledged the
military value of the NRA's effort and supported the group's
appeal for funds. In 1925 the Prince of Wales praised the organization at a fundraiser:

> Let us tell the world about ourselves fearlessly. We
> like rifle shooting. It really is our hobby. But it is
> something more. Each and every one of us knows
> that war has not ceased, that the continent of Eu-
> rope is a seething pot of jealousy and distrust and
> envy and hatred, and that we may be fighting for
> our honour, our very existence as a nation, within a
> very short time. We love the rifle because it is a
> weapon and because it is not only the right but the
> duty of every citizen to be armed and trained in the
> use of arms. We are not just sportsmen. Let us em-
> phasize the truth. Let us tell all our fellow citizens
> once and for all that we are not on the same plane
> as the golfer or the footballer. We stand, with the
> Navy, the Army, the Air Force and the Territorial
> Army.[68]

Nevertheless, seven years later, despite diminishing levels
of armed crime, the Home Office issued new instructions to
the police, tightening restrictions on firearms certificates. The
original 1920 guidelines had found it "a good reason for having a revolver if a person lives in a solitary house, where protection against thieves and burglars is essential, or has been

exposed to definite threats to life on account of his performance of some public duty." In 1937 the home secretary decided: "As a general rule applications to possess firearms for house or personal protection should be discouraged on the grounds that firearms cannot be regarded as a suitable means of protection and may be a source of danger."[69]

The Second World War

The Prince of Wales's premonition about the likelihood of a European war proved well founded. War returned in September 1939. The following spring, after the German invasion of Holland and Luxembourg, the British chiefs of staff launched plans for a home defence force. Now the goal was to arm, not disarm Englishmen. "Every Briton between 17 and 65 years of age who had ever handled a weapon and did not suffer from any physical disabilities" was eligible to serve as a Local Defence Volunteer in a Home Defence Force.[70] It was a return to the seventeenth-century militia. Within twenty-four hours of Anthony Eden's call for volunteers, 250,000 men in England, Scotland, and Northern Ireland had come forward. Eventually 1.5 million men joined the renamed Home Guard.[71] The government claimed it was not its policy to arm civilians, but urged those "who felt they had the time to train" to volunteer for the Home Guard before vacancies were filled by a new scheme—conscription. Many men were armed at first only with sticks, old rifles, sabres, and even pikes.[72] The government pleaded with British subjects and foreigners for weapons with which to arm the volunteers. Thousands of guns were donated, and rifle clubs were converted into training centers for recruits. A group of Americans, stirred by the plight of British civilians, formed the American Committee for Defence of British Homes. From June 1940 this group and thousands of other Americans contributed sporting rifles, shotguns, pistols, binoculars, and ammunition to the cause.[73] Thanks to American weapons ordered by the British government and these gifts, the 1.5-million-man Home Guard was soon armed "on a scale of one rifle for every two men." With these weapons, an official study attested, the country "had been enabled to face with confidence the threat of immediate invasion."[74] Yet fears remained about equipping the growing numbers of men, and in February 1941 Parliament was reminded that the "Home Guards could not fight against a tommy gun with a claymore or a pike." As late as May 1945 the government was still asking civilians to give or sell it their automatic pistols "because no such weapons were made in the United Kingdom and the government relied on the United States and on civilian owners in this country to meet their requirements."[75] Since members of the Home Guard were a military unit in the service of the Crown, they were exempt from the need to obtain a firearm certificate.[76] On December 4, 1941, three days before Pearl Harbor, the War Office gratefully accepted a gift of revolvers for the Home Guard from the people of the state of New York.[77] Later that month weapons from the American Committee for Defence of British Homes were presented to a London battalion.

While the British turned to armed civilians in the emergency, at least one American on the scene was doubtful it would work in the United States. Asked his opinion of the British resort to use of a Home Guard, a citizen militia, General Raymond E. Lee, based in Britain in 1941, replied:

> the British system, in his opinion, was not for us.
> Whatever the usefulness and wisdom of issuing le-

thal weapons in large quantities to the average citizen or working man in this country [Great Britain],
in his opinion, we can't think of doing so in the
United States. Of course, there are many places
where it would be all right, but the trouble is that
one could not discriminate, so what about the myr-
iads of foreigners, suspicious characters, strikers,
Communists, and thugs who would find themselves
with rifles and machine guns in their hands in
Pittsburgh, Jersey City, Detroit, Fall River, and other
centers of dissension and subversion.[78]

Lee's response is particularly ironic given the contributions of
weapons the Home Guard received from individual Americans and the number of private arms in the hands of the citizens of each country both then and today.

With national survival at stake, the British government
worried less about an armed Home Guard than about the col-
lapse of morale among the general population. In October
1940 members of the Grenadier Guards at Wanstead were ordered to be in readiness "to help the police in the event of rioting or severe bombing in the East End of London."[79] No riots occurred. On the contrary, the Home Office found that
many Londoners felt a "mild chagrin" when the focus of the
air attacks moved elsewhere.

Did the wide distribution of firearms between 1939 and 1945
increase armed crime? On the contrary, during the war crime
dropped despite the enormous numbers of military men assembling in England during the buildup for the Normandy
invasion. In the London area there was less crime in 1940 than
in 1939 and less in 1941 than 1940. Thefts of cars fell "to almost

nothing," bicycle thefts fell, and, possibly as a consequence of the blackout, burglary during the evening declined dramatically. The *Evening Standard* late in 1941 reported an increase in casual violence, but women out at night claimed they were not in danger.[80] The violent crime that did occur continued the "longstanding feature" of close association with alcohol.[81] The war did cause some novel crime problems. Toward its end almost a tenth of London crime was attributed to deserters. By 1942 homeless men were roaming the streets. Three armed Canadian deserters held up a bank in Leicester Square. This incident led to a police operation in which the papers of some 1,400 people were examined and 100 arrested. Despite the claim of lower moral standards during the war, the crime that did occur has been described as not a crime wave but at most "a crime ripple."[82]

Peace and Disarmament

With the return of peace the government's aim was once again to remove guns from private hands. Efforts were made to ensure that the weapons servicemen had as souvenirs were not brought back to Britain. Yet in 1946, when a six-week amnesty was conducted to permit people to surrender illegally held firearms, some 75,000 weapons were handed in, including 59,000 pistols and 1,580 machine guns or submachine guns.[83] With peace came vigorous enforcement of stringent controls on firearm certificates, as silently modified in 1937. The abrupt switch must have been disconcerting. The home secretary was soon peppered with questions about the police failure to renew lapsed certificates. On October 17, 1946, his response gave Parliament a rare public glimpse of the secret directive: "I would not regard the plea that a revolver is wanted for the protection of an applicant's person or property as necessarily justifying the issue of a firearm certificate."[84] Individual cases, particularly those of well-heeled applicants who appealed the decision to deny them certificates, cropped up in the newspapers. In January 1946, only months after the end of the war, Colonel Sir Frederic Carne Rasch, a deputy lieutenant of Essex and chairman of the Chelmsford Justices, appealed the refusal by the chief constable of Essex, a Captain F. R. J. Peel, to renew a firearms certificate that permitted Rasch to have ammunition. Rasch told the appeals committee he had been allowed to keep a .45 pistol for protection. "I live in a rather large, rambling house with my wife. It is in an isolated position. There is no cottage within 200 yards. I am over 67, and, therefore, not very useful with my fists. Only a short time ago a house was broken into in my neighbourhood and a person was badly hurt."[85] Rasch won his appeal. In January 1951 the Reading Divisional Court discussed the question of whether it was a good reason within the meaning of the Firearms Act for a householder to possess firearms and ammunition to protect himself and his property against armed burglars. In this instance the chief constable of Reading appealed against the decision of the recorder at Reading Quarter Sessions to overrule him and allow Sir John Henry Maitland Greenly to have a permit to get ammunition for an automatic pistol.[86] The chief constable's attorney, a Mr. Glazebrook, said he did not think Sir John Greenly's reason for wanting the ammunition—protection of home and property—was a good one, although that was the reason put forward by 75 percent of the applicants. The lord chief justice replied that it depended on individual circumstances, whereupon Glazebrook presented the justification invoked by government spokesmen from that day to this: "while it was the policy of the police not to arm themselves and to prevent burglars being armed, there was good reason why householders should not be armed." The chief justice replied, "If criminals changed their policy and were not armed, it would be a good reason." Glazebrook retorted that a minority of criminals were armed. "Moreover," he continued, "this sort of thing would provide arsenals from which burglars could take arms." The chief justice and his two colleagues were not persuaded and dismissed the constable's appeal, adding that this was a matter of discretion for the chief constable, but the applicant had the right to appeal to quarter sessions.

The incident raises two interesting points. First, the justices and 75 percent of applicants were unaware that the Home Office was instructing the police to deny certificates for weapons intended to protect home and property. And second, Glazebrook's rationale for the denial, that the police were disarmed, ignores the reason for their lack of weapons. It was not to persuade criminals to do without weapons. There were laws that severely punished criminals who carried firearms during a crime. The police were unarmed because the English people in the nineteenth century would not have tolerated an armed police establishment. Despite the scepticism of the Reading Divisional Court, the notion that an unarmed police force ought not to have to confront armed criminals and that criminals might steal weapons from law-abiding subjects has become an argument for disarming the public.

One further illustration of the obsessive police scrutiny of private firearms is the case of Sheriff Hamilton at Dunfermline, who dismissed the appeal of Colonel Gavin Brown

Thomson of Fife against the chief constable, who had refused him permission to take a sporting rifle to Germany, where he was to be stationed, on the grounds that it constituted the "export of firearms" from Britain to Germany.[87]

The return of peace did not produce a rash of gun-related crimes, despite fears to that effect voiced in Parliament from time to time. In response to a question on the issue in November 1952 the lord chancellor provided figures for cases in the Metropolitan Police district in which firearms were present though not necessarily involved. These numbers were as follows: 1948, 48; 1949, 28; 1950, 39; 1951, 14; and, for the first nine months of 1952, 17. Although Lord Lawson muttered, "Undoubtedly, the public mind is much disturbed on this question at the present moment," the figures actually showed a declining rate of armed crime.[88] Not for the first or last time, press attention had created an impression at odds with the actual state of affairs.

Looking back over the first half of the twentieth century, what conclusions can we draw about the relationship between firearms, violence, and the law in England? Several key points seem clear. First, the rate of armed crime was exceedingly low as the century began, and it continued to decline. Armed and violent crime was rare and getting rarer. The easy availability of firearms before 1920, indeed the availability of guns in the centuries before that, did not increase armed crime and may have deterred crimes, since armed civilians had peacekeeping responsibilities. Second, the Firearms Act of 1920, which took away the traditional right of individuals to be armed, was not passed to reduce or prevent armed crime or gun accidents. It was passed because the government was afraid of rebellion and keen to control access to guns. This was a longstanding goal. Nevertheless, in times of grave national peril such as the First and Second World Wars, the government armed the people so they could protect themselves and the state. The Home Guard of the Second World War had 1.5 million members. They did not misuse that trust. Nevertheless, once the emergency was over, administrations were anxious to remove privately held weapons. English governments had long wanted, and finally obtained, complete discretion over which Englishmen might be armed. The old notion that people had a duty to protect themselves and their neighbours, so central a part of English law enforcement and of the English constitution over many centuries, was reversed. Government, in its expanding control of numerous aspects of community life, now found guns inappropriate for individual defence. Personal safety could and ought to be left to the state. Unarmed civilians and unarmed police could convince criminals that it was unnecessary to carry guns. It was a serious gamble, but one that Parliament was prepared to accept on the assumption that law-abiding individuals, such as themselves, could still be armed, and the more accurate premiss that armed crime was negligible.

6

1953–2000: Only the Criminals Have the Guns

There is an easily identifiable police attitude towards the possession of guns by members of the public. Every possible difficulty should be put in their way. No documentation can be too rigid, no security requirement too arbitrary, which prevents guns coming into the hands of criminals.

—POLICE REVIEW, October 8, 1982

ENGLAND IS NO LONGER a peaceable kingdom. Scholars of criminology have traced a long decline in interpersonal violence since the late Middle Ages until an abrupt and puzzling reversal occurred in the middle of the twentieth century.[1] Indeed, a 1997 study comparing crime rates in eleven industrialized countries found the figures for England and Wales among the highest.[2] And a statistical comparison of crime in England and Wales with crime in America, based on 1995 figures, discovered that for three categories of violent crime—assaults, burglary, and

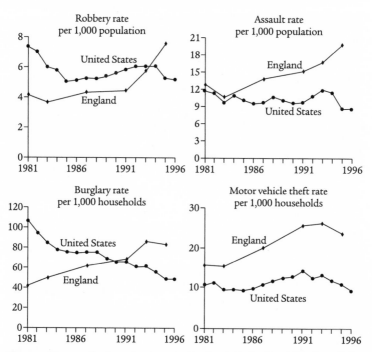

Figure I. Rates of selected crimes in England (including Wales) and the United States, 1981–1996. *Source:* Patrick A. Langan and David P. Farrington, *Crime and Justice in the United States and in England and Wales, 1981–96* (Washington, D.C.: U.S. Department of Justice, Bureau of Justice Statistics, 1998), p. 2.

robbery—the English are now at far greater risk than Americans (see Figure I). Whereas in America there were 8.8 assaults per 1,000 persons in 1995, in England and Wales there were 20 assaults per 1,000. Robberies in England and Wales were 1.4 times higher than in America and far more likely to take place while residents were at home. Burglary was nearly double the American rate. Although figures for rape and homicide are still substantially higher in the United States, they have been sharply declining since 1992 while English rates have been steadily rising.[3]

How do firearms figure in this sharp upturn in violence? Guns were freely available during the many years of rapidly declining levels of violence but were seldom used in anger. Few murders were premeditated, and those committed "in hot blood" usually made use of implements lying about or fists and feet. Although guns seldom contributed to violent crime, they may have helped keep it in check by deterring would-be burglars and muggers. By contrast, violence has increased as guns and all other potential weapons have been ever more tightly restricted. As the numbers of legal firearms have dwindled, the numbers of armed crimes have risen. Guns in the hands of average, law-abiding Englishmen had rarely been used for criminal purposes. Illegal guns in the hands of modern criminals are increasingly used. The London Metropolitan Police in the first six months of 1991 recorded 1,431 indictable offences in which firearms were involved, the majority of which were armed robberies.[4] Such figures raise a host of questions, the most pressing being how this increase in violent crime came about and what policies the government has used, clearly without success, for the past fifty years. I cannot answer the more vexing problem, why the English have become more brutal toward one another, but will concentrate on the more modest goal of assessing the relationship between firearms, the law, and violent crime.

The Escalating Crime Rate

The renowned criminologist Sir Leon Radzinowicz, musing sadly in 1977 on the "great growth of crime everywhere," chose England as "a good point of departure." He recalled how in 1959 he had described the criminal statistics for England and Wales as "grim and relentless in their ascending monotony." At that time the volume of crime recorded annually had risen from one half to three-quarters of a million offences in just over 10 years. That rapid pace was quickly eclipsed: "We had passed the million mark within five years," he reported and in 1977 "the annual total exceeds two million." Looked at another way, in 1900 police in England and Wales had recorded fewer than 3 crimes for every 1,000 people; in 1974 they recorded almost 4 crimes for every 100 people, over thirteen times as many indictable offences.[5]

With 1901–1905 serving as a baseline for crimes of violence, malicious woundings were up 174 percent by 1938 and 386 percent by 1948. Murder rose 74 percent by 1938 and 110 percent by 1948; felonious woundings had risen 127 percent by 1938 and 194 percent by 1948; and robbery increased by 117 percent in 1938 and 449 percent in 1948.[6] Of course the 1930s were a period of deep economic depression, and 1948 was just after the Second World War, both typically periods of increased crime. But from 1948 to 1963 the figures rose again, often even more steeply. The murder rate fell somewhat after 1948 but by 1961 was still up 94 percent from the beginning of the century and by 1963 up 98 percent. Felonious woundings went up 440 percent by 1961 and 450 percent by 1963. The rise of malicious woundings was steeper still—up 1520 percent by 1961 and 1779 percent by 1963—and robbery rose 959 percent by 1961 and 1013 percent by 1963. These trends have continued. Contact crime for the years 1991–1995 increased by 60 percent in rural areas, by 48 percent in urban areas, and by an astounding 91 percent in inner cities.[7]

Radzinowicz found similar increases up to the 1970s in Germany, France, Sweden, and the Netherlands and suggested various causes—"a reflex of affluence," more opportunities for crime, more anonymity, social breakdown.[8] Neither Radzinowicz nor other criminologists cited the availability of guns or other weapons as a factor in either the cause of crime or its deterrence.[9] In 1954 there were only twelve cases of robbery in London in which a firearm was used, and on closer inspection eight of these were only "supposed firearms."[10] But armed robberies in London rose from 4 in 1954, when there were no controls on shotguns and double the number of licenced pistol owners, to 1,400 in 1981 and to 1,600 in 1991.[11] In 1998, a year after a ban on virtually all handguns, gun crime was up another 10 percent.[12] Murders with guns dropped in 1999, from an average of 62 a year to 54 a year; and armed robberies have declined along with robberies in general. But despite the new handgun ban the number of incidents of "guns used for violence against the person" has increased steadily, prompting a House of Commons report deploring "a generally increasing trend in the misuse of firearms."[13]

Law, Disorder, and Public Safety

To understand the approach the British government has taken to violent crime and to the right of the individual to self-defence, it is important to recall the problems it faced after the Second World War. Many wartime government powers—such as food and price controls, and control over exports—continued for some years. Food rationing, for example, lasted until 1953. The Labour government felt a duty to sort out every major problem, and there were plenty of problems in postwar England. In response to a series of economic crises, the government promoted regional development for especially distressed areas. Between 1945 and 1951 it built 1.35 million houses.[14] A number of industries including the steel industry were nationalized. It launched a variety of programs that created a true welfare state. The Family Allowances Act gave families a weekly payment for all children after the first, while the public was protected against the vagaries of life with a National Insurance Act, the Industrial Injuries Act, and a National Health Insurance Act. The standard of living for much of the population rose to new levels of comfort. Perhaps having successfully run so much of the economy during the war, and having stretched its authority into new areas afterward, perhaps with its cradle-to-grave attention to the individual's welfare, when the issue was crime and individual protection the government had no compunction about insisting that it have what amounted to a monopoly on the use of force. Where the greater good was at stake, a disarmed public must have seemed more important than any one individual's safety. Coincidentally, this new power would help suppress internal disturbances—which may, as in 1920, have been the actual aim. At any rate, the English public, accustomed to government's handling of so much in their lives, seemed neither especially surprised nor moved to protest.

Postwar periods customarily produce higher crime rates, and the years following the Second World War were no exception. Nevertheless, English men and women felt there was a new and worrying element to the surge. What became known as juvenile delinquency was on the rise, and the blame turned to a generation raised during the trauma of war. These new offenders were often organized in gangs armed with chains, brass knuckles, and switchblade knives. In November 1948 the House of Lords pondered the changed world that was postwar Britain. *The Times* reported the discussion under the headline "Causes and Cure of Crime: Moral Standards in National Life." Subtitles for the speeches give the gist: "Homely Virtues Vanishing," "A Moral Problem," "Grave Figures for 1948," "Lack of Respect for Courts." The Lords were alarmed at a great increase in crime between 1938 and 1947, especially the very large percentage of crimes committed by those under twenty-one They generally agreed about the causes: first came the war, then the increased cost of goods that made them worth stealing, the "breakdown in home life," and finally "the growing loss of respect for the law." Viscount Simon added "a decreasing respect for the rights of the individual regarding private property." In his reply the lord chancellor focussed on the loss of respect for the courts, especially the juvenile courts, and took issue with their approach: "There was an idea that every child so dealt with was entitled to his first crime much as it used to be said that a dog was entitled to his first bite." Then he added "another factor of immense importance . . . that large areas could not really claim any longer to be a Christian country." He seems to have had the increasing numbers of divorces in mind. The Lords agreed that the Home Office, the Ministry of Education. and church leaders should work together to tackle the problem.[15] If such discussions took place, they singularly failed to return Britain to a peaceable kingdom.

The British government was fully prepared to revamp old policies or adopt new ones in the name of crime prevention. Government strategies from the 1950s to the present have tackled the problem from three directions: disarming the people, treating juvenile offenders leniently, and reducing prison sentences and police personnel, both with the aim of cutting costs. All three tactics seem to have fuelled the rise in violent crime. The first of these, police monopolization of the use of force, has the most immediate relevance to the relationship between violent crime and privately owned guns.

Disarming the People

The disarming of the populace was well on its way by 1950, thanks to ever more stringent interpretation of the 1920 Firearms Act. A series of secret instructions to police from the Home Office continued to reduce the number of acceptable reasons for being permitted to own a gun. The 1937 instructions had cautioned: "As a general rule applications to possess firearms for house or personal protection should be discouraged on the grounds that firearms cannot be regarded as a suitable means of protection and may be a source of danger."[16] In 1964 another set of instructions asserted: "It should hardly ever be necessary to anyone to possess a firearm for the protection of his house or person . . . this principle should hold good even in the case of banks and firms who desire to protect valuables or large quantities of money; only in very exceptional cases should a firearm be held for protection purposes." Five years later the Home Office instructions proclaimed: "It should never be necessary for anyone to possess a firearm for the protection of his house or person."[17] Since 1969 the number of certificates issued for purposes other than defence—usually sport—has also been deliberately cut, again as a result of secret Home Office policy. From 1989 to 1996, for example, while population and crime increased the number of firearms certificate holders declined by 20 percent.[18] The Home Office instructions on criteria for issuing gun certificates were classified until 1989, despite a 1972 report questioning whether decisions to grant certificates, "a matter of considerable importance to the general public," should remain "a matter for individual decision of chief officers and courts" and complaining that the criteria were "nowhere set out in any statute or other legal instrument."[19] There was no public debate or consultation at any stage in the implementation of this Home Office policy, which thwarted the intent of the Firearms Act and effectively removed the 1689 right of Englishmen to have arms for their defence. The only reason accepted for having firearms was gun sports, and sports are not constitutionally protected. In 1997 N. P. Chibnall, private secretary to the Royal Courts of Justice, clarified the legal situation when asked whether the Bill of Rights was still in force in its entirety. He pointed out that although there had been amendments to some provisions in the Bill of Rights, "The particular provision allowing protestant subjects to bear arms for their defence suitable to their condition and as allowed by law has not been amended, but it is of course subject to the numerous restrictions on the right to bear arms of different kinds, including firearms contained in subsequent legislation." Chibnall added that the use of firearms "for purely sporting purposes is not protected by the Bill of Rights."[20]

Were the government and civil service on good legal ground when they altered the intention of a statute and eliminated a constitutional right without legislative amendment? T. S. R. Allan, in a penetrating essay on the administration of the law, writes: "The whole of our public law . . . is premised on the view that the statutory powers of officials and public authorities are confined by the words of the relevant statute, properly construed. No one may be obliged to act contrary to his own wishes—whether for the public good or his own—because government ministers or officials think it desirable."[21]

Notwithstanding government controls on firearms, the ancient common-law notions of self-defence and the actual duty to intervene to protect others remained in force and in mind. Two statutes, the Prevention of Crime Act of 1953 and the 1967 Criminal Law Act, altered the law behind those traditional concepts, perhaps forever. Repeated government lectures on the foolishness of taking independent action in the face of an assault on oneself or others, of the need to let the experts—the police—handle such matters, did the rest.

The government unveiled this new approach, one in line with its expanded powers and pretensions, in 1953 with the Prevention of Crime Bill. This was designed to ban public carriage of all offensive, or potentially offensive, weapons and to transfer to the police sole responsibility for the protection of individuals. The first parliamentary debate on the measure was on February 26, when it came to the Commons for its second reading. The secretary of state for the Home Office, Sir David Maxwell Fyfe, argued that the public was upset over a level of violent crime that he claimed was "roughly treble the prewar rate." While he conceded "many of these offences do not necessarily involve the use of offensive weapons," the bill focussed exclusively on such weapons. English governments had long sought to prohibit private individuals from carrying firearms in public places, but the new approach went far beyond that goal and was, as Fyfe himself admitted, "drastic."[22] With the stated goal of preventing crime, the bill prohibited the carrying of any sort of weapon or potential weapon "without lawful authority or reasonable excuse." A constable could arrest without warrant anyone he had "reasonable cause to believe to be committing an offence" under the act if he was "not satisfied as to the person's identity or place of residence, or had reason to believe it was necessary to arrest him to prevent the commission of any other offence in which an offensive weapon might be used."[23]

Definitions were crucial. "Public place" was defined as any highway or other place to which at the time the public had or was permitted to have access. The definition of "offensive weapon" was more complex. There were three categories: the first two were articles "made or adapted for use for causing injury to the person," the third, more vaguely, any article "intended by the person having it with him for such use by him."

Not only did the bill greatly extend police power and open the way to arbitrary arrest, but also, as in the vagrancy act, it shifted to the person arrested the burden of proving his innocence. This, together with confusion over the third category of so-called offensive weapons—common articles carried for the purposes of using against another person—caused considerable dismay. Fyfe repeatedly insisted that the good citizen had nothing to fear. The bill was for his protection. "We have," he reminded the Commons, "a long and honourable tradition which rests on confidence derived from experience of the good sense and judgment of the police: and beyond the police lie the courts which, we may be sure, will not frivolously or vexatiously convict under this Bill." Fyfe was closely questioned about his contention that violent crime had risen sharply. Just two weeks earlier the government had defeated an effort to reinstate corporal punishment for some types of violent crimes by insisting that crime rates were declining.

And although one member regarded the bill as "only another extension of the firearms acts," many others were struck by "the enlargement in an important way of the power of the police." Four objections were raised repeatedly in both the Commons and the Lords:

> It created a new crime, hitherto unknown to the law.
> It gave new power in certain circumstances to arrest without a warrant a person in a public street.
> It was vague in some of its terms.
> It put the burden upon a person who might be innocent to stand in the dock and prove his innocence.

As an M.P. for Southgate summed it up, the bill "in some ways goes against all our concepts of justice—that is, by presuming guilt before it has been proved—offends us in many ways." It would be far better and simpler, another M.P. pointed out, to impose a greater penalty after trial if a weapon had been used or carried.[24] It is significant that rather than taking that route, the government preferred to ban the public from carrying any item of use for self-defence. Moreover, any article carried for defence was thereby branded an offensive weapon intended to cause harm. Since individuals were not to be permitted to protect themselves, the burden for their protection was left solely to the police. Ministers never explained why this dramatic reversal of centuries of common law was preferable to imposing a greater penalty on criminals who used weapons. Their decision is all the more remarkable since until 1953 the criminal use of firearms and other offensive weapons was negligible.[25] During this first debate the Commons spent little time considering the impact of the bill on the basic right of self-defence and what that might imply for the crime rate. The subject did come up twice but was quickly dismissed. Mr. Bell, an attorney, posed the example of a man in possession of "a neutral object" such as a walking stick for defending himself against possible attack, but concluded: "I do not think that this small category of cases will cause much difficulty." A representative from Northern Ireland, Lieutenant Colonel H. M. Hyde, told of a woman employed in the House of Commons whose route home led across a heath where attacks had occurred. She had armed herself with a knitting needle and just a month earlier had been able to drive off a youth who tried to snatch her handbag by jabbing him "on a tender part of his body." Hyde asked whether it was to be regarded as an offence to carry a knitting needle or other object for self-defence. The attorney general, Sir Lionel Heald, was asked to deal with the issue of the innocent person, afraid for his safety, who carried some means of protection. He expressed his belief that if "in a special case" someone "really has justification for carrying a weapon . . . because he lives on a lonely common and so on . . . he would be found to have a reasonable excuse" but insisted that "we ought not to mind discouraging members of the general public from going about with offensive weapons in their pockets, even for their own protection." He added: "It is the duty of society to protect them, and they should not have to do that . . . the argument of self-defence is one to which perhaps we should not attach too much weight."[26] This was an extraordinary statement given the government's contention that the bill was needed to combat a crime wave.

Heald's advice not to attach "too much weight" to the issue of self-defence was ignored by the Commons in their final debate a month later. Michael Higges offered an amendment that nothing in the act should make it an offence for a person to carry a weapon whose only purpose was to defend himself or persons with him against unlawful attack. He asked whether it was the intention of Parliament that a person whose only motive was that of self-protection, or protection for his wife and children, should be prosecuted and punished for carrying some implement in case of attack. Although the government wanted to discourage people from carrying weapons even for protection, there were plenty of people in England "who may have good reason for carrying some means of protecting themselves." He felt it wrong that in "this important matter" so much should depend upon the facts of the case and reasonableness of magistrates, leaving the accused to prove his innocence. Ronald Bell, who seconded the amendment, argued that self-defence should be excepted from the purview of the bill. He echoed Blackstone's argument for the natural right of self-defence, that although society ought to undertake the defence of its law-abiding members,

> nevertheless one has to remember that there are many places where society cannot get, or cannot get there in time. On those occasions a man has to defend himself and those whom he is escorting. It is not very much consolation that society will come forward a great deal later, pick up the bits, and punish the violent offender . . . A Bill of this kind, which is for the prevention of crime, ought not to strike at people doing nothing but taking reasonable precautions for the defence of themselves and those whom it is their natural duty to protect.

Fyfe, speaking for the government, dismissed the concern about self-defence as "a normal matter in the law." But, he added, the government did not "wish to lend themselves to the support of the proposition that it is right or necessary for the ordinary citizen to arm himself in self-defence. The preservation of the Queen's peace is the function of the police, and . . . it would be a great pity if anything were done explicitly by statute to condone actions which imply the inability of the forces of law and order to maintain the Queen's peace."[27]

The amendment was withdrawn. When it was clear that the bill would pass, another member asked that the act not be permanent. "This bill, which is unusual, which gives the authorities special powers and which lays the onus of proof on the accused, is not in the general interests of the British people, who have the traditional rights of freedom."[28] The proposal was rejected.

In the House of Lords there were from the outset opposition to and deep scepticism about the Prevention of Crime Bill. Although the government conceded that the bill would not stop determined criminals, it insisted that law-abiding citizens would not be harassed. Police would need a reasonable cause to believe a citizen was carrying a weapon before accosting him, and could arrest him only if they were not satisfied as to his identity or residence. In the government's view the carrying of offensive weapons was "anti-social." The Lords were then given the modern rationale for disarming law-abiding citizens: "the more the ordinary citizen arms himself, the more excuse is there for the person who intends to perpetrate something unlawful to arm himself so that he can achieve his end." The government felt "the task of protecting citizens of the country should be left to the police." Lord Saltoun moved that discussion of the bill be postponed for six months.[29] He agreed that criminals would not pay attention to this law, especially since the penalties involved were small, but the law-abiding would be hurt by it. The object of a weapon was to assist weakness to cope with strength and it was this ability that the bill was "framed to destroy." "I do not think," he added, "any government have the right—though they may very well have the power—to deprive people for whom they are responsible of the right to defend themselves." He warned, "unless there is not only a right but also a fundamental willingness amongst the people to defend themselves, no police force, however large, can do it." Saltoun branded the government position on self-defence a "revolutionary doctrine" and cited legal authority for the obligation of the individual not only to defend himself but to assist the police when asked.

"Not at all happy about this Bill," Lord Jowitt assumed he spoke for the whole House in his alarm over "the drastic powers" given to the police. Saltoun suggested that the bill be made annual so Parliament could see how well it worked. Lord Derwent maintained that any article used for defence should automatically become a defensive, not an offensive weapon and, like Jowitt, endorsed the idea of a time limit. Others agreed. Since the bill was supposedly the result of public clamor it seemed to some lords "panic legislation." As one lord reminded his colleagues, "it is one of the duties of this House to try and save the nation from what may be its own precipitate folly." The lord chancellor rejected the notion that this was panic legislation and pointed out that the home secretary had considered the bill's duration and concluded that "it should find a place in our permanent law."[30] Saltoun's amendment to postpone debate failed by a vote of three to sixty.

Later in April, with the Lords sitting as a committee,

Saltoun moved another amendment, this time to insert language to enable persons suffering from bodily weakness or infirmity to carry a weapon for self-defence.[31] He noted that at the turn of the century, when "nobody thought anything about a man who had to go home at night carrying something with which to protect himself," London had far less crime than in 1953. But there was opposition to the scope of his amendment, and Saltoun withdrew it.[32]

Despite rejecting these amendments the Lords remained chagrined by the bill. At the final reading on May 15 Lord Jowitt hoped that eventually it might become possible to repeal it: "I can only hope that the process of time will show that the powers are unnecessary." Lord Saltoun had a final warning for his colleagues: "This Bill is going through and therefore there rests upon your Lordships the duty of watching carefully how the Government discharge the new responsibility they have undertaken and if you are not satisfied, of drawing public attention to it from time to time."[33]

The second transformation in the common law on self-defence arose from the impact of the Criminal Law Act of 1967. The aim of that statute was to overhaul criminal law by abolishing the old division of crimes into felonies and misdemeanours. In the process the common-law standard that threatened persons must, in certain circumstances, retreat before resorting to deadly force was altered. Instead the act simply authorized a person to use such force as "is reasonable in the circumstances" to prevent a crime or assist in the arrest of offenders or suspected offenders.[34] Although the act made no reference to the right of personal defence against an unjustifiable attack, it did specifically modify common law. As interpreted by modern legal authorities the former "technical rules about the duty to retreat" have been superseded and that issue is now "simply a factor to be taken into account in deciding whether it was necessary to use force and whether the force was reasonable."[35] The Court of Appeal formulated the current rule as follows:

> It is not, as we understand it, the law that a person threatened must take to his heels and run . . . but what is necessary is that he should demonstrate by his actions that he does not want to fight. He must demonstrate that he is prepared to temporise and disengage and perhaps to make some physical withdrawal, and that is necessary as a feature of the justification of self-defence is true . . . whether the charge is a homicide charge or something less serious.[36]

This revision would seem to strengthen the rights of those who kill or injure someone in self-defence, but the reverse has been the case. Everything has turned on the understanding of what constitutes "reasonable" force against an attempt to commit a crime. Extreme force has been held not to be justified in an instance in which there was an attempt merely to attack or destroy property. The legal position seems to be that the only thing someone threatened with robbery can do by way of defence is "to give the robber blows and *threaten* him with a weapon."[37] An attack on one's own home, still one's castle at common law, also leaves the homeowner limited in his or her defence, since the intruder might only be threatening property, and any use of what might be seen as excessive force to protect the home will be considered unreasonable.

The combination of these two statutes, which put so much emphasis on the interpretation of "reasonable," has thrown the law on self-defence into disarray and seriously disadvantaged individual citizens. One scholar found it "unthinkable" that in drafting the Criminal Law Act of 1967 "Parliament should inadvertently have swept aside the ancient privilege of self-defence. Had such a move been debated it is unlikely that members would have sanctioned it." Still, she is optimistic that we can "expect the legislature to consider the wider problems posed by the use of force. In view of the inadequacy of existing law, there is some urgency here."[38] Her article was published more than twenty-five years ago, and nothing has yet been done.

How have these two statutes disadvantaged victims of attack? During debate on the 1953 act the government had assured Parliament that a law-abiding person would not be hurt by it and that it would be reasonable to carry an article for protection when travelling in dangerous areas. But although the defence of having a reasonable excuse for carrying some such article remains available, prosecutors have vigorously pursued possible breaches while the courts have given reasonable excuse "a restricted interpretation."[39] Consider the following case:

> The defendant was stopped by police running on a
> road on the evening of May 15, 1973 and found to be
> carrying a length of polished steel, a two foot
> length of cycle chain, a metal clock weight and a
> studded glove. He said he had these for his protec-

tion because he had been threatened by a gang of youths. He was charged under the 1953 Act. At his hearing it was determined that on several occasions a group of youths had chased him or threatened him with assault. He had reported these incidents to the police. The justices found at his hearing that he believed there was an imminent threat against him. This fear proved well-founded for sixteen days later he was attacked and beaten so badly he was hospitalized. The justices held he had a reasonable excuse for carrying the weapons and did not convict.

The prosecutor appealed the case to the Queen's Bench Divisional Court. This court decided that the defendant did not need to carry all four weapons for protection and that a reasonable excuse to carry a weapon must be related to an imminent and immediate threat of danger at the time they are carried. The regular and routine carrying of weapons was not sanctioned. The judges found no reasonable excuse and sent the case back to the lower court with a direction to convict.[40] The fact that the defendant was in real fear every time he went out or that he had notified the police who failed to protect him cut no ice with the Queen's Bench justices. They were applying the principle enunciated by Lord Widgery in the case of *Bryan v. Mott* that for the carrying of a weapon to be "reasonable" the "threat . . . must be an imminent particular threat affecting the particular circumstances in which the weapon was carried."[41] Lord Widgery also determined that it was reasonable for a man who actually had been attacked to carry something to defend himself for a day or two, "perhaps a little longer," but stretching this to seven days was "very close to the borderline."[42]

Even when an individual has used an implement to save his life when no other help was available, he is still likely to be prosecuted. This happened to Eric Butler, a fifty-six-year-old British Petroleum Chemicals executive.

> In March 1987 two men assaulted Butler in a London subway car, strangling him and smashing his head against the door. No one in the car came to his aid. Later Butler testified "My air supply was being cut off, my eyes became blurred and I feared for my life." In desperation he unsheathed a sword blade in his walking stick and slashed at one of them "as my last means of defence," stabbing the man in the stomach. The assailants were charged with unlawful wounding but Butler was also tried, and convicted of carrying an offensive weapon.[43]

Merely threatening to defend oneself can also prove illegal, as an elderly lady discovered. She succeeded in frightening off a gang of thugs by firing a blank from a toy gun, only to be arrested for the crime of putting someone in fear with an imitation firearm.[44] Use of a toy gun for self-defence during a housebreak is also unacceptable, as a householder found who had detained with an imitation gun two men who were burgling his home. He called the police, but when they arrived they arrested him for a firearms offence.[45]

The problem of self-defence is not the only troublesome aspect of the 1953 act. As M.P.s had feared, there has been considerable difficulty about the legality of carrying ordinary articles that are neither made nor adapted for causing injury. Among the items that courts have found illegally carried with offensive intentions are a sheath knife, a shotgun, a razor, a sandbag, a pickaxe handle, a stone, and a drum of pepper. An Edinburgh taxi driver was charged for carrying two feet of rubber hose with a piece of metal inserted at one end as protection against violent passengers, even though some taxi drivers had been attacked and seriously hurt in that city.[46] A tourist who had used her pen knife to protect herself when some men attacked her was convicted of carrying an offensive weapon.[47] Possession of a broken milk bottle was held to be illegal although the defendant had intended to use it to commit suicide. As Smith and Hogan explain in their criminal law textbook, "*Any* article is capable of being an offensive weapon." They do add that if the article is unlikely to be able to cause an injury, then the onus of proving the necessary intent to do so will be "very heavy."[48] Of course an article unable to cause an injury would be useless for self-defence.

The 1953 act also has some strange anomalies that prejudice anyone planning to protect himself or herself. In his textbook on criminal law Glanville Williams has given the example of a man carrying a wrench for protection. If he intended to use it merely to frighten an attacker rather than to strike him, it would not be an offensive weapon. If used on the spur of the moment when an attack took place it would not be an offensive weapon under the act. If a person wasn't carrying a wrench but snatched one from an assailant or spied one and used it when attacked, he would not be guilty of having it with him, and it would not be an offensive weapon. But it would be an offence to carry a wrench for protection, since self-defence, according to the Prevention of Crime Act, is not considered a reasonable excuse for having such an article in a public place.[49]

Why isn't self-defence a reasonable excuse? According to

Williams, the English are not allowed to make a habit of carrying a weapon or other article for defence, because every weapon could be used for that purpose and "the excuse could be used by thugs as well as by honest men."[50] The English government and society have staked a great deal on the theory that criminals might decide they needed to be better armed to commit felonies if ordinary citizens were able to carry some means of protection. As A. J. Ashworth explained it, the law also assumes that the carrying of a weapon "manifests a willingness to cause (or at least, to threaten) injury, and that the carrier therefore constitutes an identifiable source of danger to public order." This prohibition gives police the authority to intervene at an early stage. In addition, noted Ashworth, it is thought that "a sceptical approach to 'innocent' explanations for carrying an article offensive *per se* is amply justified by the threat to public order which even a weapon originally brought out for an innocent purpose might present." However, he argued, this offence is a "preparatory crime," which goes much wider than the usual law of attempts and "almost inevitably requires proof of an intent to commit a particular category of crime against a particular person." The 1953 act specifies neither the magnitude nor the injury nor even a particular victim. Such a broad prohibition brings with it "the need . . . to preserve a balance between public protection and individual liberty."[51]

Thoughtful legal experts have been chagrined at the failure to provide that balance. There is also concern that by requiring the accused to prove his innocence the 1953 act is a departure from the "golden thread" of English criminal law "for which no special justification has been advanced."[52] Two cases described by Glanville Williams, both of which occurred after

Ashworth wrote, would seem to justify his plea for balance between public protection and individual liberty.

> In 1978 a man, O'Shea, feared he was about to be set upon by a gang of youths. While defending himself, he accidentally killed one. The court rejected his plea of self-defence and sentenced him to four years in prison. On appeal his sentence was affirmed.

> In 1980 Shannon was attacked by a bully—a heavily built man who had previous convictions for violence and had threatened Shannon's life. Shannon fought back and witnesses described the fight (evidently one-sided) as "pretty frightening." Shannon testified he was held by the neck and was being dragged down and "kneed." He lashed out with a pair of scissors and inflicted a fatal blow. The jury heard a great deal of questioning about how Shannon happened to be carrying scissors, an issue irrelevant to the charge. In the event the jury found him guilty of manslaughter. The Court of Appeal reversed the decision, not because of the verdict, but because of a fault in the judge's charge.[53]

These cases, which seem to deny individuals a right to use deadly force, even accidentally, in self-defence, puzzle and disturb legal scholars. Williams has noted that "for some reason that is not clear, the courts occasionally seem to regard the scandal of the killing of a robber (or of a person who is feared to be a robber) as of greater moment than the safety of the robber's victim in respect of his person and property." He argued that the requirement that an individual's efforts to de-

fend himself be "reasonable" was "now stated in such miti-
gated terms as to cast doubt on whether it still forms part of
the law."[54] Given the narrow interpretation of reasonable excuse, Smith and Hogan maintain that a new state of affairs
prevails that "may qualify the important principle that a man
cannot be driven off the streets and compelled not to go to a
public place where he might lawfully be because he will be
confronted by people intending to attack him. If he decides
that he cannot go to that place unless armed with an offensive weapon, it seems that he must stay away. He commits an
offence if he goes armed."[55]

Since 1953 it has been the government's contention that
prevention of violence is the responsibility of the police. People are not to take matters into their own hands. Indeed, they
are more likely to get hurt or to hurt someone else if they attempt such a response. If fearful for their safety they are to
contact the police. If they witness a crime they are not to intervene, but to alert the police. The old common-law duties to
protect oneself, one's family, and one's neighbours and to intervene to stop a crime have been vigorously discouraged. In
1958 Lord Chesham assured the House of Lords that the government supported "the British principle that it is the right
and duty of each citizen to preserve the peace and bring male-
factors to justice, with the corollary that the police are merely
paid to act on the citizens' behalf."[56] In the interest of the
public good crime prevention is to be, and increasingly has
been, left to the constable. Yet Ashworth politely asked:
"When the law is unable to provide adequate protection of an
individual, might it not be permissible for him to carry a
weapon in order to defend life and limb? In the scope of the
defence of 'reasonable excuse,' we encounter an issue which is

constitutionally as fundamental as the justifications for the offence itself. Public order is at stake, certainly. But so is individual liberty—in some cases, the very right to life."[57]

Treating Juvenile Offenders Leniently

The aftermath of the Second World War brought to fruition in England an attitude toward offenders that is part of a general European trend, important for its impact on violent crime and remarkable because leniency toward criminals contrasted starkly with severity toward the law-abiding citizen's right to protect himself or herself.[58] For reasons both philosophical and economic, fewer criminals have been incarcerated than before the war, and those who have been imprisoned were given shorter sentences and seldom served more than a fraction of those.[59] The official response to concern about the increase in juvenile crime was to treat juveniles more leniently in hopes of rehabilitating them. The Criminal Justice Act of 1948 endorsed this policy. When the Commons took up the issue of juvenile offenders, Mr. Royle opposed "the principle that any court should have the power to sentence any person under 17 years of age to imprisonment as we know it now" and argued that since the school-leaving age was fifteen they should be counted as children to the age of sixteen. Mr. Hynd agreed that the people they represented would generally "regard with horror the prospect of boys and girls being sent to prison under the age of 17."[60] Earl Winterton disliked the use of the word "children," since boys of seventeen served in the army and navy, but he suggested that the bill be modified so that young persons could not be sent to prison unless there was no other way to deal with them.[61] Ultimately Parliament decided that the Criminal Justice Act of 1948 should go even further. It forbade a court to impose imprisonment on anyone under twenty-one unless it felt there was no other way to deal with the offender.[62]

The results of these policies toward juveniles have not been reassuring. Police in the 1950s complained of "teddy boy" gangs who were "against everybody and everything" and who "resort[ed] to violence at the slightest disagreement." A study of crimes of violence in London from 1950 to 1960 found that although the majority of those convicted were over twenty-one, in each year studied the increase among young offenders was greater than that of other groups. Two-thirds of violent sexual attacks, assaults on police, and attacks in public places were committed by offenders under twenty-five.[63] The aim of protecting juveniles from the harsh environment of prison was laudable, but alternative means of reform were not sufficiently successful to prevent an increase in juvenile crime or to protect the law-abiding public.

Reducing Sentences and Police

More lenient policies have had little better success in reforming criminals. During the 1950s nearly half of the offenders from every age group had previous records for nonviolent crimes, and 40 percent of these had three or more previous convictions. This trend brings us to the second shift in government policy, the use of alternatives to prison for offenders of all ages.[64] It became government policy not to incarcerate those who committed nonviolent crimes and to release violent offenders more quickly. Prisons were overcrowded, new ones are expensive, and keeping someone jailed costs money.

And so a 1990 Home Office White Paper, "Crime, Justice and Protecting the Public," argued for more of the strategies that for forty years had failed to stop, let alone reverse, steeply increasing rates of crime. It recommended that courts combine community service, probation, and curfews so that more offenders convicted of property crimes could be punished in the community, on the grounds that punishment in the community was better not only for the offender but also for the victim. Maximum penalties for theft and for burglary, except in the case of burglary in homes, were to be further reduced. Courts were to be required to consider a report by the probation service before giving "a custodial sentence" and "to give reasons for imposing a custodial sentence, except for the most serious offences." More use was to be made of financial penalties, especially compensation to victims. The report did recommend making time served in prison closer to the actual sentence, so that "all prisoners [would] serve at least half their sentences in custody" and prisoners serving sentences of four years or more would no longer get parole "if this would put the public at risk." This recommendation was presumably meant to placate the public, for the report noted that people were less tolerant of violence and wanted severer punishment. On the other hand, the report also claimed that there was a "growing awareness that prison is usually not the best way of dealing with many less serious property crimes."[65]

Almost all these White Paper suggestions merely confirmed what had become standard practice. Courts seldom imposed maximum penalties even for serious crimes if it would involve more than five years' imprisonment. More than 90 percent of those convicted of statutory wounding between 1950 and 1960 were sentenced to less than half the maximum term, and 60 percent of those imprisoned were sentenced to less than two years for offences carrying maximum terms of ten years or more. Not only did prisoners routinely serve only one-third of their sentences, but the average length of those sentences declined from 1957 to 1960.[66] Some offences were also downgraded. For instance, from 1993 the police increasingly charged assault offenders with "common assault" rather than the far more serious "wounding."[67] By contrast, the penalty for possession of a firearm or imitation firearm during the commission of a crime or at the time of apprehension was seven years, a harsher penalty than for rape or for most other violent crimes. By the late 1980s the courts began giving longer sentences for rape and serious violence, presumably in response to public concern. In 1987 80 percent of those convicted of serious violent crimes received sentences of at least five years, compared with only 30 percent in 1984, and rape offenders were made to serve one-half instead of one-third of their sentences.[68] Even in dealing with violent offenders the courts relied more on fines than on any other method.[69]

In 1996, as crime continued to soar, yet another official report outlined yet another government strategy on crime control. The authors boasted that crime had declined from 1992 to 1995, but what that meant was that the rate of increase had fallen. The report criticized the 1990 approach and called for "honesty in sentencing": a prisoner must serve the full term ordered by the court, and automatic early release would be abolished.[70] Longer prison terms have followed. As a result of that policy, coupled with rising crime, the prison population in England and Wales grew from 1995 through 1999 to 125 inmates per 100,000 inhabitants, well above the European Union average of 87 per 100,000.[71] Even so, honesty in sentencing did not really mean serving a full sentence, merely the insistence that prisoners earn their release. And although the report called for an automatic life sentence for a second conviction for a serious crime, the authors maintained that the "great advantage of a life sentence is its flexibility."[72] Indeed, two years after the 1996 report the government was still encouraging courts to send fewer criminals to prison and to use community-based alternatives.[73]

Recent studies make it clear that the number of previous offenders at large is even greater than the new policies would suggest, because for five main categories of violent crime—murder, rape, robbery, assault, and burglary—fewer and fewer offenders are apprehended. Between 1981 and 1995 the risk of alleged murderers' being caught fell 12 percent.[74] For rape it fell by 63 percent, for robbery by 40 percent, for assault by 66 percent, and for burglary by 78 percent. This meant that in 1995, the year before the government report just cited, a murderer in England had a 50 percent chance of being convicted, but a rapist only a 10 percent chance. And whereas in 1955 a robber had a one-in-two chance of being caught, by 1975 this had slipped to a one-in-three chance, and, by 1995, to less than a one percent chance of conviction.[75] There is little to deter the criminal. Comments of police inspectors in a 1960 Royal Commission report still hold more than forty years later: "Year by year since 1954 crime has risen throughout the country, and the sharp increases in crimes of violence against the person and against property are particularly disquieting" and have led to the "belief in some quarters that crime pays, and the criminal statistics of the past few years lend strength to this belief."[76]

The decline in rates of apprehension is not a result of limited police powers. English police may not be routinely armed, but they can stop and search anyone they believe may have an offensive weapon, illegal drugs, or stolen property. They can conduct warrantless searches. They can hold a suspect for a time without permitting him access to a lawyer, and evidence they gather illegally is not automatically excluded. One reason for the decline in rates of apprehension has been an unwillingness or inability to hire more police. During a period in which crime quadrupled in London, police numbers did not increase at all, and in many areas they fell.[77] The *Sunday Times* in April 2000 found Southampton, a city of 215,000, frequently able to muster only 7 officers to patrol the streets and only 10 officers for duty on evening shifts, often fewer. In Reading, with 200,000 people, the number of police on duty sometimes fell to 10, and in Herefordshire some emergency callers "will not see a police officer for three days."[78] By comparison, Lille, a French city with a smaller population than Southampton's, had 150 police on duty on a Friday night that month, and Jackson, Mississippi, with 200,000 inhabitants, had 48 officers on patrol and 44 more on hand for emergency calls. A senior officer in an English city of 175,000 was reluctant to provide information on police strength: "We could not possibly publicise the numbers. It would destroy public confidence and be an invitation for every criminal and his dog to come here." The shortage of police is even worse in the countryside where police stations have been "rationalised"—that is, closed or consolidated.[79] As a result, in 1999 more than 70 percent of rural communities had no police presence. "Thanks to inadequate funding and modern policing methods," Edward Leigh, a Conservative M.P. pointed out, "you can have one police car roaming around 600 square miles."[80] In parts of

New Forest calls to the police go to Southampton, some forty miles away. Crime has become so menacing that "fear of burglary and armed robbery" has been a factor in the closure of rural post offices.[81] In 2001 England's Police Federation was preparing to announce that it was powerless to prevent crime in some parts of British cities and presented the home secretary with the results of a specially commissioned international study that drew what a *Times* reporter described as the "most startling comparison," between London and New York. The study reports that New York City had one police officer for every 161 citizens, London one for every 290 people and, as proof of the value of the New York approach, pointed out that between 1992 and 2000 New York had a 42 percent increase in police and a 54 percent drop in crime, whereas London had a 10 percent increase in police and a 12 percent rise in crime.[82]

To respond to complaints without raising costs, the government has turned in earnest to the people. After nearly fifty years of insisting that most peacekeeping be left to the police, the authors of the 1996 report called on the public for help. To spot crime they called for formation of neighbourhood watches, business watches, vehicle watches, farm watches, and street watches. They also urged further recruitment and greater reliance upon "special constables," volunteers who serve as police in their spare time and have full powers of a police constable.[83] The increased use of closed-circuit television has been touted as a substitute for additional police personnel. Cameras in parks and business areas can record crimes on film and, it is alleged, deter would-be offenders.[84] Britain now has more surveillance cameras than any other Western country.[85] In sum, the English public have got the worst of both worlds. Self-help has been sternly discouraged. Police have been given expanded powers at the expense of civil liberties. Their government has severely restricted their right to self-defence with the assurance that society will protect them. But society has failed in that obligation and has left them at the mercy of criminals.

Use of Guns in Crime

Violent crime has been rising, but have firearms been involved? Police and government statistics point to their increased use but magnify the impact by requiring the police to list as a firearm "involved in crime" any gun "fired, used to threaten or used as a blunt instrument, or carried for possible use," as well as any firearm (even an antique one) stolen during a crime, handled, or obtained by fraud or forgery.[86] These Home Office statistics also include as "firearms involved in crime" children's airguns and imitation guns. Even with this catchall approach the number of crimes of violence in which the perpetrators were charged with carrying firearms or imitation firearms was very small and tended to increase with the overall increase in crime. In 1950 firearms were involved in 17 of 1,150 cases of violence, and in 1967 in 44 of 1,919 cases, most of which involved adolescents with air pistols.[87] If we consider only indictable crimes of violence in which a firearm was actually used, as opposed to "involved," the percentages are even more modest. In 1957 only 2.3 percent of serious crimes used firearms. In 1962 the share had risen to 3.3 percent, but this increase was accounted for "almost entirely" by incidents in which airguns were fired at victims without causing injury.[88] Of the small fraction of serious firearms offences, those in which legally owned weapons were also involved were a small fraction. For example, of the 152 homicides committed from 1992 through 1994 involving a firearm, only 22, or 14 percent, of the guns had been legally held. Theft of legal firearms is the usual reason given for reducing numbers of weapons legally held, but in only 5 percent of these 152 homicides was the weapon used believed to have been stolen.[89] There has been a similar pattern in Scotland. Of the 669 homicides from 1990 through 1995 only 44 were committed with firearms, and only 3 of these, or .4 percent, were committed with licenced firearms.[90]

Firearms Atrocities Provoke Gun Restrictions

The fact that legally owned firearms were almost never used in serious crime did not deter English governments from continuing to tighten gun controls. The number of firearm certificates has been steadily reduced, and gun licence fees have been raised.[91] From 1973 through 1978 fees for grant and renewal of a firearm certificate were increased by 714 percent and 800 percent, respectively, and for grant and renewal of a shotgun certificate by 1200 percent and 800 percent.[92] Legislation was also passed to bring other types of weapons under control and finally to ban handguns altogether.[93] The introduction of a requirement for a shotgun certificate demonstrates the way English governments have used firearms regulations to advance an agenda other than public safety, sometimes in lieu of meaningful action to protect the public.

The notion of bringing shotguns within the certificate system had been considered for some time. But when the home secretary, Sir Frank Soskice, studied the matter in 1965 he decided that requiring certificates for the over 500,000, and possibly as many as 3 million, shotguns in legitimate use would burden the police and "not be justified by the benefits which would result."[94] Before the year was out Soskice was replaced at the Home Office by Roy Jenkins, who reconsidered the matter and came to the same conclusion.[95] Then fate intervened. On August 12, 1966, two London policemen approached a parked car containing three men. One of the occupants, Harry Roberts, shot both policemen dead while an associate dashed to the waiting police car and shot the driver three times, killing him. The murder weapons were handguns. Britain's "greatest manhunt" was on.[96] Two of the culprits were quickly arrested, but the third eluded the police for three months, while the case dominated the news. The public was enraged and demanded that capital punishment, which the government had abolished provisionally the previous November, be reinstated. Instead, Jenkins announced plans "to end the unrestricted purchase of shotguns!" He claimed that "criminal use of shotguns" was "increasing rapidly, still more rapidly than that of other weapons."[97] His statistics included all sorts of offences, most involving damaged property, poaching, and threats, not armed crime. This evidence had been available to him when he had decided that requiring certificates for shotguns was an unproductive use of police time. Jenkins' motive seems to have been to divert attention from reinstatement of capital punishment. If that was his goal, he succeeded, but, as Munday and Stevenson reckon it, "at the cost of approximately half a million man hours of police time per year over the ensuing twenty years, and far more than that since 1988."[98] The new restriction was embedded in the groundbreaking Criminal Justice Bill of 1967 discussed above, where, as Part V of a complex measure, it attracted little attention in the Commons.[99] The Lords did debate it and found little justification for the new controls.[100] Many lords were convinced it would have no effect on criminals who wanted to obtain shotguns, a fact that Lord Stonham, undersecretary of state at the Home Office, conceded.[101] But Stonham gave the usual response—it would make it more difficult for a criminal to get such a weapon—and asked the Lords to support this "honest attempt, the best we can make, to deal with a real problem." The undersecretary noted the provision for certification of shotguns was "the beginning of our plans, and the one which we thought would best give us control." The bill passed without further challenge to Part V.

The following year the shotgun certification program was incorporated into the Firearms Act of 1968, which consolidated the 1920 Firearms Act, subsequent amendments to it, and a measure on airguns and shotguns that regulated purchase by youths between the ages of fourteen and twenty-one.[102] The new act also incorporated the Firearms Act of 1965, a hastily drafted measure that gave police greater powers to search and arrest without warrant, penalized carrying a firearm with intent to commit an indictable offence, created the offence of armed trespass, regulated yet again the carrying of firearms and ammunition in a public place, increased the minimum length of shotgun barrels, and raised penalties. This scatter-shot measure seems to have been designed to forestall any increase in violence that might follow the abolition of hanging.[103] Gun controls and shotgun registration were a diversion from the issue of the ending of capital punishment. The following year Jenkins pushed through controls for the more powerful type of imported airgun, although

Colin Greenwood was unable to find "a single case in which this 'specially dangerous air weapon' featured in a crime or accident."[104]

Two major firearms restrictions have been imposed since 1968, both in response to particular atrocities committed with guns. Without such provocation governments were unable to get tighter restrictions, as the Conservative government's Home Office Green Paper of 1972–73 demonstrated. Its premisses were bluntly set out in the foreword: firearms use in crime was growing; in particular use of shotguns was growing; "while determined criminals will usually manage somehow to acquire firearms, society should through legal controls . . . seek to make this as difficult as possible"; "the only effective way of doing this is to reduce society's total gun inventory"; "consequently a considerable minority of law-abiding citizens must be subjected to increased regulation and restriction of their firearms ownership and use patterns." The report and the uncheckable and problematic statistics on which it was based came under attack, and no bill was introduced.[105] Nine years later two government orders increasing gun licence fees were disallowed by the House of Commons by an overwhelming majority.[106] It took the channelling of public outrage roused by firearms atrocities to enable the government to enact more draconian restrictions. Before considering these new acts three important points deserve to be highlighted. First, very few legally held weapons, even stolen ones, were used in crime. Second, English governments were quick to concede that criminals "will usually manage somehow to acquire firearms," but nonetheless insisted that the only effective way to reduce the number of firearms used in crime was to impose ever tighter restrictions on those fewer and fewer legally held weapons. The only effort to reduce the pool of illegal firearms has been an occasional amnesty during which they could be handed in. Finally, without some spectacular massacre, the English public was satisfied that the high level of firearms restrictions was sufficient.

Two atrocious massacres, both perpetrated by men who acquired their firearms legally, did occur during the thirty years after the 1968 Firearms Act. The outrage over each was channeled into enactment of stricter firearms regulations. The first of these two crimes was the Hungerford massacre of August 1987. Michael Ryan was a twenty-seven-year-old former paratrooper and resident of Hungerford, a town of eight thousand. On that summer day he dressed in a combat jacket and, brandishing a gun in each hand, went on a shooting spree. His first victim was a woman having a picnic with her children in Savernake Forest. He returned home to kill his mother and their dog and then wandered out, eventually killing sixteen people and wounding another fourteen before taking his own life. As *The Times* put it, Ryan had "stalked Hungerford, dealing out death and injury at his personal whim."[107] The ordeal ended eight hours after it started when Ryan, trapped in a secondary school, shot himself. The public was shocked that this deranged killer had got his cache of weapons legally. There was less focus on the fact that he was able to deal out "death and injury at his personal whim" for eight hours because a disarmed community and a disarmed police force did not have the means to stop him. Armed police had to be brought in from outside.

Several days later another mass shooting took place in Bristol. A cry went up for more firearms controls, and by late 1987 the government introduced a bill that became the 1988 Firearms Act. That act has been regarded with some justification as the final eradication of the Englishman's constitutional right to have arms for his defence, because shotguns, the last type of firearm that could be purchased with a simple show of fitness, were brought under more stringent controls, similar to those on pistols and rifles.[108] The Conservative government had hesitated to "impose a 'good reason' requirement on the possession of shotguns," for fear of "massive noncompliance . . . a very large number of guns will simply disappear."[109] Pressure from the Labour party apparently overcame government caution.[110] The result was a modified version of the "good reason" requirements for handguns, with police required to grant a certificate unless they could show that the applicant had no good reason for having a shotgun. In practice, however, police have tended to impose their own "good reason" requirement. The act also imposed a security condition that enabled the police to demand costly security arrangements before granting a certificate, and for the first time shotguns were to be registered. A ragbag of restrictions culled from the rejected 1972–73 Green Paper were included. No research or evidence was presented that these measures would solve any particular problem. Government logic on the efficacy of the act was as follows. Hungerford could have no "absolute guarantee against Ryan," nor could "changes to statutory law . . . prevent criminals from gaining access to guns"; nevertheless with the new act Parliament could "hope to reduce the risk of tragedy and make it more difficult for criminals to get guns" and "shift the balance substantially in the interests of public safety."[111] This ambivalence was echoed in Parliament. Members argued that since most "professionally organised criminals find no difficulty in obtaining unlawful weapons in the so-called black market . . . we should not deceive ourselves into believing that a more punishing regime for the shooting community will somehow prevent another crime, or the tragedy of Hungerford, because it will not." One M.P. pointed out that Ryan might have seized a bus and rammed it into a queue of people, killing as many; another warned about the "bureaucracy of incredible proportions relative to the practical results" that stricter controls would mean. But the American example, with its large numbers of firearms homicides and suicides, was cited as a model the English did not wish to follow.[112] No one pointed out that Britain's firearms restrictions were already the strictest of any democratic country's. No tactic was suggested to reduce criminal access to illegal firearms other than an amnesty for handing in guns. No one drew attention to the painfully slow police response to the emergency. On the contrary, M.P.s for Hungerford and Bristol congratulated the police for "their speedy and well-coordinated action."[113] The 1972–73 Green Paper, with its removal of the last right of Englishmen to have arms for their defence, its extension of police powers to stop and search, its emphasis on restrictions without proof of benefit and of admittedly marginal value, became law with little scrutiny. The public wanted action to prevent mass murder. Parliament gave them new restrictions and subjected them to greater police powers.

The second massacre occurred nine years later. On the morning of March 13, 1996, Thomas Hamilton, a suspected pederast known to the police and known to be mentally unstable, walked into a primary school in Dunblane, Scotland. In a matter of minutes he shot sixteen young children and their teacher and wounded ten other pupils and three other teachers before killing himself.[114] Scotland has its own legal system, but Scots are subject to legislation passed for the United Kingdom, including firearms legislation. Hamilton had held a firearm certificate for some years, although according to all the rules he should never have been granted one. Indeed, he had been refused membership in several gun clubs. The evidence presented to Lord Cullen, who chaired the formal inquiry, revealed that the police had been asked to revoke his gun licence but despite seven investigations had done nothing. The Cullen Commission received evidence and advice from a wide range of groups and individuals and considered a great array of proposals. The Home Office presented statistics that it claimed demonstrated a direct correlation between the number of guns owned and the rates of criminal violence in Britain and the United States, Europe, and Australia. These statistics have been attacked as seriously distorted; areas in England, America, and Switzerland with the highest rates of gun ownership were in fact those with the lowest rates of violence.[115] Indeed, using Home Office statistics for the same set of countries James Hawkins found that *"firearms* homicide correlates closer with *car* ownership than it does with firearms ownership." The Home Office chose not to submit its data on firearms ownership by constabulary area in England, which showed a *negative* correlation.[116] Among other submissions to the commission was a statement from the Labour party, which found crimes from legal firearms "unacceptably high," although only 9 percent of homicides were caused by firearms of which just 14 percent had been legally held.[117] Before Dunblane, firearms homicides in Scotland had been rarer still. Of the 669 homicides between 1990 and 1995, only 44 were committed with firearms, and of these only 3, or .4 percent, involved licenced firearms.[118]

In the end the Cullen Commission recommended a variety of new controls on gun clubs, better police procedures with more emphasis on the fitness of the applicant to have a firearm, and "consideration" of restrictions on self-loading pistols and revolvers.[119] John Major's Conservative government had decided to accept the Cullen recommendations and not to ban handguns. The Labour party proposed that single-shot .22 handguns, which needed to be reloaded after each shot, should remain legal. But a media frenzy and an emotional campaign by parents of Dunblane victims, denouncing opponents of a complete handgun ban as accomplices in murder, hardened the views of both parties. Major was also under pressure from the Scottish secretary, Michael Forsyth, the M.P. for the area around Dunblane, who threatened to resign unless a ban was imposed. Major agreed to ban handguns above .22 caliber while requiring .22 caliber handguns to be stored at shooting clubs.[120] This policy resulted in the Firearms Act of 1997.[121] A few months later Tony Blair and the Labour party swept into office with a huge majority and insisted upon going the Conservatives one better by removing the exemption for .22 caliber handguns and imposing a complete handgun ban. Efforts to exempt Britain's Olympic target-shooting team and handicapped target shooters were defeated. The Firearms Act (No. 2) 1997, a measure unprecedented in a democratic country, initiated a nearly complete ban on handguns. Owners of pistols were ordered to hand them in. The penalty for possession of an illegal handgun is ten years in prison. The crime of one berserk individual led to the punishment of some 57,000 law-abiding gun owners. While Home Office minister Alun Michael would boast, "Britain now has some of the toughest gun laws in the world,"

Lord Stoddard lamented the introduction of collective punishment into English law.[122]

The Illegal Arsenal

Just how many guns are still available in this disarmed nation? It is surprisingly difficult to determine even the number of legal firearms. One certificate may cover several weapons, and there is no obligation to notify the police when a gun is sold or disposed of. Greenwood found a national average in the late 1960s of 1.34 firearms per certificate.[123] A larger question is to what extent gunowners complied with each new restriction. Since illegal as well as legal firearms must be considered in an assessment of the relationship between arms and violence, it is essential to address the issue, however speculatively. The 1870 licencing act was unenforceable, and each new effort to subject weapons already in private hands to new requirements added to the underground cache. J. A. Stevenson's research has convinced him that compliance has never exceeded 25 percent, if it even approached that level. Police made compliance less likely by openly and systematically reducing the numbers of certificates issued. The 216,281 certificates in England and Wales in 1968 had been reduced by a third, to 138,400, in 1993.[124] In the three years after it became necessary to have a good reason to get or renew a shotgun certificate, the number of certificates granted fell by 157,000.[125]

Once restrictions made it easier to obtain an illegal than a legal weapon, many firearms were underground from the outset. As with the "dark figure," or unreported crimes, it is impossible to be exact about the size of this illegal arsenal, but there have been some educated guesses. We can be relatively certain, for instance, of the numbers of pump-action and self-loading shotguns that went underground after the 1988 act. As the Conservative government had feared, there was "massive noncompliance," and "a very large number of guns" did "simply disappear."[126] Some 300,000 pump-action and self-loading shotguns were sold in the years just prior to the new act, but at most only 50,000 were submitted to proof with restricted magazines, handed in to police, or obtained certificates.[127] A quarter of a million shotguns simply disappeared. In November 1997 the Home Office reported that as a result of the new handgun ban some 142,000 handguns had been turned in, a total far short of the original police estimate of 200,490 handguns legally held.[128]

How large is this illegal pool of weapons? Firearms turned in during amnesties can provide some notion of the remaining illegal pool. In three amnesties before the Second World War nearly 39,000 firearms were handed over.[129] From 1946 through 1968 four additional amnesties garnered approximately 212,088 weapons.[130] Thousands of additional firearms have been turned in every year to police. For example, from 1946 through 1969 some 58,006 weapons were surrendered to the London Metropolitan Police alone, only a negligible number of which were legally held.[131] Colin Greenwood pointed out that pistols were the largest class of weapon surrendered and that 75 percent of those turned in during 1969 were illegally held. Few of these pistols were taken from criminals; most came from law-abiding people. Despite increasingly strict control of pistols since 1920, the proportion of pistols to all firearms surrendered has been relatively constant, the source "by no means drying up." Looking at pistols turned in to the Metropolitan Police from 1949 through 1969 and calculating the likely number of weapons per certificate, Green-wood reckoned that legally held pistols in the London area accounted for only one-twelfth the number of the illegal pistols actually surrendered; thus "the number of illegally held pistols in circulation far exceed[ed] the number held on firearms certificates."[132] Nor does London seem to have been exceptional, for he found a similar pattern in a sample of fifteen police forces.[133] Combining guns turned in at amnesties with others handed in to police yields the amazing total of 523,568 firearms surrendered to the police from 1946 to 1969, of which 237,380 were illegal pistols. Fifty years of stringent controls failed to deprive the illegal market of handguns.

In the 1980s A. B. Bailey of Oxford took a different tack to try to gauge the size of the illegal firearms pool. Bailey theorized that if 50 percent of the illegal pool were surrendered in any one year there must be about 800,000 illegal pistols and nearly 2,400,000 firearms of all types still in the pool. If only 25 percent of illegal firearms were surrendered the total illegal arsenal would rise to some 4 million unlicenced weapons. Michael Yardley, a research psychologist, considers 4 million a low estimate.

Munday and Stevenson see this illegal pool of firearms as distinct from the small black market of guns actually used in crime. From 1988 to 1992 firearms figured in some way in fewer than fifty homicides and slightly over 4,000 robberies a year.[134] The real number of weapons used in crime, however, is even smaller than this, since at least a quarter of these were imitation guns or airguns and some weapons are used repeatedly. Criminals can even hire a gun, then return it to a criminal armourer.[135]

The upshot is that the illegal pool of firearms in England in the year 2000 may have been some 4 million weapons, many held by otherwise law-abiding people. The penalties they would suffer if these were discovered are severe. Eighty years of firearms controls have failed to eliminate or even substantially reduce that arsenal.

Have Strict Gun Laws Lowered Rates of Violent Crime?

Many, if not most, Americans believe that England's strict gun laws have led to its low rates of violent crime. Half of that equation is certainly incorrect. There were remarkably low rates of violent crime before the first of the gun laws. One did not lead to the other. Still, it is important to know whether the many English firearms acts of the twentieth century have been beneficial: have they worked? The short answer is no, not if the goal was to reduce the use of firearms in crime, to make it more difficult for criminals to obtain guns, to "shift the balance substantially in the interests of public safety."[136] Armed crime, never a problem in England, has now become one. Handguns are banned, but the kingdom has millions of illegal firearms. Criminals have no trouble finding them and exhibit a new willingness to use them. In the decade after 1957 the use of guns in serious crime increased a hundredfold.[137] While almost 90 percent of murders in 1994 were still committed "by the time-honoured means of sharp or blunt instruments, hitting, kicking, or strangling, burning, drowning or poisoning," firearms became more common in robberies.[138] In 1904, before passage of gun restrictions, there were only 4 armed robberies a year in London. By 1991 this had increased 400 times, to 1,600 cases. From 1989 through 1996 armed crime increased by 500 percent at the very time the number of firearms certificate holders decreased by 20 percent.[139] No wonder J. Q. Wilson concluded: "The very great restrictions placed by English law on the private possession of firearms has apparently not impeded the increase in robbery . . . Despite legal restrictions, the steady shift from unarmed to armed robbery has proceeded apace—where there is a will, there is a way."[140]

Any impact the gun laws might have had on crime ought to show up in statistics on the type of guns used in committing offences. If the laws have worked at all, fully automatic weapons, which are prohibited, and handguns, which have been restricted for eighty years, should be less available than shotguns and powerful airguns, which were placed under controls more recently.[141] Yet in 1967 shotguns, though just put under some control, were used in only 21.3 percent of armed robberies while pistols were used in 45.6 percent.[142] Twenty years later these proportions were little changed.[143] Convenience, not arms controls, seems to have dictated the choice of weapon.

If the aim of the arms restrictions was to disarm the law-abiding public rather than criminals, the firearms acts were generally successful. The ancient constitutional right of Englishmen "to have arms for their defence" exists only on paper. That right of a free person to be armed, long regarded as a badge of citizenship, is now considered a grave menace to public order. However, English governments have gone far beyond this in their zeal to monopolize force by prohibiting any implement an individual might use to protect himself. In so doing they have effectively removed an even more basic right, *the* most basic right of all, the right of personal security, again in the name of public order. These policies have had a perverse impact. If they did not cause the unprecedented surge in violent crime, they certainly abetted it. There is now little to deter criminals, who are in the enviable position of being protected by the majesty of the law and of the courts from the risk of confronting victims armed even with walking sticks, let alone firearms, are shielded from any resistance by their victims that might qualify as "unreasonable force," and whose chances of arrest and punishment are minimal.

Government created a hapless, passive citizenry, then took upon itself the impossible task of protecting it. Its failure could not be more flagrant. When a 1995 study of criminal victimisation asked people in eleven industrialized countries how safe they felt walking alone in their area after dark, "those in England and Wales were most anxious (32 percent felt a bit or very unsafe)."[144] They are right to be afraid. The proportion of households that had a completed or attempted burglary was highest in England. Those at greatest risk of contact crime—defined as robbery, assaults, and sexual assaults against women—were the people of England and America, where the rate was double that of Northern Ireland. On victims' views of the seriousness of crime, residents of England and the Netherlands were "most pressured by crime." One in ten English respondents felt very likely to be burgled in the coming year, the highest percentage of the eleven countries. When it came to reporting crime, the view that "the police would not help" was mentioned most often in France, England, the Netherlands, and Switzerland. For what the study calls "overall victimisation," England tied with the Netherlands for the highest. Since 1995 violent crime in England dropped in some categories before climbing once again, while rates in America have continued to decline. In fact, in a clear demonstration of the futility of gun bans, English armed crime rose 10 percent in 1998, the year after the ban on handguns. Home Office figures for April 1999 through March 2000 showed that violent crime increased 16 percent, street robberies by 26 percent—the highest ever—muggings by 28 percent, and robberies in London by nearly 40 percent.[145] Although the overall crime rate fell slightly from 1996 through 2000, violent crime more than doubled.[146] Even before these latest rises the overall crime rate in England was 60 percent higher than that in America.[147] In October 2000 it was announced that for the first time in mainland Britain an English police force had introduced armed foot patrols, the aim being to combat rising gun crime.[148] Other forces in urban centers began to follow Nottinghamshire's example and by May 2001 were considering increasing the number of officers routinely armed.[149]

A snapshot of what the rise in violent crime has meant to individuals was provided by Mark Steyn in a *Spectator* essay on November 28, 1998. Steyn described a meeting he attended in the prosperous village of Kineton, in Warwickshire, where people pleaded for more police protection. A representative from Stratford-upon-Avon district council "attempted to allay residents' fears by talking about video surveillance cameras for the village green and promising to speak to Warwickshire Constabulary so that they could send an extra patrol car through the village every second Tuesday." Steyn continued, "By the time the meeting ended, night had fallen and I emerged from the hall to find the picture-postcard village transformed into a besieged fortress, the shop fronts disfigured by ugly aluminum shutters." He angrily concluded,

"All they can do is advise you to barricade yourself in behind more and more alarms and window locks. Why not try something else?"[150] Two years later, with no policy change and crime rates higher still, Steyn described a series of brutal robberies and the fear pervading the daily life of rich and poor alike. His sister-in-law, in her comfortable manor house in a prosperous part of rural England, lay awake at night "listening to yobbo gangs drive up, park their vans, and test her doors and windows before figuring out that the little old lady down the lane's a softer touch."[151]

The case of Tony Martin, a fifty-five-year-old Norfolk farmer, epitomizes what the English policy of strict weapons controls and government monopolization of protection has produced. Martin had already suffered repeated burglaries in his "remote and squalid Victorian farmhouse" when Brendon Fearon, ringleader of a burglary gang from Nottinghamshire, and Fred Barras, a sixteen-year-old repeat offender, broke into his home on the night of August 20, 1999. Martin was awakened at ten, when the intruders smashed in his window. He slipped downstairs with his unregistered shotgun as the two men were busily filling a bag with small silver items, and opened fire, hitting Fearon in the leg and killing Barras. Martin was charged with murder, attempted murder, and possession of an illegal shotgun. At his trial the prosecutor accused Martin of lying in wait for the burglars, shooting them like "rats in a trap." The jury heard testimony that an underworld contract of £60,000 had been offered on the farmer's life. On April 19, 2000, Tony Martin was sentenced to life in prison for murder. He was given an additional ten years for wounding Fearon and another twelve months for possessing a shotgun without a certificate. When the verdict was read, members of the teenage burglar's family "roared in approval," a female relative shouting at Martin: "I hope you die in jail." Martin's eighty-six-year-old mother said she was "devastated, shocked and upset. Because of this verdict, decent people will not be able to sleep at night." The county's chief constable admitted that Martin had suffered so many losses that he believed it "a waste of time" working with the police. Mr. Justice Owen summed up his view of the result to the court: "It seems to me that this case does serve as a dire warning to all burglars who break in to the houses of other people. Every citizen is allowed to use reasonable force to prevent crime. Burglary is a crime. The householder in his own home may think he is being reasonable but that can have tragic consequences."[152]

A public furor in Martin's favor followed the verdict and prompted the opposition Conservative Home Affairs spokesperson Ann Widdecombe to launch a "bash a burglar" campaign. But in Widdecombe's view Martin used excessive force. What would have been appropriate? If he had used a stick to beat Barras across the head—presumably without doing much damage—and kept him quiescent until the police arrived, she said, "then good for him." How he was also to manage to keep his other intruder quiescent she didn't say. Even Labour Home Secretary Jack Straw has called for an end to the "walk on by" culture.[153] Opposition politicians have begun to take another look at the state of self-defence law and to consider how it might be changed. When William Hague, leader of the Conservative party, promised that the next Conservative government would "overhaul the law" to provide greater protection for those confronting burglars he was accused of adopting a "lynch mob mentality."[154] Police spokesmen have opposed any change. The chairman of the Police Federation argued "that the law didn't need to change, it was merely a matter of how this word 'reasonable' is interpreted by judges, juries and magistrates." And Crispian Strachan, chief constable of Northumbria, insisted that offering greater legal protection to people who tackled intruders "risked generating American levels of violent assault and killing in Britain." "I've heard comparisons to America," he continued, "where there is a slightly lower rate of domestic burglary but a very high rate of violent crime and murder. That is because they have a right to defend themselves at all costs. I would not want to see that introduced here."[155] Both Strachan's comparison of crime rates and his description of American law are misleading and dated stereotypes. A final note on the Martin case. After the verdict two jurors came forward claiming to have been intimidated into finding Martin guilty by their fear of retribution and the presence of a group of men sitting in the public gallery staring at the jury. In an unprecedented move, three Appeal Court judges have ruled that for the first time in British history questions may be put to the jury after a trial.

In October 2001 appeal court judges reduced Martin's sentence from murder to manslaughter. Accordingly his life sentence was reduced to five years and his ten-year sentence for wounding Fearon to three years, to run concurrently. The judges' decision was based not upon new evidence presented that bolstered his claim of self-defence, but upon a finding of diminished responsibility because he had been abused as a child. Lord Woolf, speaking for the judges, said, "Martin used a firearm which he knew he was not entitled to have in a manner which was wholly unjustified. There can be no excuse for this, though we treat his responsibility as being reduced." Martin will be eligible for parole in about a year. Fearon has already been freed. In commenting on the court's decision, the editor of *The Spectator* noted that the ruling did "absolutely nothing to put right a fundamental injustice in English law: that somebody using excessive force in self-defence can be convicted of the same offence as a serial killer who slits the throats of old ladies in cold blood."[156]

Thus an English farmer, living alone, has been sentenced to life in prison for killing one professional burglar and to ten years for wounding another when the two broke into his home at night. Had Martin been living in England in the nineteenth century or in any state in America, in France, or in Germany today, he would not have been tried for murder.[157] Jurors felt constrained, and in some cases intimidated, into convicting him. So far has England veered from its constitutional tradition and the basic right of the law-abiding subject to personal security. Dicey's warning a century ago has proven prophetic: "Discourage self-help, and loyal subjects become the slaves of ruffians."[158]

7

More Guns More Crime or More Guns Less Crime?
The American Case

To disarm noncriminals in the hope this might indirectly help reduce access to guns among criminals is a dangerous gamble with potentially lethal consequences.

—GARY KLECK, "Guns and Violence," 1995

Notice that "safer society" means "the society with fewer violent-encounter deaths for nonaggressors" and not "the society with fewer violent-encounter deaths overall."

—LANCE STELL, "The Legitimation of Female Violence," 1991

O N JUNE 26, 2000, *The Mirror*, a London daily, advised readers to brace themselves for the latest annual crime figures, which were expected to show an astonishing 19 percent increase in violent crime and an even more astounding 38 percent increase in robberies in London.[1] Yet the next evening, when American television viewers were cautioned that violence in England was worse than in the United States, *The Mirror* leapt to the kingdom's defence, reporting that "Britain reacted with fury and disbelief" to the American claim. Those same Home Office officials about to release statistics testifying to a record increase in English crime, together with British "tourist chiefs," condemned the American report as "fanciful." Further on in the article readers discovered that even before the latest increases England had overtaken America in every major category of violent crime except murder and rape.[2] The general outrage at the American report in the face of nearly half a century's spiralling crime rates confirmed Mark Steyn's observation: "Old impressions die hard. Americans still think of Britain as a low-crime country. Conversely, the British think of America as a high-crime country." "Neither impression," Steyn added, "is true. The overall crime rate in England and Wales is 60% higher than that in the United States"[3] The original *Mirror* article's warning had been near the mark. On July 18 the government revealed the largest twelve-month increase in assaults and street robberies for a generation. *The Telegraph* summed it up: "There was a 26 per cent increase in street robberies—the highest ever. Offences of violence rose by 16 per cent, the biggest increase for at least 10 years, and the most serious assaults went up by almost 13 percent . . . Some urban areas, such as Greater London and the West Midlands, recorded an increase of nearly 40 per cent in robberies."[4] A year later the *Sunday Times* would report that over the past four years violent crime in England and Wales had more than doubled.[5] Still, old impressions die hard. The English and American peoples still share notions of England as the peaceable kingdom, of America as the violent republic. But the truth of this particular comparison matters deeply because of its policy implications. The Anglo-American contrast is cited repeatedly as proof that more guns means more crime. England's reputation for modest rates of violent crime has been paired with its reputation for strict gun laws, laws that are now the most stringent of any democracy's. America, by contrast, is branded a "gun culture." About half of all American households own firearms.[6] Half of the equation is incorrect. The peacefulness England used to enjoy was not the result of strict gun laws. When it had no firearms restrictions England had little violent crime, while the present extraordinarily stringent gun controls have not stopped the increase in violence or even the increase in armed violence.[7] By opting to deprive law-abiding citizens of the right to keep guns or to carry any article for defence, English government policy may actually be contributing to the lawlessness and violence afflicting its people.

But what of the American side of the premiss? The English case demonstrates that fewer guns do not mean less crime, but do more guns mean more crime? Are America's 75–86 million gun owners with their 200–240 million firearms a cause of crime; do they and their weapons have no impact one way or the other; or do their weapons deter violence?[8] England's rates of interpersonal crime have soared as its gun laws have become stricter. America's rates of violent crime also rose until 1991. Since then they have declined dramatically every year, sinking in 1999 to a thirty-year low.[9] The American murder rate has been described as "in startling free-fall."[10] The homicide rate had fluctuated by about 20 percent between 1974 and 1991, but in 1999 criminologist Franklin Zimring found that "we're pushing beneath that bottom so that we have a structural change in the level of homicide risks in American cities

. . . It's a real turning point in American lethal violence."[11]
Gun homicides accounted for the entire decline in homicides
from 1997 through 1998.[12]

During these years of declining crime rates, American
firearms legislation became far more permissive on the state
level, and rather less so on the national level: a majority of
states now give law-abiding citizens the right to carry concealed weapons while the federal government has imposed
new, if limited, national controls.[13] The stark differences in
law and public policy between England and America make a
genuine comparison all the more valuable for sorting out the
relationship between guns and violence in a manner that may
be useful to both countries.

The English have been reluctant to reconsider the premiss
behind seventy years of failed arms policies. Not so Americans, who seldom hesitate to question first principles. They
are in the throes of a highly charged debate over the role that
guns play in violent crime and the policy implications of that
role. Sharp policy splits among multiple and overlapping jurisdictions make the American scene considerably more con-
fusing than the English. Federal laws have been based largely
on the supposition that more guns mean more crime. Accordingly legislation such as the Brady Act and the ban on guns
defined as assault weapons aim to restrict access to handguns
and powerful automatic weapons.[14] Beyond this each of the
fifty states has its own policy for individual purchase, possession, and carrying of guns, based on its own theory of the link
between guns and violence and its own constitution. Even
some cities have firearms polices. No jurisdiction has, or can,
completely forbid the purchase of guns, but requirements for
their purchase and carriage differ widely. On the theory that

more guns mean more crime, Washington, D.C., has banned handguns for residents, and New York City and Chicago allow only a few privileged residents to own them. The small town of Morton Grove, Illinois, also banned handguns. Six states refuse to permit any citizen to carry a concealed weapon. By contrast, the theory that armed citizens not only protect themselves but deter crime has gained acceptance in recent years and led state after state to permit residents to carry concealed weapons. In 1994 four states passed legislation allowing all law-abiding adults the right to carry concealed handguns, ten others did so in 1995, and in 1996 another three states followed suit. Eight others had had such legislation on the books for years. To date thirty-three states, a clear majority, are required to grant residents who meet the basic standards the right to carry concealed weapons. One of these, Vermont, has no gun laws.[15] Vermont also has the lowest crime rate in the nation. The little community of Kennesaw, Georgia, a suburb of Atlanta, requires every home to have a firearm for protection. This jigsaw of divergent practice and experience makes for confused statistics and tricky comparisons, since no state or city can seal its borders. The subject is of such moment that scholars from various fields have resolutely waded into this morass in an effort to clarify the relationship between firearms and violence. The more reliable and sophisticated of these studies can help us assess the American case. But first, some history.

America's Firearms History in Brief

The contrasts between a disarmed England and a well-armed America are so great that it is hard to believe the two share a constitutional legacy. Their respective bills of rights recognize the right of citizens to have firearms.[16] As we have seen, the language of the English right confined it to Protestants and then to what was thought "suitable to their condition and as allowed by law." In practice all law-abiding Englishmen had a right to be armed. The language of the American Second Amendment is more sweeping: "A well-regulated militia being necessary to the security of a free state, the right of the people to keep and bear arms shall not be infringed." Its initial clause refers to the necessity for "a well-regulated militia," but it goes on to grant "the people," regardless of religion or condition, a right "to keep and bear arms" that "shall not be infringed." Even more important than its broader language, the American right is constitutionally entrenched and cannot be removed by a simple vote of the legislature or behind-the-scenes policy of the civil service. But it has been threatened from a different quarter. Since the 1960s those determined to limit firearms have insisted that the Second Amendment never protected an individual right, that its purpose was to ensure state control over state militia or to protect a "collective right" for militia members to be armed.[17] Even if there was once an individual right, they insist that it is now an anachronism. The collective-right interpretation first became attractive in the early twentieth century, when fears about armed blacks in the South and millions of immigrants pouring into northern cities provided an incentive to narrow the scope of the Second Amendment so that weapons could be denied to suspect groups.[18] American authorities of the time, like their English counterparts, were haunted by the specter of disorder and revolution.

Early in the twentieth century both countries passed firearms legislation, the English the 1903 Pistols Act and in 1920 the landmark Firearms Act. The first American federal gun law didn't pass until 1934, but before that discriminatory laws in the South kept blacks disarmed, and in 1911 New York State passed the Sullivan Law, which made it a felony to carry a concealed weapon without a licence or to own or purchase a handgun without obtaining a certificate. The Sullivan Law, like the 1920 Firearms Act, made the granting of a certificate discretionary, but unlike the English statute its jurisdiction was limited to one state and it affected only handguns. During the 1920s Americans were dismayed as mobsters armed with submachine guns fought for possession of the market in illegal alcohol. Public attention remained fixed on the dangers of automatic weapons during the 1930s thanks to the exploits of such flamboyant depression-era scoundrels as "Pretty Boy" Floyd, George "Machine Gun" Kelly, and Bonnie Parker and Clyde Barrow. The result was passage of the first federal gun-control legislation, the National Firearms Act of 1934. This statute required registration, police permission, and a tax for possession of automatic weapons, sawed-off rifles, and shotguns and silencers, all weapons closely linked to criminals. The Roosevelt administration had meant to include a plan for registration of all handguns for a nominal one-dollar fee but dropped the idea when the firearms industry, rural police chiefs, and the National Rifle Association objected to it.[19] More than thirty years were to pass before widespread riots and three political assassinations again led to demands for stricter firearms legislation. The Gun Control Act of 1968 limited mail-order sales, the purchase of firearms by felons, and the import of military weapons. Robert Cottrol finds this statute "something of a watershed," for since its passage the debate over gun control and the right to be armed have become "semi-permanent features" of late twentieth-century American life.[20] In the 1990s federal legislation banned a list of "assault weapons" and through the Brady Act required background checks before the purchase of a firearm. Public concern about crime also led to greater insistence that there was no individual right to be armed. But a scholarly consensus, based on twenty years of research, has concluded that the Constitution does guarantee an individual right.[21] Americans have guns, but they also have gun control; reputedly some 20,000 laws grace the books of American states and municipalities. There is no statistical evidence for this suspiciously round number, but its wide acceptance does illustrate that while firearms are not banned they are certainly subject to controls.

Are International Comparisons of Crime Sound?

Is a comparison between English and American crime rates as striking as it seems? English police frequently dismiss such comparisons as invalid, at least comparisons in which English crime rates appear higher. The police are correct to the extent that international comparisons are tricky. We need to accommodate differing definitions for particular crimes and different methods of calculation, not to speak of different social and economic settings and different techniques for dealing with incorrigibles. But comparisons are eminently worthwhile, because they shed light on the way each country maintains order. More important, any comparison that reveals a more effective way to reduce crime must be worthwhile. Once we have sorted through all the variables, a battery of intriguing questions awaits us. There is no doubt that guns play a much larger role in American than in English crime. According to 1996 police statistics, they were used in only 7 percent of English murders but in 68 percent of American murders, and the American murder rate in 1996 was six times the English rate.[22] Victim surveys found that 4 percent of English robberies were armed robberies, compared with 28 percent of U.S. robberies.[23] Yet with the exception of murder and rape, since 1995 American rates of violent crime have been lower than English rates. English thugs were quite capable of perpetrating offences without guns, although gun crimes also rose in England. When it comes to homicide, however, the English have historically had a very low murder rate.[24] Despite the large pool of illegal firearms in Britain today, and the large legal pool in the past, criminals made little use of guns.[25] In fact although violent crime has risen sharply in England in the last five years, an international study found that the murder rate has remained low, with London's among the lowest of all European capitals'.[26] On the other hand, New York City's homicide rate has been at least five times higher than London's for two hundred years. For most of that time there were no serious firearms restrictions in either city. "Even without guns," Eric Monkkonen writes, "New Yorkers still managed to out-stab and outkick Liverpudlians by a multiple of 3 and Londoners by a multiple of 5.6."[27] If the heterogeneous American population, with its rags-to-riches ethos, seems more prone to violence than the English population, is the availability of any particular sort of weapon only incidental? Or have guns made America's rate of violence higher than it would otherwise have been? Many insist that they have, that criminals have easy access to lethal weapons and that ordinary people who own a firearm are likely to seize it during a quarrel. Some in the medical community have dubbed firearms a health hazard. According to Richard Maxwell Brown, however, Americans are more violent, not because of firearms, but because of legal standards of self-defence. He believes that England's low homicide rate is attributable to a common-law duty to retreat when attacked, while America's rate is high because Americans believe that common law allows the individual to stand his ground and kill in self-defence.[28] Americans certainly have far more latitude to protect themselves than the English, along with better means to do so. Whatever the cause, if Americans are more violent, could guns play an important role in deterring crime, rather than increasing it? States that have concealed-carry laws certainly assume this. This does not mean that everyone needs to be armed. In his pioneering study, John Lott explains this rationale:

> Deterrence matters not only to those who actively take defensive actions. People who defend themselves may indirectly benefit other citizens . . . cab drivers and drug dealers who carry guns produce a benefit for cab drivers and drug dealers without guns . . . homeowners who defend themselves make burglars generally wary of breaking into homes. These spillover effects are frequently referred to as "third-party effects" or "external benefits." In both cases criminals cannot know in advance who is armed.[29]

Which brings us to another question: Has the adoption of these nondiscretionary concealed-carry laws worked, or has the freedom some thirty-three states allow millions of residents to carry concealed handguns caused a bloodbath as every irritated American reaches for his weapon? American experiments with dramatically different gun policies can provide valuable information about which method works best, or indeed whether firearms policies are determinative.

The Variables behind Statistics

The first variables that must be tackled are the crime figures themselves. National definitions of crimes differ. The American homicide rate includes both murder and nonnegligent manslaughter as well as shootings in self-defence. The Federal Bureau of Investigation (FBI) instructs American police to list homicides as murder even if the case isn't subsequently prosecuted or if it eventually proceeds on a lesser charge.[30] These American reporting practices make the recorded U.S. homicide rate as high as possible without including peripheral crimes such as attempted murder. In Britain, by contrast, the homicide figure "is massaged down to a bare minimum." It includes murder, infanticide, manslaughter with diminished responsibility, and common-law manslaughter but, like the United States, not attempted murder. Three statutes have changed the way the English calculate homicide, all of which reduce the total figure. The Road Traffic Act of 1956 removed from the category of manslaughter motor-vehicle homicide caused by dangerous driving. A year later the Homicide Act divided murder into capital and noncapital, created separate responsibility for each individual involved, and devised a new category of diminished responsibility. These changes altered the way the police recorded and dealt with homicides and the decisions courts and juries made. But the unique feature of British homicide statistics, that of massaging the figure down, was initiated by the Home Office in 1967, when ministers were anxious that homicide figures be kept to a minimum to prevent pressure to reinstate capital punishment. The scheme they hit upon works this way. Each homicide case is tracked through the courts. If a homicide is eventually reduced to a lesser charge or determined to be an accident or self-defence, it is removed from the statistics. The result is to reduce the English homicide rate by as much as a quarter and in recent years by an average of 12 percent.[31] If Howard Taylor, an economic historian, is correct, however, the practice of deliberately underrecording and even underprosecuting murder in England has been going on for more than a century. Taylor argues that since murder trials were very expensive, the extraordinarily level rate of recorded murder from the mid-nineteenth century up to 1966 was due to the fact that "prosecutions for murder were among the most strictly rationed of all crimes." Cases that meant exceeding the budget for prosecution went back to ratepayers and the police to prosecute and were, he suggests, "perhaps dismissed, or deals done to reduce charges to wounding, assault etc." Such cases did not appear in the statistics as murder. Those suspected murders reported to the director of public prosecutions were not officially recorded as a murder "known to the police" until the investigation or trial was concluded. Moreover, Taylor adds that most murders "did not get as far as a report to the Director of Public Prosecutions. Because the discovery of a suspicious death and its subsequent investigation and prosecution could make a large dent in a police authority budget, it was an open secret that most murders went uninvestigated." He cites the 1899 *Judicial Statistics* that coroners' juries "return as deaths by accidents or misadventure or from natural causes many cases which are really homicides. Among the 1,981 'open verdicts' returned in 1899 were no doubt many homicides . . . [which] are never cleared up . . . many of the persons guilty of murder are unknown, or, if known, are not apprehended." As additional evidence he points out that whereas murders stayed surprisingly constant up to 1967, statistics for other violent deaths such as suicides and accidents rose sharply.[32] This is not to deny that the American murder rate is far higher than the English, but that the English rate is, and may long have been, artificially low.

Attempted murder is excluded from both countries' homicide rates. The United States includes attempted murder in its figures for aggravated assault, while the English figures do not, thus enlarging the U.S. figures for aggravated assault. The English figure for attempted murder is low and convictions for it rare, but the English have very high figures for "wounding," and some homicide attempts may be slipped into that category. In 1996, for example, the police recorded only 674 attempted murders but 174,583 woundings.

Rape is the other violent crime much more common in America than in England. Even for rape, for which reporting is problematic, definitions warp the figures. In 1981 to be categorized as rape in England an incident had to involve only a male offender aged fourteen or over, a female victim, and penetration of the vagina by the penis. No husband could be accused of raping his wife. Not until 1994 was English law changed to include male victims, spouses, and anal intercourse. In America rape includes offenders of both sexes, victims of both sexes, and all sorts of sexual acts. For both murder and rape the American rates are far higher but declining, while the English rates are rising. As measured by police statistics the U.S. murder rate in 1981 was 8.7 times the English rate but had dropped to 5.7 times the English rate by 1995. The U.S. rate for rape in 1981 was 6 times the English rate but only 1.4 times the English rate in 1996 after English law defined rape more comprehensively.[33]

The major discrepancy in definition between the two countries involves assaults. England distinguishes between the offence of wounding, in which actual or serious bodily harm is involved, and the lesser offence of common assault, in which a victim may be punched, kicked, or jostled with no serious injury. The U.S. distinguishes between aggravated assault, in which murder has been attempted and the victim has serious wounds or is knocked unconscious, and simple assault, in which the victim suffers bruises but no weapon was used. Although the definitions are not perfectly compatible, there seems little option but to compare the English crime of wounding with the American crime of aggravated assault.

Major disparities also come from a less obvious quarter, the rates at which victims report crimes to police and the rates at which the police record those reports. Reporting by English and American victims varies for different crimes. A greater proportion of assaults is reported to American police than to English police, some 54 percent compared with 40 percent. More burglaries are reported to English police than to Americans, some 66 percent compared with 50 percent, but slightly more robberies are reported to American police than English. There is a lopsided disparity in the rates at which police of each nation officially record the crimes reported to them. Patrick Langan and David Farrington found: "Compared to police in England, police in the United States more often record as crimes those alleged offenses that are reported to them."[34] In America the police recorded 78 percent of robberies reported to them, the English police only 35 percent, and in 1998 the latter's share had fallen to 30 percent. As for burglaries, from 1981 to 1995 the percentage of reported burglaries recorded by American police rose from 58 percent to 72 percent, while the English rate fell from 70 percent to 55 percent. Despite this considerable English underreporting, the English crime rate in 1995 for most violent crime was still substantially higher than that of the United States. In both nations police are recording a greater percentage of crimes reported to them than in the past, but the English police still grossly underreport crimes. In 1995 the English police were recording only 46 percent of all reported crimes, "bringing England in 1995 to about the level the United States was in 1973 (43%)." As a result of lower English reporting and lower English recording of crime *The 1998 British Crime Survey* found four times as many crimes occurred as police records indicated.[35]

The Social and Economic Setting

The disparities in reporting of crimes are rooted in the cultural and ethnic differences between the peoples as well as in their different legal definitions and recordkeeping. Until recently America has been more violent than England. The American murder rate from knives alone, for instance, is twice the English murder rate for all weapons.[36] Eric Monkkonen argues that "high American violence is not simply a matter of weapon availability." Indeed guns were available to the English for most of the two hundred years he is considering, but they were seldom used in murders. Monkkonen concludes:

"Even without guns the United States would still be out of step, just as it has been for two hundred years."[37] Just why this is so is debatable. From its founding America has been a land of immigrants, whereas England had little immigration from the eleventh-century Norman invasion until the middle of the twentieth century. The racial and ethnic tensions and demographic differences this produced, the problems of acculturation as each new group worked its way into the American mainstream, and America's less stable culture have had an unfortunate impact on crime.[38] Further, for a host of reasons a disproportionate share of America's violent crime has been committed by blacks.[39] In 1991 of some 160.8 million white American adults 396 per 100,000 were in prison on any given day.[40] Of the 20.6 million black adults 2,563 per 100,000 were in prison. Of the 5.6 million adults of other races some 643 per 100,000 were in prison. Although for policy reasons England incarcerates far fewer criminals, the proportions for each race are comparable. In 1991 of the 36.7 million white adults on any given day 102 per 100,000 were in prison, while of the 750,000 black adults about 667 per 100,000 were in prison. Of the 1.2 million adults of other races some 233 per 100,000 were in prison. In both the United States and England the incarceration of blacks is about six times that of whites, the incarceration rate of other races about two times the white rate. This unfortunate racial disparity plays a large role in the very high American homicide rate, which is "to a great extent, a black phenomenon."[41] Both murderers and their victims are disproportionately black. In 1994 African Americans composed 12 percent of the American population but made up 56 percent of those arrested for murder.[42] There were 5,106 black offenders compared with 4,445 whites, and 5,527 black victims compared with 5,371 white victims. Whatever racial antagonisms exist, blacks generally killed blacks, and whites killed whites.[43] Immigration and race also play a role in English crime. Only a small proportion of the increase in England's crime rate can be due to immigrants, but Scotland Yard has generally refused to disclose the race of criminals in crime statistics. The results of a study on race and crime that Scotland Yard undertook more than twenty years ago "are closely guarded." J. Q. Wilson reckons that if the findings were likely to have changed the popular perception that increased muggings were attributable to West Indians, the data would have been released.[44] In July 2000, just after publication of embarrassingly higher crime figures, Scotland Yard broke with precedent and disclosed that shootings in the black community accounted for nearly three-quarters of gun crime in London. Sixty-eight percent of these shootings involved black gunmen attacking black victims, mostly in disputes over drugs.[45]

Not only race but socioeconomic factors appear to be more instrumental causes of homicide than the availability of guns. A study of international homicide undertaken by the Office of Health Economics (OHE) in London and published in 1976 found that the American homicide rate at the time was higher than in any European country but much lower than in Mexico and other countries with rigorous gun controls. The OHE concluded: "One reason often given for the high numbers of murders and manslaughters in the United States is the easy availability of firearms . . . But the strong correlation with racial and linked socio-economic variables suggests that the underlying determinants of the homicide rate are related to particular cultural factors."[46] One of those factors is the lucrative market in illegal drugs, another the impact of single-parent and troubled homes. A Detroit investigation discovered about 70 percent of juvenile homicide perpetrators did not live with both parents, and that young black males from single-parent homes were twice as likely to engage in crime as young black males from two-parent families.[47] On the other hand, the breakdown in the family is comparable in England and America.

American homicide is also primarily an urban phenomenon, and urban areas are far more likely to have restrictive gun control. All of which leads to the question of who owns those 200 million firearms in America and what impact their weapons have on them and on crime.

Gun Owners

The America media tend to portray the typical gun owner as an ill-educated, boorish "redneck," a vigilante who relishes shooting creatures great and small. Studies by the National Institute of Justice, an arm of the Department of Justice, found American gun owners disproportionately rural, southern, male, and Protestant, but also disproportionately white-collar workers and affluent or middle-class.[48] Gun ownership is also higher among middle-aged people and among married people. When the "personality profiles" of gun owners were examined they were found to be little different from the rest of the population, although gun owners are more likely to approve the use of defensive force to help victims.[49] Additional information comes from exit polls taken at elections in 1988 and 1996 that asked questions about gun ownership. The results revealed a general increase in gun ownership, from 27.4 to 37 percent, between those dates, with a 70 percent increase in the share of women owning firearms.[50] In 1996 gun ownership by whites exceeded that by blacks by about 40 percent. Blacks may have underreported their guns, but John Lott, author of the most extensive study of the impact of gun laws, argues that even a black gun-ownership rate of 100 percent could not explain "by itself" the difference in the black and white murder rates. The sole exception to the increase in gun ownership was among those living in urban areas with a population over 500,000. While rural areas have the highest gun-ownership rates and the lowest crime rates, Lott found that cities with more than 500,000 people have the lowest gun-ownership rates and the highest crime rates.[51] "If firearms ownership, or legislative regime, were determinant," J. A. Stevenson concludes, "the American homicide rate should be almost entirely a white phenomenon and a suburban or rural phenomenon. It is, of course, quite the opposite."[52]

More striking than any distinction between gun owners and nonowners is the difference between both groups and owners of illegal guns. Since probably fewer than 2 percent of handguns and well under 1 percent of all guns will ever be involved in a single violent act, the problem of criminal gun violence is concentrated within a very small group.[53] A government study of adolescents discovered that 74 percent of those owning illegal guns commit street crimes, 41 percent use drugs, and all are far more likely than not to be gang members. But it also found that boys who own legal firearms "have much lower rates of delinquency and drug use and are even slightly less delinquent than nonowners of guns."[54]

Is a Gun a Health Risk?

"That gun in the closet to protect against burglars will most likely be used to shoot a spouse in a moment of rage," a *Phila-*

delphia Inquirer article told readers in 1988. "The problem is you and me—law-abiding folks."[55] From at least the 1930s experts also assured the public of a gun's uselessness against intruders. H. C. Brearley, a homicide scholar in the 1930s, claimed: "Those most experienced in such matters generally agree that it is almost suicidal for the average householder to attempt to use a firearm against a professional burglar or robber."[56] These two common notions about gun use, fostered by the media, police, and the governments of England and America, go to the root of the relationship between guns and violence.[57] Are gun owners more likely to kill someone they know, or to injure themselves than to find their guns helpful for protection? Will the presence of a gun make them aggressive? To the last question three psychologists who conducted laboratory tests of word-and-picture associations would answer yes.[58] FBI figures appear to support these fears, for they show that people are frequently killed by someone they know.[59] But crime statistics and an investigation into whom the FBI puts into the category of "people they know" lead to a different conclusion. First, crime records reveal that rather than gun homicides' being the work of peaceful people in a moment of rage, some 90 percent of adult gun murderers have prior criminal records stretching back over an average of six years or more and involving four major adult felony arrests.[60] These are not "law-abiding folks." Juvenile murderers as well as most of their victims also have criminal backgrounds. Boston records for 1990–1994 showed that 76 percent of juvenile victims and 77 percent of juveniles who murdered other juveniles had prior criminal arraignments. Victims had an average of 9.5 criminal arraignments, offenders an average of 9.7.[61]

But what of domestic homicides? A study by Arthur Kellerman and others published in the *New England Journal of Medicine* claimed to demonstrate that keeping a gun in the house "was strongly and independently associated with an increased risk of homicide."[62] The gun was a health hazard. Kellerman and his associates used a sample of 444 homicides that occurred in the victims' homes in three counties and a control group of people who lived near the deceased and were the same sex, race, and age range. Among other flaws in their methodology, the authors failed to mention the key point that in only 8 of the 444 homicides had the gun involved been kept in the home.[63] Four other physicians, in a study published in 1975, examined records for Cuyahoga County, Ohio, from 1958 through 1973 to determine the value of a gun for protection. They counted 148 fatal gun accidents during those fifteen years, of which 78 percent were in the home and 23 involved burglars, robbers, or intruders killed by people defending their homes. The methodology was again faulty. The authors made a basic mistake of counting all 148 deaths, not just the 115 in the home, in the numerator. Worse, they counted as a valid defence with a gun only the rare instances in which an intruder was killed, and never even established whether any of the recorded accidents were defensive uses. Their conclusion, published in a distinguished medical journal, was that since by their reckoning there were six times as many fatal gun accidents in the home as burglars killed, "the possession of firearms by civilians appears to be a dangerous and ineffective means of self-protection."[64]

Police records are a more reliable indicator of whether a gun in the home has led an otherwise peaceful citizen to shoot someone, and of the real cost of accidents. According to records from Detroit and Kansas City, Missouri, in 90 percent of domestic homicides police had been called to the home at least once in the two years before the murder, and in 54 percent of the cases they had been called five times or more.[65] "Most family murders are preceded by a long history of assaults," another study has concluded; intrafamily homicide "is typically just one episode in a long-standing syndrome of violence."[66] Again these are not ordinary "folks" whose domestic peace is unpredictably shattered by gun violence. How, then, is one to understand the FBI finding that most killings are of family, friends, or others "known to the murderer"? Into the category of those known to each other police put members of rival gangs—most murders arise from gang-related turf wars over drugs—drug pushers and buyers, prostitutes and their clients, bar customers, gamblers, even cab-drivers killed by customers.[67]

Accidents with guns are also a cause for concern, especially those highly publicized accidents involving children. In 1988, the last year for which handgun figures were available, there were 200 accidental deaths caused by handguns throughout America. Interestingly, 22 of these accidents were in states with concealed-carry laws and 178 in states without them.[68] Firearm accidents involving children have actually declined in America by 55 percent since 1930, despite the great increase in numbers of firearms.[69] In 1996 there were 1,134 accidental deaths from all firearms in the entire country. Of these some 42 were children, 17 up to the age of four and 25 from five to nine years old. That same year 1,915 children died in car crashes and another 489 were killed when struck by cars, 805 drowned, and 738 were killed by fire. Nearly twice as many children drowned in the bathtub or died from ingesting household poisons than died from all gun accidents.[70] If guns had no legitimate purpose, even one death would be one too many. On the other hand, if they do play a part in personal protection there is an important, countervailing reason for maintaining an item that might hurt a child. Kitchen knives, household chemicals, and bathtubs continue to be found in every home.

The question is whether there *is* a countervailing reason to keep a firearm. Do guns play a real role in protecting their owners or are individuals, as is often argued, more likely to hurt themselves or someone else than their attackers? There are risks of erroneous killings when someone acts in what he believes to be self-defence. One such incident was the well-publicized mistake when a Louisiana man shot a Japanese student who came to his door in a Halloween disguise and pretended to threaten him. Fortunately, there are only about thirty of these mistaken killings a year in the entire nation. Over the same period the police erroneously kill five to eleven times more innocent people.[71]

But are guns useful for protection? They clearly are one of the few means by which the weak can defend themselves against the strong, women against men, a lone man against two or more attackers. Still, the oft-stated claim is that defensive gun ownership is a "dangerous self-delusion."[72] According to Handgun Control, Inc., if you are attacked the best defence against injury "is to put up no defense—give them what they want or run." But criminological studies have established that victims who resisted with a gun or other weapon were only half as likely to be hurt as those who put up no resistance, while nonresisters were not only more likely to be hurt but far more likely to be raped or robbed.[73] Even in the grave situation in which a victim with a gun is confronting a robber with a gun, the National Crime Victim Survey found that armed victims were still far less likely to be injured than those who resisted in other ways, and slightly less likely to be hurt than those who didn't resist at all.[74] Some 98 percent of the time armed citizens merely have to brandish their gun to stop an attack.[75] Contrary to popular belief, criminals take the gun away from the victim in less than one percent of such confrontations.[76]

There is also plenty of anecdotal evidence of successful defensive gun use. One such case involved George Smith, aged seventy. A frequent patron of a small variety store in a working-class neighborhood of Indianapolis, Smith was there when two robbers entered and pointed a gun at him. He pretended to faint, and one robber went into the back room while the other stayed by the cash register. When the proprietress screamed from the store's back office, Smith picked himself off the floor, drew the gun he was carrying, shot the intruder who had threatened him, and then wounded his accomplice as he fled. The store had been robbed twice before in the past two years, and the last time the owner, Jerry Moore, and Smith, who had been outside the shop, had been wounded. Smith had been hospitalized for weeks. "So he bought a gun. Two years later, when intruders came again, Smith was ready." No charges were filed, since the police agreed that Smith had acted in self-defence.[77] In another incident the *New York Times* reported, "Burglar Puts 92-Year-Old in the Gun Closet and Is Shot."[78] Without firearms neither Smith nor the ninety-two-year-old would have been able to defend themselves.

Although anecdotes abound, statistics on defensive use of firearms are harder to come by. The chief difficulty in calculating the effectiveness of resistance with a firearm is that the majority of defensive uses of a firearm are not reported to or by the police. Police statistics report the shootings of victims or felons, but not the many times when the mere brandishing of a firearm scared away attackers.[79] Even studies that include questions on the subject are unlikely to get accurate responses. There are important variations in the way questions are asked and differences in the time period covered. Moreover, responders have every reason to be cautious about providing information on a defensive gun use that may have involved their illegally carrying a gun in or through a public space, as well as defensive use that might result in police questions. Fifteen national polls of defensive gun use, including polls by the *Los Angeles Times,* Gallup, and Peter Hart Research Associates, Inc., found between 700,000 and 3.6 million defensive uses annually. One survey, the large and normally reliable National Crime Victimization Survey, conducted by the Census Bureau for the Justice Department, found only about 82,000 uses in 1988 and 110,000 in 1990.[80] The NCVS survey is sharply at odds with the other fourteen and almost certainly represents a serious underestimate, probably because sensitive questions were asked by a law enforcement agency, the survey was not anonymous, and thousands of otherwise law-abiding people own guns without the necessary permit or state licence.[81] Interestingly, the testimony of incarcerated felons supports the large number of defensive gun uses. Thirty-four percent of the felons interviewed in a landmark study admitted to having been "scared off, shot at, wounded or captured by an armed victim."[82] Gary Kleck and Marc Gertz point out that since as many as 400,000 people a year claim to have "almost certainly" saved a life by using their guns for defence, the result "cannot be dismissed as trivial." If only one-tenth of these people are correct, "the number of lives saved by victim use of guns would still exceed the total number of lives taken with guns."[83]

Do Armed Citizens Deter or Increase Crime?

There are various ways to look at the issue of the impact of firearms on crime. One is simply comparing numbers of guns owned with the numbers of crimes committed. When a group of researchers did such a study they found that in the years 1973–1992 the number of firearms in American homes nearly doubled, with a 110.2 percent increase in handguns and a 73.3 percent increase in all firearms.[84] If guns were the primary cause of homicide, or even one of the main causes, the homicide statistics ought to reflect this immense increase. Indeed, this time span includes the peak year for homicides, 1980. But the murder rate failed to reflect the jump in numbers of guns. In 1973 the homicide rate was 9.4 per 100,000; twenty years later, when the supply of guns had risen by another 77.6 million, the homicide rate had declined to 8.5 per 100,000. Moreover, the number of homicides committed with firearms dropped, from 68.5 percent of homicides in 1973 to 58.7 percent in 1985, went up to 68.5 percent in 1992 but down again in 1994, when another 9,392,279 guns had been purchased.[85] Raw crime numbers simply did not rise with the dramatic increase in privately owned firearms.

A second way to test the relationship is to consider the impact of the concealed-carry laws now in force in thirty-three states (Figure 2). These provide clear evidence that armed citizens do not increase crime. States debating the adoption of nondiscretionary concealed-weapons laws were continually warned of the terrible violence that would be unleashed if hundreds of thousands of citizens were permitted to carry handguns. What would these people do during a quarrel or after a traffic accident? Fears of a bloodbath, especially in large, densely populated states, have proved unwarranted. In all the decades of experience with concealed-carry laws in an increasing number of states, there is only one recorded incident of the use of a permitted handgun in a shooting following a traffic accident, and that was determined to be a case of self-defence. Florida's concealed-carry law took effect on October 1, 1987. From that date until the end of 1996 over 380,000 licences were issued, only 72 of which were subsequently revoked because the holders had committed crimes, few of which involved the permitted guns.[86] During Virginia's first nine years of experience with the concealed-carry system not a single permit holder was involved in a violent crime.[87] After the first year of Texas' concealed-carry law more than 114,000 licences had been issued and only 17 revoked, while a year after Nevada's law went into effect police could not document "one case of a fatality that resulted from irresponsible gun use by someone who obtained a permit under the new law."[88] In South Carolina only one person who received a pistol permit since 1989 "has been indicted on a felony charge . . . That charge . . . for allegedly transferring stolen property last year, was dropped by prosecutors after evidence failed to support the charge." North Carolina has not had a single permit revoked as a result of use of a gun in a crime. Not only has no permit holder anywhere ever shot a police officer, but there have been cases in which permit holders have used their guns to save officers' lives.[89]

These large numbers of ordinary citizens carrying firearms

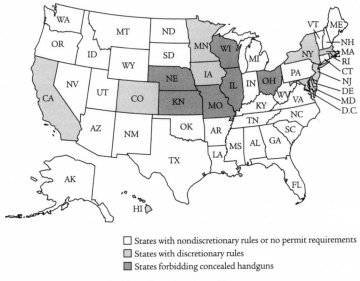

Figure 2. State concealed-handgun laws as of June 2000

have not increased the crime rate. But have they actually deterred crime and lowered it? Have more guns, as John Lott
contends, meant less crime? We know that in both England
and America the areas of densest firearms ownership—rural
and suburban areas—have less crime than the urban areas,
where legal firearms are rare. Criminals on their own testimony prefer victims who are unarmed: evidence of this shows
up in burglaries. In Britain and Canada, where few potential
victims will be armed, almost half of all burglaries are "hot
burglaries," that is, with the residents at home, whereas in the
United States only 13 percent are "hot burglaries."[90] Convicted
felons admit that they worry more about armed victims than
about the police.[91]

Measuring deterrence is necessarily an inexact exercise,

since it involves incidents that don't happen. Yet the overall impact of firearms policies can be tested by comparing jurisdictions before and after they adopt concealed-carry laws, and comparing those that have such laws with those subject to more restrictive firearms policies. The most frequently cited study of the impact of concealed-carry laws, the work of three criminologists at the University of Maryland, was published in March 1995. The authors examined five counties in three states for the years 1973–1992.[92] They concentrated exclusively on urban areas, picked counties without explaining their selection, and failed to take account of other variables that might have an impact on crime rates. In an article titled "The False Allure of Concealed Guns," the *New York Times* reported that these researchers found that homicides increased after concealed-carry laws were enacted but "did not conclude that the new laws had caused the increases," only that "they found strong evidence that the laws did not reduce gun homicides."[93] Whatever the researchers found or failed to find in their five counties, the newspaper stuck to its message of the hazards of carrying a gun by citing a study of fifty-one incidents in which police officers were killed, 85 percent without firing their weapons and 20 percent with their own weapons. The University of Maryland study was a start, but not sufficiently inclusive in terms of either the districts examined or the factors considered. For example, such factors as the demographic curve and increase in illegal drugs also have a significant impact on the crime rate.[94] A much larger study that examined 170 cities for a single year, 1980, found that private gun ownership can deter crime, but again the methodology included no other variables that might affect the crime rate and lacked longitudinal perspective.[95]

The most comprehensive investigation in terms of scope, duration, extensiveness of data, and control for key variables is that undertaken by economist John Lott. Lott's study is the first to analyze systematically all 3,054 counties in the United States over an extended period (from 1977 to 1992) to determine whether concealed-carry legislation saved or cost lives. He found that these laws coincided with fewer violent crimes—that is murders, aggravated assaults, and rapes—although property crimes rose, perhaps from what is known as the substitution effect. When concealed-carry laws went into effect in a county, Lott found that murder rates fell by 8 percent, rapes by 5 percent, and aggravated assaults by 7 percent. Not all counties were effected equally: the decline in violent crime was steepest in high-crime areas. When counties with almost 600,000 people passed a concealed-carry law the murder rate fell by 12 percent, or 7.4 times more than for the average county of 75,773 people. This result is not surprising, since the ability of potential victims to be armed is more crucial in high-crime areas and it is in these areas that policing is often inadequate. It is these urban areas and the most vulnerable groups—minorities, the elderly, and women—which are often the most insistent upon gun control, who have benefitted most from concealed-carry laws.[96] When Lott broke down his data by income and by the percentage of a county population that was black and therefore often more susceptible to crime, he found that with the concealed-carry laws both higher-income areas and counties with more blacks had particularly large declines in crime. He also compared the crime rates for states that had concealed-carry laws with states that had restrictive laws (including the District of Columbia). He found the rate of violent crimes 81 percent higher in states that did not have concealed-carry laws. If lives were saved by con-cealed-carry laws, he reckons they were lost in states and counties without such deterrence. Using 1992 figures, Lott es-timated that if the counties without nondiscretionary hand-gun laws had been required to issue handgun permits that year, murders in the United States would have declined by about 1,400, rapes by 4,200, aggravated assaults by 60,000, and robberies by 12,000. On the other hand there would have been 240,000 more property crimes, a rise of 2.7 percent.[97] If these figures are correct, the value of concealed-carry laws in deterring violent crime is significant and portentous. Lott has since updated this work, using 1996 statistics and including the ten additional states that adopted concealed-carry laws in 1994 and 1995.[98]

But what of other measures to reduce crime? How effective are harsher sentences for crimes committed with guns and waiting periods and background checks for gun purchasers? In an attempt to increase control on gun dealers, the 1994 Vio-lent Crime Control and Law Enforcement Act imposed new licencing regulations that had reduced their numbers by 56 percent within three years.[99] The same act raised licence fees from $30 to $200 for new licences and $90 for renewals. Might the impact of these other measures be at least partly responsi-ble for the decline in violent crime in Lott's concealed-carry counties? When he analyzed the impact of these measures Lott discovered that harsher sentencing reduced aggravated assault and robbery, but that its impact on other violent crimes was inconsistent.[100] There is no evidence that the re-duction in numbers of gun dealers had a positive impact.[101] Mandated waiting periods yielded inconsistent results, ac-tually raising the rates of murder and rape while lowering those for aggravated assault and burglary. The best-known of recent gun-control measures, the Brady Act, which mandates a background check before sale of a gun, took effect in 1994. Although the present decline in violent crime began in 1991, well before the Brady law was instituted, the Clinton administration has given that act considerable credit for the decline in violence by preventing thousands of gun purchases. Since determined felons are less likely to try to get a gun through normal channels, the best test of the Brady Act is not how many people were prevented from buying guns at first application—most rejections were for technicalities—but whether crime fell as a result of the law.[102] When Lott tested counties for the impact of the Brady Act he found it "associated with significant increases in rape and aggravated assaults," while the declines it brought about in murder and robbery were "statistically insignificant." Such analyses of the efficacy of various firearms strategies are essential to wise policy decisions. They also demonstrate that the impact attributed to concealed-carry laws was not merely a reflection of the beneficent effect of other gun laws.

Lott's results have been unwelcome. His methods and the figures used in his groundbreaking study have been closely scrutinized. His approach is thorough, broadly based, careful, reasoned, and scholarly. No one else has analyzed data for every county in the United States over an extensive period to test the relationship between guns and violent crime. He has made his data available to all academics who requested it, and has provided a detailed response to criticisms of his methods in a second edition of his book.[103] But instead of applauding his efforts many gun-control advocates have virulently attacked him, intent solely upon discrediting his results. The unrelenting assault on Lott's work, on the distinguished journal that published his original article, and on the foundation that funded his research, is indicative of the unfortunate emotional level at which much debate over firearms policy in America is conducted and the obstinate refusal of many of those involved to consider unwelcome facts.[104] But it is essential to the public interest to understand the actual relationship between guns and violence in order to implement policies that best enhance the safety of law-abiding people.

The decline in America's rate of violent crime is attributable to many factors. The American judicial system has played a key role in preventing crime. A person committing a serious crime in the United States is more likely to be caught, more likely to be convicted, and more likely to be incarcerated than his or her counterpart in England.[105] Moreover, for every major category of violent crime American offenders are sentenced to longer periods of incarceration and subsequently serve more time in prison than offenders in England. Since 1981 an offender's risk of being caught, convicted, and incarcerated has been rising in the United States but falling in England.

A close examination of the English and American systems makes it easier to appreciate why English rates of crime are rising while American rates are falling. Whatever the old stereotype and whatever its own imperfections, the American legal system provides its citizens with better protection against crime than does the English system. The American judicial system is tougher and more efficient. At the same time it embodies a more liberal approach to the rules of self-defence and permits the means for that defence. Americans today possess the right "to have arms for their defence" that the English were guaranteed in the English Bill of Rights three hundred years ago. The English themselves no longer have this right. The decline in violent crime in the United States and its rise in England serve to underline the fact that guns in and of themselves are not a cause of crime. Moreover, there is evidence that armed civilians, as thirty-three states believe, do reduce crime.

8

The Right Equation

... the Bill of Rights still remains unrepealed, no practice or custom, however prolonged, or however acquiesced in on the part of the subject, can be relied on by the Crown as justifying any infringement of its provisions.

—BOWLES V. BANK OF ENGLAND, 1913

CRIME HAS MANY CAUSES. But guns, in and of themselves, have been singled out by many in England and the United States as a direct cause of criminal violence. Less prominent in these discussions, and absent in traditional crime statistics, is the deterrent impact of an armed public. Of course deterrence is, if not quite as complex as crime, also not attributable to a single cause. Deterrence can take many avenues besides, or in addition to, permitting ordinary citizens to protect themselves with guns or with other weapons. Efficient apprehension, conviction, and punishment of offenders help. So too do laws that permit persons attacked or whose homes are invaded to defend themselves and their possessions with the necessary vigor. Nondiscretionary concealed-handgun laws have had a significant role in deterrence of violent crime in America and provide individuals with the means to protect themselves in the way common law intended. Not every citizen needs to be armed for the deterrence to work. Simply knowing that some people are, and not knowing who, makes criminals hesitant to commit violent crimes. As John Lott points out, "Citizens who have no intention of ever carrying concealed handguns in a sense get a 'free ride' from the crime-fighting efforts of their fellow citizens."[1] Those who are armed protect themselves and others.

The American debate is not over. The rift remains between the majority of state jurisdictions wedded to policies based on the premiss that more guns mean less crime, and those still convinced that more guns mean more crime. But Americans are scrutinizing first principles, and even as the argument continues the American rate of violent crime continues its steady decline. The English debate is just beginning. And as it does, a nation in which law-abiding citizens have been effectively disarmed of all weapons for nearly fifty years, their rights of self-defence severely circumscribed, dependent upon inadequate police protection, their judicial system reluctant to incarcerate those offenders it is able to apprehend, affords only minimal deterrence. The result is a rate of violent crime soaring to record levels. The props of crime prevention that worked so well in the late nineteenth century have all been removed. Four hundred years of increasing civility have been reversed. The safety of the individual has taken a back seat to a government agenda that prefers a passive, if vulnerable, populace, a government that demands a monopoly of force that it can succeed in imposing only upon law-abiding citizens. The English government has never investigated the impact of its basic policies or seriously considered alternatives. The "guns equals violence" equation remains unquestioned, indeed vehemently defended in the face of the tragic failure of policies crafted upon it. In England fewer guns have meant more crime. In America more guns have meant less crime.

People have a natural right of self-defence that Blackstone fervently believed no government could deprive them of, since no government could protect the individual in his moment of need. "One has to remember that there are many places where society cannot get, or cannot get there in time," the Commons were reminded during debate over the 1953 Prevention of Crime Act. "On those occasions a man has to defend himself and those whom he is escorting. It is not very much consolation that society will come forward a great deal later, pick up the bits, and punish the offender."[2] Is English society safer or more secure for this sacrifice of personal security? Not if safer society means the society with fewer violent encounters for nonaggressors, rather than the society with fewer violent encounters overall.[3]

We have yet to consider one additional thesis about the relationship between guns and violence: the possibility that guns make no difference, that violence is not caused or cured by their availability. There is evidence in both the English and the American cases that guns, by themselves, do not cause violent crime. During the years when the English had plentiful access to firearms, violent crime declined to an enviable low. The availability of guns did not increase crime and may have deterred it. In America there are a variety of causes for high rates of violence independent of the availability of guns. There are deeper causes of both crime and social civility than the presence or absence of firearms. But firearms have not been a neutral factor. The latest studies demonstrate that they can form part of an effective deterrence against predators and ensure a safer community.

The principal aim of society, William Blackstone affirmed, "is to protect individuals in the enjoyment of those absolute rights, which were vested in them by the immutable laws of nature." He defined those absolute rights, those "great and primary" rights, as personal security, personal liberty and private property. The very first is personal security. The great jurist was well aware that at times individual rights were trampled upon, even great and primary rights, but he was convinced that the English constitution was sufficiently resilient to restore them.

> The absolute rights of every Englishman . . . as they are founded on nature and reason, so they are co-eval with our form of government; though subject at times to fluctuate and change: their establishment (excellent as it is) being still human. At some times we have seen them depressed by over-bearing and tyrannical princes; at others so luxuriant as even to tend to anarchy . . . But the vigour of our free constitution has always delivered the nation from these embarrassments, and, as soon as the convulsions consequent on the struggle have been over, the ballance of our rights and liberties has settled to it's [sic] proper level, and their fundamental articles have been from time to time asserted in

parliament, as often as they were thought to be in danger.[4]

Blackstone was an optimist. But in the past that optimism has been well founded. Allowing individuals the means to protect themselves and also thereby to deter crime is not without some potential cost to the general quiet. But as a more modern English jurist, Browne-Wilkinson, pointed out in a 1985 opinion: "It is implicit in a genuine right that its exercise may work against (some facet of) the public interest: a right to speak only where its exercise advanced the public welfare or public policy . . . would be a hollow guarantee against repression."[5]

Appendix: Firearm Licences in England and Wales

Beginning in 1870 the British government required owners of firearms who intended to use or carry them off their private premises to purchase an annual licence. The Gun Licence Act remained in force until 1967. Licence fees obtained by the government provide a minimum estimate of private gun ownership during that period. Henry Neuburger, an English economist and statistician in the British civil service, used these returns to determine how the numbers of licenced firearm owners varied between 1871 and 1964. Professor Gary Mauser of Simon Fraser University, an economist and expert on firearms statistics, kindly undertook an analysis of Neuburger's work for this book.[1]

The sophisticated econometric model Neuburger created, based upon the number of gun owners per 100,000 people in the general population, used three variables: the general economic conditions, involvement in hunting, and the number of military personnel in the country. Hunters were required to obtain a game permit but did not need also to purchase a gun licence. Warfare increased exposure to firearms and interest in them, and British officers were required to purchase their own sidearms.

Not only is the model Neuburger created statistically significant, but all the independent variables are significant. Neuburger found the possibility that any of the variables were significant purely as a result of chance less than one in 1,000. As Figures A.1, A.2, and A.3 demonstrate, private gun ownership rose and fell with other consumer goods as well as with the numbers of hunters and military personnel. These trends are distinctly different from depictions of rising rates of violent crime in England in the twentieth century. Given the numbers of gun licences, there is no correspondence between the numbers of private firearms owners and the increase in rates of violent crime.

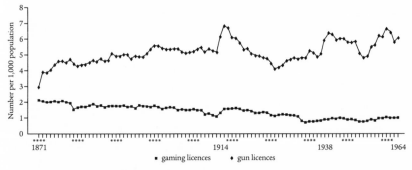

Figure A.1. Gun and game licences, 1871–1964

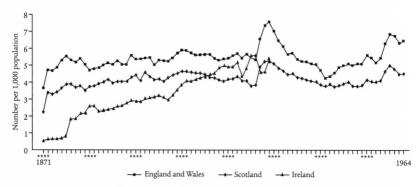

Figure A.2. Gun, firearm, and shotgun licences, 1871–1964

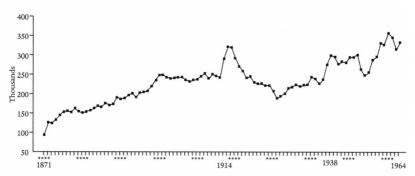

Figure A.3. Number of guns in the United Kingdom, 1871–1964

Notes

Introduction

Epigraph: A. V. Dicey, *Introduction to the Study of the Law of the Constitution,* 8th ed. (1915; reprint, Indianapolis, 1982), p. 341.

1. See, for example, Franklin Zimring and Gordon Hawkins, *Crime Is Not the Problem: Lethal Violence in America* (Oxford, 1997); Craig A. Anderson, Arlin J. Benjamin Jr., and Bruce D. Bartholow, "Does the Gun Pull the Trigger? Automatic Priming Effects of Weapon Pictures and Weapon Names," *American Psychological Science* 9 (July 1998): 308–314; Arthur Kellerman et al., "Gun Ownership as a Risk Factor for Homicide in the Home," *New England Journal of Medicine,* October 7, 1993, pp. 1084–91.

2. Anderson, Benjamin, and Bartholow, "Does the Gun Pull the Trigger?" p. 308.

3. For example, in his study of homicide in thirteenth-century England James Given judged England the only country in northern Europe that produced such thorough homicide records at such an early date; James Buchanan Given, *Society and Homicide in Thirteenth-Century England* (Stanford, 1977), p. 4.

4. See, for example, Thomas A. Critchley, *The Conquest of Violence: Order and Liberty in Britain* (London, 1970); J. M. Beattie,

"The Pattern of Crime in England, 1660–1800," *Past and Present*, no. 62 (February 1974); E. P. Thompson, *Whigs and Hunters: The Origin of the Black Act* (New York, 1975); Douglas Hay et al., eds., *Albion's Fatal Tree* (London, 1975); J. S. Cockburn, ed., *Crime in England: 1550–1800* (London, 1977); David Philips, *Crime and Authority in Victorian England: The Black Country, 1835–60* (London, 1977); Lawrence Stone, "Interpersonal Violence in English Society, 1300–1980," *Past and Present*, no. 101 (November 1983): 22–33; J. A. Sharpe, *Crime in Early Modern England: 1550–1750* (London, 1984); Thomas A. Green, *Verdict According to Conscience: Perspectives on the English Criminal Trial Jury, 1200–1800* (Chicago, 1985); Martin Wiener, *Reconstructing the Criminal: Culture, Law and Policy in England, 1830–1914* (Cambridge, 1990). Most relevant for this study is Colin Greenwood's groundbreaking work, *Firearms Control: A Study of Armed Crime and Firearms Control in England and Wales* (London, 1972), which appeared just as the interest in crime in English history was beginning.

5. A group of scholars has been actively assessing the experience of those states that have opted for right-to-carry laws to reduce crime. See, for example, John R. Lott Jr. and David B. Mustard, "Crime, Deterrence, and Right-to-Carry Concealed Handguns," *Journal of Legal Studies* 26 (January 1997): 1–68. See also Chapter 7 of this volume.

6. For the history of this practice and its conversion into a right see Joyce Lee Malcolm, *To Keep and Bear Arms: The Origins of an Anglo-American Right* (Cambridge, Mass., 1994).

7. Michael Bellesiles takes issue with the idea that firearms played a role in colonial and early national America and denies that they were available to any but wealthy Englishmen. However, the sources cited do not support the thesis. See Michael Bellesiles, *Arming America* (New York, 2000), and my reviews in *Reason Magazine*, January 2001, pp. 49–51, and in *Texas Law Journal* 79 (May 2001): 1657–76.

8. There has been a lively debate over whether the Second

Amendment grants an individual the right to be armed. Over the past decade a scholarly consensus has emerged that an individual right was intended, and leading constitutional experts have accepted that view. See especially Lawrence Tribe, *American Constitutional Law,* 3d ed. (New York, 2000), 1: 894–903; Leonard W. Levy, *Origins of the Bill of Rights* (New Haven, 1999), pp. 133–149.

9. See, for example, Sir Leon Radzinowicz and Joan King, *The Growth of Crime: The International Experience* (London, 1977); Sir Leon Radzinowicz, *A History of English Criminal Law and Its Administration from 1750,* 5 vols. (London, 1948–1986); Nigel Walker, *Behaviour and Misbehavior: Explanations and Non-Explanations* (Oxford, 1977); V. A. C. Gatrell, Bruce Lenman, and Geoffrey Parker, eds., *Crime and the Law: The Social History of Crime in Western Europe since 1500* (London, 1980); Paul Brantingham and Patricia Brantingham, *Patterns in Crime* (New York, 1984).

10. Brantingham and Brantingham, *Patterns of Crime,* figs. 10–1 and 10–2, pp. 253, 254. This finding was based upon the United Nations report *Crime Prevention and Control: Report to the Secretary General* (New York, 1977).

11. Terence Morris, *Crime and Criminal Justice since 1945* (Oxford, 1989), p. 154.

12. Terence Morris and Louis Blom-Cooper, *A Calendar of Murder: Criminal Homicide in England since 1957* (London, 1964). The sole exception is a note that in 1960 the girlfriend of a convicted robber/murderer had been able to purchase another shotgun immediately after the crime "with no apparent difficulty." Morris and Blom-Cooper comment that this was an instance of "the laxity of the present law"; p. 219 n.

13. Robert Sindall, *Street Violence in the Nineteenth Century: Media Panic or Real Danger?* (Leicester, 1990).

14. Walker, *Behaviour and Misbehaviour,* pp. 112–113, 125–126, 143.

15. Peter Squires, *Gun Culture or Gun Control? Firearms, Violence and Society* (London, 2000), pp. 1, 10, 15, 16, 223.

16. Franklin E. Zimring, "Reflections on Firearms and the Criminal Law," *Journal of Criminal Law and Criminology* 86 (Fall 1995): 1.

17. Sir Stephen Tumin, *Times Literary Supplement,* March 21, 1997, p. 15.

18. In their introduction to *The Civilization of Crime: Violence in Town and Country since the Middle Ages* (Chicago, 1996) editors Eric A. Johnson and Eric H. Monkkonen explain: "Three decades ago, it could have been said that historians of crime were far more optimistic about studying everything around crime than about studying crime itself. The latter pursuit was considered elusive primarily because empirical estimates concerning crime's volume and severity seemed to be unattainable, at least for crime in earlier ages;" p. 2. V. A. C. Gatrell, "The Decline of Theft and Violence in Victorian and Edwardian England," in Gatrell, Lenman, and Parker, *Crime and the Law,* p. 249.

19. R. A. I. Munday and J. A. Stevenson, *Guns and Violence: The Debate before Lord Cullen* (Brightlingsea, Essex, 1996), p. 309.

20. This view was first presented by Kitsuse and Circourel in 1963. See Munday and Stevenson, *Guns and Violence,* pp. 78–83.

21. Howard Taylor's provocative article on this subject makes a strong case for the pivotal impact of budgetary concerns on the prosecutions and recording of crime. See "Rationing Crime: The Political Economy of Criminal Statistics since the 1850s," *Economic History Review* 60 (August 1998): 569–590.

22. Munday and Stevenson, *Guns and Violence,* p. 83.

23. Keith Bottomley and Clive Coleman, *Understanding Crime Rates: Police and Public Roles in the Production of Official Statistics* (Farnborough, 1981), p. 101.

24. *The Times* (London), September 27, 1990, and October 30, 1992.

1. The Middle Ages

Epigraph: J. S. Cockburn, "Patterns of Violence in English Society: Homicide in Kent, 1560–1985," *Past and Present* 130 (February 1991): 105.

1. See Eric A. Johnson and Eric H. Monkkonen, eds., *The Civilization of Crime: Violence in Town and Country since the Middle Ages* (Chicago, 1996), p. 5.
2. For a fuller discussion of this issue see James A. Sharpe, "Crime in England: Long-Term Trends and the Problem of Modernization," in Johnson and Monkkonen, *The Civilization of Crime*, pp. 17-34.
3. See James A. Sharpe, "Debate: The History of Violence in England: Some Observations," *Past and Present*, no. 108 (August 1985): 214-215.
4. J. S. Cockburn, "The Nature and Incidence of Crime in England 1559-1625: A Preliminary Survey" in *Crime in England: 1550-1800*, ed. Cockburn (London, 1977), p. 49.
5. Sharpe, "Debate."
6. Barbara Hanawalt, *Crime and Conflict in English Communities, 1300-1348* (Cambridge, Mass., 1979), pp. 19-20.
7. See, for example, Joyce Lee Malcolm, *To Keep and Bear Arms: The Origins of an Anglo-American Right* (Cambridge, Mass., 1994), p. 65.
8. 4 William and Mary c. 8. See W. S. Holdsworth, *A History of English Law*, 2d ed., 12 vols. (London, 1924-1938), 6: 405-406 and n. 5.
9. Lawrence Stone, "Interpersonal Violence in English Society: 1300-1980," *Past and Present*, no. 101 (November 1983): 25.
10. For divine visitation as a cause of death see James A. Sharpe, *Crime in Seventeenth-Century England* (Cambridge, 1983), p. 125.
11. See J. A. Sharpe, *Crime in Early Modern England, 1550-1750* (London, 1984), p. 170, on the continuities between the pattern of serious crime in the late Middle Ages and in the early modern period. Once government statistics begin to be published the continuity of this pattern is marked.
12. Alan Macfarlane seems something of an exception. In *The Justice and the Mare's Ale: Law and Disorder in Seventeenth-Century England* (Oxford, 1981), he argued that early modern England

was exceptionally free from violence. He came to this conclusion, however, from a close study of a single village. See Stone's critique in "Interpersonal Violence," pp. 22–23.

13. Thomas A. Green, *Verdict According to Conscience: Perspectives on the English Criminal Trial Jury, 1200–1800* (Chicago, 1985), p. xv.

14. Stone, "Interpersonal Violence," p. 29.

15. Cockburn, "Patterns of Violence," p. 76.

16. Sharpe, *Crime in Early Modern England*, p. 60.

17. Sharpe, "Crime in England," p. 22. Sharpe points out that there were massive variations in homicide rates during the Middle Ages, from 5 per 100,000 in thirteenth-century Bristol to 110 per 100,000 in fourteenth-century Oxford. He also cautions that the uncertainty of early population figures makes determining rates difficult.

18. T. R. Gurr, "Historical Trends in Violent Crime: A Critical Review of the Evidence," *Crime and Justice: An Annual Review of Research* 3 (1981): 300.

19. Sharpe, "Crime in England," p. 22. Where historians differ is how to account for this long decline in violent crime, or, put another way, this increasing civility. Some have begun to turn with increased interest to the works of the sociologist Norbert Elias, whose descriptions of the "civilizing process" coincide with their findings. Elias' 1930s works argued that control of individual impulse was linked to the growth of powerful states and courts in Europe, that violent behavior became increasingly controlled by the state, which gained for itself a monopoly over violence. He argued that the state forced unarmed men in pacified social spaces to restrain their violence. See Johnson and Monkkonen, *The Civilization of Crime*, pp. 4–5.

20. See Johnson and Monkkonen, *The Civilization of Crime*, p. 6.

21. William Blackstone, *Commentaries on the Laws of England*, 4 vols. (London, 1765-1769; University of Chicago facsimile, 1968), 4: 5.

22. Sharpe, "Crime in England," p. 22.

23. Hanawalt, *Crime and Conflict*, table 3, p. 66.

24. Ibid., pp. 97–98.

25. Pollack and Maitland write of the early common-law rule on a killing in self-defence: "The Man who commits homicide by misadventure or in self-defence deserves but needs a pardon." See Frederick Pollack and Frederic William Maitland, *The History of English Law before the Time of Edward I*, 2 vols., 2d ed. (Cambridge, 1968), 2: 479.

26. Sir James Fitzjames Stephen, *History of the Criminal Law of England*, 3 vols. (London, 1883), 3: 45–46.

27. See Edward Coke cited by O. Hood Phillips, *The Principles of English Law and the Constitution* (London, 1939), p. 153.

28. J. H. Baker, *An Introduction to English Legal History*, 2d ed. (London, 1979), p. 429.

29. See T. A. Green, "The Jury and the English Law of Homicide," *Michigan Law Review* 74 (January 1976): 482; George Crabb, *A History of English Law; or an Attempt to Trace the Rise, Progress, and Successive Changes of the Common Law* (Burlington, Vt., 1831), p. 306. There has been much confusion about the different standards for self-defence, with the strict standards for a plea of self-defence during a sudden argument being misunderstood as also applying in other circumstances. Baker found a somewhat different division after 1512, with the three types of killing being killing with malice; killing without malice, which he dubbed chance medley; and accidental or excusable killing. He noted that after a case in 1600 the doctrine of chance medley faded away, and the test of manslaughter in such cases became not hotbloodedness but the presence or absence of provocation. See Baker, *English Legal History*, pp. 429–430.

30. Crabb, *History of English Law*, p. 306.

31. Blackstone, *Commentaries*, 3: 3–4.

32. Ibid., p. 4.

33. Crabb, *History of English Law*, p. 306.

34. Anonymous, "Newgate Sessions, 1369," in *A Selection of Cases upon Criminal Law*, ed. Joseph H. Beale, 4th ed. (Cambridge, 1928), p. 443.

35. See Crabb, *History of English Law*, pp. 305–306.

36. Thomas A. Green pointed out that as early as the seventh century slayers of outlaws or "manifest felons" who refused to surrender were protected by the law against retaliation by the kin of the slain; "Jury and English Law of Homicide," p. 437, n. 87. According to John Henry Stephens, self-defence is calculated to hinder the perpetration of an atrocious crime "and where the slayer is himself free from all blame . . . is not only a matter of excuse, but of justification"; *New Commentaries on the Laws of England (Partly Founded on Blackstone)*, 4 vols., 5th ed. (London, 1863), 4: 138. For Blackstone's list of justifiable homicides see *Commentaries*, 4: 178–80. On the issue of the necessity to retreat, Blackstone's contemporary Sir Michael Foster wrote: "our law nowhere imposes the duty of retreat upon one who without fault himself is exposed to a sudden felonious attack, and . . . the duty of withdrawal or retreat is imposed upon him alone who is the first aggressor, or who had joined in a mutual combat." See Rollin M. Perkins and Ronald N. Boyce, *Criminal Law*, 3d ed. (Mineola, N.Y., 1982), p. 1121 n. 45.

37. Green suggested that initially making the homicide of a felon justifiable rather than excusable homicide may have been an attempt "to harness the ancient custom of private retaliation, perhaps because it could not be entirely prevented, by legitimating it solely where the wrongdoer refused to submit to the judicial process." He added: "as the judicial system and the test for refusal to submit to it developed, these slayings came to be seen as on behalf of the law." Green, "Jury and English Law of Homicide," pp. 436–437.

38. The requirement to raise a "hue and cry" dates from at least

the thirteenth century. A writ of 1252 explained that upon the raising of the cry neighbours were to turn out with weapons they were bound to keep. The requirement that householders stand watch can be traced to an ordinance of 1233. The system was consolidated in the Statute of Winchester, 1285. See Pollock and Maitland, *History of English Law*, 1: 565-566.

39. Howel's Case, from *Select Pleas of the Crown*, ed. F. W. Maitland, vol. 1, Selden Society (London, 1888), p. 94.

40. Rex v. Leonin and Jacob, Worcestershire Eyre, 1221, in Maitland *Select Pleas*, p. 85.

41. See Green, "Jury and English Law of Homicide," p. 436.

42. Blackstone, *Commentaries*, 4: 180.

43. A. V. Dicey, *Introduction to the Study of the Law of the Constitution*, 8th ed. (1915; reprint, Indianapolis, 1982), p. 346.

44. Ibid., pp. 343-344.

45. Foster, *Discourse II. Of Homicide*, quoted in Dicey, *Law of the Constitution*, 2: 273, 274.

46. Ibid., p. 347.

47. See Green, "Jury and English Law of Homicide," pp. 436-437.

48. 1 Edward III, c. 5. Translation from F. W. Maitland, *The Constitutional History of England*, ed. H. A. L. Fisher (Cambridge, 1968), p. 277.

49. Baker, *English Legal History*, p. 429. 24 Hen. VIII c. 4 (1532). On slaying in defence of a family member rather than oneself see Green, "Jury and English Law of Homicide," pp. 434-435 and n. 81. Also see Green, *Verdict According to Conscience*, p. 30. The use of "mansion" here does not appear to have the modern meaning of a grand house, merely that of a dwelling.

50. Green, *Verdict According to Conscience*, p. xv.

51. Ibid., p. 38. Hanawalt found that larceny, burglary, and robbery together constituted 73.5 percent of indictments between 1300 and 1348; *Crime and Conflict*, table 3, p. 66.

52. Green, *Verdict According to Conscience*, pp. xv, 38, and 38 n. 29.

53. Green, "Jury and English Law of Homicide," p. 432.

54. Of robbers who committed murder 50.4 percent were acquitted, but of those found guilty some 42.6 percent were executed; James Buchanan Given, *Society and Homicide in Thirteenth-Century England* (Stanford, 1977), p. 133.

55. Green, "Jury and English Law of Homicide," p. 432.

56. Given, *Society and Homicide*, pp. 41, 48, 73–75.

57. Hanawalt, *Crime and Conflict*, p. 101.

58. Given, *Society and Homicide*, p. 189.

59. Hanawalt, *Crime and Conflict*, p. 100.

60. Given, *Society and Homicide*, pp. 175–6.

61. In London 61 percent of homicides took place on the street. See Hanawalt, *Crime and Conflict*, p. 101.

62. Ibid., p. 99.

63. Given, *Society and Homicide*, pp. 116–117, 119.

64. The share was 9.4 percent. See Given, *Society and Homicide*, p. 106.

65. Hanawalt, *Crime and Conflict*, pp. 229, 232–233. Hanawalt found little evidence that crime figures increased during times of political turmoil, although she did find some impact in 1328, during the turbulent reign of Henry III, when his mother, Isabella's, release of prisoners in 1328 coincided with an increase in crime. See pp. 225–226.

66. Every English county with surviving records from that period experienced a higher crime rate than during the previous decade. There was a similar increase in national violence during the English campaigns of Crécy and Calais in 1345–46; ibid., pp. 234–235.

67. Ibid., pp. 225, 235–236.

68. Ibid., pp. 242 and 243.

2. The Tudor-Stuart Centuries

Epigraph: "Proceedings in the Case of Ship Money between the King and John Hampden, Esq., 1637," in *A Complete Collection of State-Trials* (London, 1780), vol. 5, p. 125.

1. John Briggs, Christopher Harrison, Angus McInnes, and David Vincent, eds., *Crime and Punishment in England: An Introductory History* (New York, 1996), p. 22.

2. James A. Sharpe, *Crime in Early Modern England* (London, 1984), pp. 49, 54.

3. Briggs et al., *Crime and Punishment*, table 2.1, p. 29.

4. Sharpe, *Crime in Early Modern England*, p. 56.

5. Catherine Ferguson found between 1660 and 1692 some 687 indictments for theft as opposed to 73 for murder; "Law and Order on the Anglo-Scottish Border, 1603-1707" (Ph.D. diss., St. Andrews University, 1980), pp. 78-80.

6. Sharpe, *Crime in Early Modern England*, pp. 170-171.

7. J. S. Cockburn, "The Nature and Incidence of Crime in England 1559-1625: A Preliminary Survey" in *Crime in England, 1150-1800*, ed. Cockburn (London, 1977), pp. 56-57; Lawrence Stone, "Interpersonal Violence in English Society, 1300-1980," *Past and Present*, no. 101 (November 1983): 24.

8. James A. Sharpe, *Crime in Seventeenth-Century England* (Cambridge, 1983), p. 138.

9. S. C. Pole, "Crime, Society and Law-enforcement in Hanoverian Somerset" (Ph.D. diss., Cambridge University, 1983).

10. Stone, "Interpersonal Violence in English Society," p. 29.

11. Sharpe, *Crime in Early Modern England*, p. 22; James B. Given, *Society and Homicide in Thirteenth-Century England* (Stanford, 1977), table 3, p. 39.

12. Cockburn, "Nature and Incidence of Crime," p. 56.

13. J. M. Beattie, "The Pattern of Crime in England, 1660-1800," *Past and Present*, no. 62 (February 1974): 61.

14. 2 James I c. 8.

15. William S. Holdsworth, *A History of English Law*, 2d ed., 12 vols. (London, 1924-1938), 8: 436.

16. Coke quoted in O. Hood Phillips, *The Principles of English Law and the Constitution* (London, 1939), p. 153.

17. Holdsworth, *History of English Law*, 8: 435-436. 4 & 5 Philip and Mary c. 4, "An Act that Accessaries in Murder and divers Felonies shall not have the Benefit of Clergy," was part of the tightening of the rules for murder committed during a felony to ensure that no benefit of clergy would protect accomplices involved in a wide range of violent acts. The act stated that "all and every Person and Persons that . . . shall maliciously command, hire or counsel any Person or Persons to commit or do any Petty Treason, wilful Murder, or to do any Robbery in any Dwelling House or Houses, or to commit or do any Robbery in or near any Highway in the Realm of England . . . or wilfully to burn any Dwelling-house or any Part thereof, or any Barn . . . that then every such Offender or Offenders, and every of them being outlawed . . . or convicted of the same Offence . . . do stand mute of Malice or froward Mind, or do challenge peremptory above the Number of twenty Persons, or will not answer directly to such Offence, shall not have the Benefit of his or their Clergy."

18. Sharpe, *Crime in Early Modern England*, pp. 109-110.

19. Recent research has found that the number of single people during the seventeenth century was exceptionally high. The proportion of those never married at the age of forty to forty-four rose to 21 percent for the cohort born in 1616 and to 24 percent for that born in 1641. See Steve Hindle, "The Problem of Pauper Marriage in Seventeenth-Century England," *Transactions of the Royal Historical Society*, 6th ser., 8 (1998): 73. This high proportion of single adults may well account for the startling number of infanticides in this period.

20. Sharpe, *Crime in Early Modern England*, pp. 61-62.

21. 21 James I c. 27.

22. Sharpe, *Crime in Seventeenth-Century England*, p. 136.

23. William Blackstone, *Commentaries on the Laws of England*, 4 vols. (London, 1765-1769: reprint, Chicago, 1979), 4: 198.

24. The act that repealed the 1624 statute was passed in 1803; Sharpe, *Crime in Seventeenth-Century England*, pp. 135-136.

25. See "Judicial Statistics, 1890," Parliament, Session 1890, vol. 77.

26. Holdsworth, *History of English Law*, 8: 302-303.

27. J. H. Baker, *An Introduction to English Legal History*, 2d ed. (London, 1979), p. 430.

28. I have relied upon Holdsworth, *History of English Law*, 5: 199, for information about the legal treatment of dueling. See also Sharpe, *Crime in Early Modern England*, pp. 96-97.

29. Holdsworth, *History of English Law*, 8: 303.

30. See Joyce Lee Malcolm, *To Keep and Bear Arms: The Origins of an Anglo-American Right* (Cambridge, Mass., 1994), especially chap. 5.

31. Frances Parthenope Lady Verney, ed., *The Memoirs of the Verney Family*, 4 vols. (1892-1899; reprint, London, 1970), 4: 282.

32. John Evelyn, *The Diary of John Evelyn*, ed. E. S. deBeer, 6 vols. (Oxford, 1955), January 21, 1664. And see Verney, *Memoirs*, 4: 291, 314-315, 317.

33. Verney, *Memoirs*, 4: 286.

34. Anthony Wood, *The Life and Times of Anthony Wood, Antiquary of Oxford, 1632-95, Described by Himself*, ed. A. Clark, 5 vols. (Oxford, 1891-1900), vol. 2, February 7, 1677.

35. Verney, *Memoirs*, 4: 316.

36. Anchitel Grey, *Debates in the House of Commons from the Year 1667 to the Year 1694*, 10 vols. (London, 1763), 1: 336-337.

37. 23 Charles II c. I. See also Holdsworth, *History of English Law*, 6: 403 n. 10.

38. Holdsworth, *History of English Law*, 8: 330-331.

39. According to Holdsworth (ibid., p. 331), statutes had expanded the powers of officials to take measures to arrest rioters and rendered them liable to special penalties if they failed in their duties. He noted, "But these statutes only rendered more explicit the common law principles; and it is these principles upon which the modern common law rests."

40. 24 Henry VIII c. 5.

41. Blackstone, *Commentaries*, 4: 180-181; T. A. Green, "The Jury

and the English Law of Homicide," *Michigan Law Review* 74 (January 1976): 441.

42. C. G. Cruickshank, *Elizabeth's Army,* 2d ed. (Oxford, 1966), pp. 106-107.

43. 3 Henry VIII c. 3.

44. Cruickshank, *Elizabeth's Army,* pp. 102-104, 105.

45. 33 Henry VIII c. 9.

46. The statute of 33 Henry VIII c. 6 against handguns and cross-bows noted in its preamble that English armies would hence-forth employ firearms as well as longbows.

47. See Malcolm, *To Keep and Bear Arms,* pp. 79-80, 83-84.

48. 33 Henry VIII c. 6. The act's preamble stated that "malicious and evil disposed persons" were riding "in the King's high-ways and elsewhere, having with them cross-bows and little hand-guns . . . to the great peril and fear of the King's most loving subjects."

49. 33 Henry VIII c. 6.

50. 2 & 3 Edward VI c. 14 (1549).

51. Malcolm, *To Keep and Bear Arms,* pp. 11-14.

52. See William R. Fisher, *The Forest of Essex* (London, 1887), pp. 214-215.

53. See Malcolm, *To Keep and Bear Arms,* pp. 79-81.

54. Elizabeth M. Halcrow, ed., *Charges to the Grand Jury at Quarter Sessions, 1660-1677, by Sir Peter Leicester* (Manchester, 1953).

55. H. H. Copnall, ed., *Nottingham County Records, Notes and Ex-tracts . . . of the Seventeenth Century* (Nottingham, 1915), p. 92.

56. 6 & 7 William III c. 13.

57. See Malcolm, *To Keep and Bear Arms,* pp. 11, 79-86.

58. See Sharpe, *Crime in Early Modern England,* p. 57.

59. See, for example, Malcolm, *To Keep and Bear Arms,* pp. 33, 45.

60. For a fuller account of this effort see Joyce L. Malcolm, "Charles II and the Restoration of Royal Power," *Historical Journal* 35 (1992): 307-330.

61. See B. M. 1851, c. 8(133), (134), (135), British Library, London. And see Joyce Lee Malcolm, "The Right of the People to Keep

and Bear Arms: The Common Law Tradition," *Hastings Constitutional Law Quarterly* 10 (Winter 1983): 300–301.

62. A temporary militia act in 1661 was followed by a permanent act in 1662. Both gave wide latitude to junior militia officers to search for weapons and to disarm anyone they judged a threat. See 13 Charles II c. 6 (1661); 14 Charles II c. 3 (1662).

63. Privy Council Registers, P.C. 2, vol. 55, fol. 71 (December 1660), Public Record Office, London.

64. Ibid., fols. 187 (September 4, 1661), 189 (March 29, 1661).

65. 22 & 23 Charles II c. 25. For a detailed analysis of this act see Malcolm, *To Keep and Bear Arms,* pp. 65–76.

66. William Blackstone, *Commentaries on the Laws of England,* 4 vols., 12th ed. (London, 1793–1795), 4: 175. The requirement for voting was an income of 40 shillings.

67. Blackstone, *Commentaries,* 1st ed., 2: 411.

68. P. B. Munsche, "The Game Laws in Wiltshire, 1750–1800," in Cockburn, *Crime in England,* p. 218; Douglas Hay, "Poaching and the Game Laws on Cannock Chase," in *Albion's Fatal Seed: Crime and Society in Eighteenth-Century England,* ed. Hay et al. (London, 1975), p. 200.

69. See William LeHardy, ed., *Hertfordshire Sessions Books* (Hertford, 1930), vol. 6; J. C. Jeaffreson and William LeHardy, eds., *Middlesex Sessions Rolls* (London, 1888, 1892), vols. 3, 4; Copnall, *Nottingham County Records;* S. A. Peyton, ed., *Minutes of the Proceedings in Quarter Sessions Held for the Parts of Kesteven in the County of Lincoln, 1674–1695,* 2 vols., Lincoln Record Society Publications, nos. 25–26 (Lincoln, 1931). Note that the Lincolnshire series does not begin until 1674.

70. See S. C. Ratcliffe and H. C. Johnson, eds., *Warwick County Records: Quarter Sessions Indictment Book,* vols. 6: *1631–1674,* 7: *1674–1682,* 8: *1682–1690,* 9: *1690–1696,* Warwick County Records (Warwick, 1941, 1946, 1953, 1964).

71. William LeHardy, ed., *County of Buckingham Calendar to the Sessions Records,* 4 vols. (Aylesbury, 1933), 1: 137.

72. P. B. Munsche, *Gentlemen and Poachers: The English Game Laws,*

1671–1831 (Cambridge, 1981), p. 214, n. 45. Munsche found that even after passage of the Game Act of 1671 the statute of 33 Henry VIII continued to be used against those charged with unlawful possession of a gun in preference to the new act.

73. John Evelyn, *The Diary of John Evelyn*, ed. E. S. deBeer, 6 vols. (Oxford, 1955), 4: 411–412.

74. Cited by John Childs, *The Army, James II, and the Glorious Revolution* (Manchester, 1980), p. 106.

75. See Malcolm, *To Keep and Bear Arms*, pp. 98–99; Maurice Ashley, *James II* (London, 1977), p. 165, for an account of the revenues voted to James II.

76. James Miller, "Catholic Officers in the Later Stuart Army," *English Historical Review* 88, no. 346 (1973): 42, 46, 47.

77. See Malcolm, *To Keep and Bear Arms*, p. 101; Sir John Bramston, *The Autobiography of Sir John Bramston of Skreens*, ed. Lord Braybrooke, Camden Society (London, 1845), p. 205.

78. Gilbert Burnet, *Bishop Burnet's History of His Own Time*, 2 vols., (London, 1840), 2: 424.

79. See Malcolm, *To Keep and Bear Arms*, pp. 96–98. Parliament refused James's request for revenues for his enlarged army and prepared a bill "to make the militia usefull." This failed when James prorogued the Parliament the next day. See p. 102.

80. See Malcolm, *To Keep and Bear Arms*, pp. 104–105.

81. See Joyce L. Malcolm, "The Creation of a 'True, Ancient, and Indubitable' Right: The English Bill of Rights and the Right to Be Armed," *Journal of British Studies* 32 (July 1993): 226–249.

82. See "Grey's Debates," in *A Parliamentary History of the Glorious Revolution*, ed. David Lewis Jones (London, 1988), pp. 125–133. For a fuller discussion of the conversion of the duty to be armed into a right see Malcolm, "Creation of a 'True, Ancient, and Indubitable' Right."

83. *Commons Journal, 1688–1693*, 10: 21–22.

84. J. R. Western, *Monarchy and Revolution: The English State in the 1680's* (London, 1972), p. 339.

85. J. H. Plumb, *The Growth of Stability in England, 1675–1725* (London, 1967), p. 64.
86. See, for example, G. D. Newton and F. E. Zimring, *Firearms and Violence in American Life: A Staff Report Submitted to the National Commission on the Causes and Prevention of Violence* (Washington, D.C., 1969), p. 255; Lee Kennet and James Anderson, *The Gun in America* (Westport, Conn., 1975), pp. 25–27.
87. 4 & 5 William and Mary c. 23. (1692).
88. Thomas Coventry and Samuel Hughes, *An Analytical Digested Index to the Common Law Reports from the Time of Henry III to the Commencement of the Reign of George III*, 2 vols. (Philadelphia, 1832), 2: 1303.
89. Richard Burn, *The Justice of the Peace and Parish Officer,* 2 vols. (London, 1755), 1: 442–443; *Modern Reports; or Select Cases Adjudged in the Courts of King's Bench, Chancery, Common Pleas, and Exchequer, since the Restoration of Charles II,* vol. 10 (London, 1741), p. 26.
90. See Malcolm, *To Keep and Bear Arms,* pp. 122–134. For leading cases on this issue see Rex v. Gardner, King's Bench (1739) and Wingfield v. Stratford and Osman, King's Bench (1752).
91. Cockburn, "Patterns of Violence in English Society," p. 103.
92. Cockburn, "Nature and Incidence of Crime," pp. 85–86.
93. See Sharpe, *Crime in Seventeenth-Century England,* table 13, p. 128.
94. Sharpe, *Crime in Seventeenth-Century England,* p. 129.

3. The Eighteenth Century

Epigraph: Leon Radzinowicz, *A History of English Criminal Law and Its Administration from 1750,* 5 vols. (London, 1948–1986), 1: 77.

1. Other acts also introduced new felonies. For example, in 1710 an attempt to assassinate Robert Harley resulted in 9 Anne c. 16 ss 1, an act that made an attempt to assault or kill a privy

councillor in the execution of his duty a felony. A protest by weavers about new fashions prejudicial to their trade that involved attacks on those wearing the garments led to a statute in 1719, 6 George I c. 23 ss 11, which made it a felony to assault persons in the street and willfully and maliciously tear, spoil, cut, or deface their clothes. In 7 George II c. 21 (1734) an assault with intent to rob was made a felony punishable by transportation for seven years.

2. Quoted in Radzinowicz, *History of English Criminal Law,* 1: 77.

3. J. M. Beattie, *Crime and the Courts in England, 1660–1800* (Princeton, 1986), p. 75.

4. See J. A. Sharpe, *Crime in Early Modern England, 1550–1750* (London, 1984), p. 59 and n. 49. While the model that posited a shift in sorts of crime provoked by a shift to capitalism fitted neatly with notions of a violent Middle Ages, violent crime was never the predominant sort of crime in England, and property crime declined in these centuries. Therefore no such shift took place.

5. Between 1681 and 1791 the population nearly doubled. See Geoffrey Elton, *The English* (Oxford, 1992), p. 162, cited from E. A. Wrigley, "The Growth of Population in Eighteenth-Century England: A Conundrum Resolved", *Past and Present,* no. 98 (1983): 121–150.

6. J. M. Beattie, "The Pattern of Crime in England, 1660–1800," *Past and Present,* no. 62 (February 1974): 61.

7. 1 George I ss II, c. 5 (1715).

8. For the text of the statute see W. C. Costin and J. S. Watson, *The Law and Working of the Constitution: Documents 1660–1914,* 2 vols. (London, 1952), 1: 123–126.

9. The Riot Act was finally repealed by Schedule 3, Part III of the Criminal Justice Act of 1967. For further information on this extraordinary measure see Richard Vosler, *Reading the Riot Act: The Magistery, the Police, and the Army in Civil Disorder* (Philadelphia, 1991), pp. 1–11.

10. The most thorough study of this act is E. P. Thompson, *Whigs and Hunters: The Origin of the Black Act* (New York, 1975).

11. 9 George I c. 22 (1722), "An Act for the more effectual punishing wicked and evil disposed Persons going armed in Disguise, and doing Injuries and Violences to the Persons and Properties of His Majesty's Subjects, and for the more speedy bringing the Offenders to Justice."

12. See William Blackstone, *Commentaries on the Laws of England,* 4 vols. (1765-1769; reprint, Chicago, 1979), 4: 244; Thompson, *Whigs and Hunters.*

13. For an explanation of the game laws then in effect see Joyce Lee Malcolm, *To Keep and Bear Arms: The Origins of an Anglo-American Right* (Cambridge, Mass., 1994), pp. 13-15, 69-76. A statute of Henry VII that made it a felony to kill game in disguise or at night had been nullified since the reign of Elizabeth by humane court judgments. Coke in his *Institutes* was among those outraged by a statute so at odds with traditional forest law "by which no man might lose either life or limb for killing a wild beast." The 1671 Game Act punished the offender with the confiscation or destruction of the weapons and dogs he was forbidden to keep, payment of damages, payment of a sum not exceeding 10 shillings for the poor, and, he was if unable to pay, commitment for not longer than one month. For the graver crime of poaching at night the punishment was payment of treble damages or three months' imprisonment. Also see Thompson, *Whigs and Hunters,* p. 58. "An Act to prevent the malitious burning of Houses, Stackes of Corne and Hay and killing or maiming of Catle," 22 & 23 Charles II c. 7, passed in 1670, had made a variety of rural crimes felonies. See Malcolm, *To Keep and Bear Arms,* p. 67.

14. For a thorough account of the Black Act's legal provisions see Radzinowicz, *History of English Criminal Law,* pp. 49-79.

15. Ibid., pp. 75-76 and n. 81.

16. See 3 William and Mary c. 10 (1691).

17. See, for example, Blackstone, *Commentaries,* 4: 4. Blackstone wrote of the care the enacting of penal laws deserves. "The enacting of penalties, to which a whole nation shall be subject, ought not to be left as a matter of indifference to the passions or interests of a few, who upon temporary motives may prefer or support such a bill . . . It is never usual in the house of peers even to read a private bill, which may affect the property of an individual, without first referring it to some of the learned judges, and hearing their report hereon. And surely equal precaution is necessary, when laws are to be established, which may affect the property, the liberty, and perhaps even the lives, of thousands. Had such a reference taken place, it is impossible that in the eighteenth century it could ever have been made a capital crime, to break down (however maliciously) the mound of a fishpond, whereby any fish shall escape; or to cut down a cherry tree in an orchard."

18. See Douglas Hay, "Property, Authority and the Criminal Law," in *Albion's Fatal Tree: Crime and Society in Eighteenth-Century England,* ed. Hay et al. (New York, 1975), pp. 17–63.

19. Radzinowicz, *History of English Criminal Law,* 1: 77.

20. Sir Matthew Hale, *Pleas of the Crown* (London, 1678), vol. 1, p. 13, quoted in William S. Holdsworth, *A History of English Law,* 2d ed., 12 vols. (London, 1924–1938), 11: 561.

21. Thompson, *Whigs and Hunters,* pp. 206–207.

22. Johnson, quoted from *The Rambler,* no. 114, by Holdsworth, *History of English Law,* 11: 563.

23. "An Act for better preventing the horrid Crime of Murder," 25 George II c. 37 (1752).

24. Holland, quoted in T. C. Hansard, ed., *The Parliamentary Debates from the Year 1803 to the Present Time,* 1st ser., 20: 297.

25. Beattie, *Crime and the Courts,* p. 630.

26. Peter Ryland King, "Crime, Law and Society in Essex, 1740–1820" (Ph.D. diss., Cambridge University, 1984), pp. 28–29.

27. King, "Crime, Law and Society," pp. 29–30.

28. Blackstone, *Commentaries,* 4: 239. Blackstone noted that the setting of the bar at 12 pence had been done in the time of King Athelstan, eight hundred years earlier. Considering the great inflation since that time, Sir Henry Spelman in the seventeenth century complained "that while every thing else was risen in it's nominal value, and become dearer, the life of man had continually grown cheaper." See Blackstone, 4: 238–239.

29. Hansard, *Parliamentary Debates,* 20: 297. See Holdsworth, *History of English Law,* 11: 559; Blackstone, *Commentaries,* 3: 366.

30. Radzinowicz, *History of English Criminal Law,* 1: 72–73.

31. Ibid., p. 62.

32. Ibid. See p. 62, n. 40, for another attempt to mitigate the sentence for destroying trees, in which the committing magistrate stated that the death sentence surprised those concerned. He joined with the plaintiff and many local residents in a petition to mitigate the sentence.

33. Holdsworth, *History of English Law,* 11: 570, 571.

34. Beattie, *Crime and the Courts,* pp. 479–480.

35. 4 George I c. 11.

36. Beattie, *Crime and the Courts,* p. 628.

37. See Holdsworth, *History of English Law,* 11: 573–574.

38. Peter William Coldham, *Emigrants in Chains: A Social History of Forced Emigration to the Americas: 1607–1776* (London, 1992), p. 1; V. A. C. Gatrell, *The Hanging Tree* (Oxford, 1994), p. 10, n. 17.

39. Coldham, *Emigrants in Chains,* p. 1.

40. Gatrell, *Hanging Tree,* p. 7. Gatrell found that of those hanged in the 1820s one-third were guilty of property crimes, of which one-fifth were for burglary and housebreaking and one-sixth for robbery. One in fifty were convicted of murder, one in twenty for attempted murder, and one in twenty for rape.

41. The seven thousand hanged during these years may testify to a crime wave after the American Revolution, which was dealt

with by vigorous law enforcement and hangings. See Beattie, *Crime and the Courts,* p. 630.

42. Ibid., p. 474.

43. Ibid., p. 478.

44. See "A Summary of Capital and Transportable Offences, 1795," reprinted by Lloyd Evans and Paul Nicholls, eds., *Convicts and Colonial Society, 1788–1853* (Stanmore, New South Wales, 1976), p. 105.

45. Hansard, *Parliamentary Debates,* 20: 297.

46. J. A. Sharpe found this true for the eighteenth century but found the situation in the sixteenth and seventeenth centuries less clear. In fact he found no rise in crime with the return of peace in 1650 or with the political changes of 1660. And he found some increased crime during war, though mostly as a result of soldiers on their way to ports of embarkation and the harmful impact of foreign war on trade. See Sharpe, *Crime in Early Modern England,* pp. 57, 62–63.

47. John Styles, "Crime in 18th Century England," *History Today* 38 (March 1988): 38.

48. King, "Crime, Law and Society in Essex," pp. 68–69.

49. For a close study of this subject see Clive Emsley, *Crime and Society in England, 1750–1900* (London, 1978). On the impact of recruitment see p. 28.

50. Ibid., p. 45, n. 36.

51. Quoted in King, "Crime, Law and Society," p. 27.

52. Quoted in Emsley, *Crime and Society,* pp. 28–29.

53. Quoted in King, "Crime, Law and Society in Essex," p. 68.

54. Ibid.

55. Rudyard Kipling, "Chant-Pagan: English Irregular, Discharged."

56. William Cobbett, *Cottage Economy* (1824; reprint, London, 1980), p. 10, cited by King, "Crime, Law and Society in Essex," p. 60.

57. Sharpe's study of early modern crime points out that the

level of homicides tended to be more stable, but property crime fluctuated markedly; *Crime in Early Modern England,* p. 49.

58. King, "Crime, Law and Society in Essex," p. 34 and table 2.1.

59. See Douglas Hay, "War, Dearth and Theft in the Eighteenth Century: The Record of the English Courts," *Past and Present,* no. 95 (1982), quoted in King, "Crime, Law and Society in Essex," p. 61.

60. King, "Crime, Law and Society in Essex," pp. 64–65. See King, pp. 65–66, for the comments that follow on the size and rapidity of demobilization.

61. Sharpe, *Crime in Early Modern England,* p. 63 and fig. 4, p. 64.

62. For the decline of assaults see S. C. Pole, "Crime, Society and Law-enforcement in Hanoverian Somerset" (Ph.D. diss., Cambridge University, 1983), table IV.2, p. 179; on the decline in robbery and violent forms of property crime generally see Beattie, *Crime and the Courts,* pp. 137–139 and 140–198.

63. Lawrence Stone, "Interpersonal Violence in English Society, 1300–1980," *Past and Present,* no. 101 (November 1983): 29.

64. Sharpe, *Crime in Early Modern England,* pp. 170–171.

65. J. S. Cockburn, "Patterns of Violence in English Society: Homicide in Kent, 1560–1985," *Past and Present,* no. 130 (February 1991): 82–83.

66. Ibid., p. 86. For the seventeenth century see Malcolm, *To Keep and Bear Arms,* pp. 79–84.

67. Thomas Birch, ed., "An Account of the Number of Deaths," in *Collection of Yearly Bills of Mortality, 1657–1758* (London, 1759), cited by Eric H. Monkkonen, *Murder in New York City* (Berkeley, 2001), p. 37.

68. Marshall, cited by Monkkonen, *Murder in New York City,* p. 37.

69. Ibid.

70. 5 Anne c. 14 (1706).

71. Richard Burn, *The Justice of the Peace and Parish Officer,* 2 vols. (London, 1755), 1: 443.

72. Joseph Chitty, *A Treatise on the Game Laws, and on Fisheries*, 2d ed. (London, 1826), p. 83 and note c.

73. John Strange, *Reports of Adjudged Cases in the Courts of Chancery, King's Bench, Common Pleas and Exchequer*, 2 vols. (London, 1755), 2: 1096; Burn, *Justice of the Peace*, 1: 442–443.

74. Joseph Sayer, *Reports of Cases Adjudged in the Court of King's Bench Beginning Michaelmas Term, 25 Geo. II, Ending Trinity Term, 29 & 30 Geo. II, 1751–1756* (London, 1775), pp. 15–17.

75. Blackstone, *Commentaries*, 1: 136.

76. The right to be armed was specifically for Protestant subjects, since there was the fear that Catholics might overthrow the Protestant regime. On the other hand, Catholic subjects were permitted firearms for their personal defence and were disarmed only in times of great crisis. See Malcolm, *To Keep and Bear Arms*, pp. 122–123.

77. For the account of the crisis and parliamentary debates on this subject see William Cobbett, ed., *The Parliamentary History of England from the Earliest Period to the Year 1803*, 36 vols. (London, 1806–1820), 21: 655–656.

78. William Blizard, *Desultory Reflections on Police: With an Essay on the Means of Preventing Crimes and Amending Criminals* (London, 1785), pp. 59–60.

79. Pole, "Crime, Society and Law-enforcement," table IV.1, p. 170, and pp. 168–173, 176–183.

80. Beattie, *Crime and the Courts*, p. 107 and table 3.4, p. 108.

81. Beattie, "The Pattern of Crime in England," p. 61.

82. Pole, "Crime, Society and Law-enforcement," p. 173.

4. The Nineteenth Century

Epigraph: V. A. C. Gatrell, "Crime, Authority and the Policeman-state," in *The Cambridge Social History of Britain: 1750–1950*, vol. 3: *Social Agencies and Institutions*, ed. F. M. L. Thompson (Cambridge, 1990), p. 246.

1. Ibid., pp. 290–291. The number of homicide trials dropped by

70 percent from the mid-1830s to the prewar years, while reports of homicides dropped by 53 percent from the late 1860s and early 1870s to 1911–1914. Gatrell judges that the decline in homicide is proven by the decline in reports, "a decline which probably understated the real decline since the reporting even of homicide became more reliable with time." See V. A. C. Gatrell, "The Decline of Theft and Violence in Victorian and Edwardian England," in *Crime and the Law: The Social History of Crime in Western Europe since 1500,* ed. Gatrell, Bruce Lenman, and Geoffrey Parker (London, 1980), p. 286.

2. T. C. Hansard, ed., *The Parliamentary Debates from the Year 1803 to the Present Time,* 4th ser., February 27, 1895, 30: 1661.

3. The Militia Act of 1757 sought to put the militia upon a more efficient basis, but it was unpopular and county quotas often were not met. The burden of service fell disproportionately on the poor, as the wealthy could hire substitutes. A Supplementary Militia Act passed in 1796 increased the total numbers and tried to make county quotas more equitable.

4. In November 1830, according to Lord Broughton, Sir James Graham thought "a revolution almost inevitable." See John Cam Hobhouse, *Recollections of a Long Life,* ed. Lady Dorchester, 6 vols. (1909; reprint, New York, 1968), 4: 59. And see David Eastwood, "The Age of Uncertainty: Britain in the Early-Nineteenth Century," *Transactions of the Royal Historical Society,* 6th ser., 8 (1998): 94.

5. Gatrell, "Crime, Authority and the Policeman-state," p. 250. Gatrell argues that since 1805 the judicial system had been generating "spurious evidence . . . that crime was increasing alarmingly." But it was not crime, he points out, but the prosecution rate that had increased.

6. Kingsley, quoted in F. C. Mather, *Public Order in the Age of the Chartists* (Manchester, 1959), p. 1.

7. 34 George III c. 54 (1794).

8. 36 George III c. 7 (1795).

9. 36 George III c. 8 (1795).

10. For the background of the yeomanry corps I have relied upon Mather, *Public Order in Age of Chartists*, pp. 142–147.

11. 42 George III c. 90. The new militia act was also meant to ensure that more able individuals would serve. Since it still permitted men to hire substitutes (ss XL–XLII), it failed to achieve that goal. The act stated that no peer or person in other forces would be required to serve in the militia and exempted the Thames watermen and poor men with more than one child born in wedlock.

12. *The Times*, August 6, 1803, cited by H. J. Blanch, *A Century of Guns: A Sketch of the Leading Types of Sporting and Military Small Arms* (London, 1909), pp. 4–5. According to a "Specification of Arms" issued by the Ordnance in 1794, a new musket could be purchased for £1 16s 10 1/2d, a new pistol for £2 11d. See Howard L. Blackmore, *British Military Firearms* (London, 1961), pp. 63–64. Used equipment would have been far less costly.

13. See Mather, *Public Order in Age of Chartists*, pp. 142–146.

14. John Lord Campbell, *Lives of the Lord Chancellors and Keepers of the Great Seal of England*, 7th ed., vol. 9 (New York, 1878), pp. 131–132. Campbell was active in the Commons on reforming the law and served as solicitor general and attorney general.

15. 60 George III c. 1 (1819).

16. 1 George IV c. 2 (1819).

17. Hansard, *Parliamentary Debates*, December 1819, 41: 1126.

18. Ibid., cols. 1128, 1130–31, 1136.

19. For an account of this event and of the trial, Rex v. George Dewhurst et al., that followed, see Joyce Lee Malcolm, *To Keep and Bear Arms: The Origins of an Anglo-American Right* (Cambridge, Mass., 1994), pp. 166–168.

20. Rex v. George Dewhurst and Others, in *Reports of State Trials*, ed. John Macdonnell, n.s., vol. 1 (London, 1888), p. 538.

21. For the trial record see ibid., pp. 529–608. For the comments of the Crown's attorney see p. 538.

22. Ibid., p. 576.

23. Ibid., pp. 601-602.

24. The population at the time rose by only half. See Howard Taylor, "Rationing Crime: The Political Economy of Criminal Statistics since the 1850s," *Economic History Review* 51 (August 1998): 569.

25. See Gatrell, "Theft and Violence," pp. 239-243.

26. Burdett, quoted in Hobhouse, *Recollections of a Long Life,* 4: 74.

27. Ibid., 2: 121.

28. Mather, *Public Order in Age of Chartists,* p. 9.

29. John Charlton estimates that 1842 was the bleakest time for working people "since the coming of an industrial society." See Charlton, *The Chartists: The First National Workers' Movement* (London, 1997), p. 32.

30. Mather concludes that the Chartists had ready access to firearms; *Public Order in Age of Chartists,* pp. 17, 19, 20.

31. Ibid., p. 19 and n. 2.

32. Stephen, quoted in ibid., p. 17.

33. Ibid., p. 18. Despite their training the Chartists seem not to have become effective fighters, and Mather found them easily frightened. See pp. 20-21.

34. Ibid., p. 25.

35. Ibid., p. 20. Mather cites Home Secretary Lord John Russell's remarks on the subject in May 1839. And see John Stephenson, ed., *London in the Age of Reform* (Oxford, 1977), p. 186.

36. Hobhouse, *Recollections of a Long Life,* 4: 57.

37. Russell, quoted in Mather, *Public Order in Age of Chartists,* pp. 40-41.

38. Colin Greenwood, *Firearms Control: A Study of Armed Crime and Firearms Control in England and Wales* (London, 1972), p. 16. Of weapons sold in London during the first six months of 1848, for example, the group labelled "Mechanics, Labourers, etc." who were believed to be or known to be Chartists bought 122 long guns, 162 pistols, 22 swords, and 18 other

weapons. These figures do not include weapons bought out-side London or secondhand. Such sales seem to have been common, for the *Stockport Advertiser* reported in April 1839: "in our Market Place, on Saturday, war like weapons of every description were openly disposed of, by two individuals." The same newspaper referred earlier to an individual who sold pistols at 3 shillings a brace in the New Mills district. In April 1839 young Chartists were borrowing muskets from nearby farms. For these and other anecdotal and statistical reports see Mather, *Public Order in Age of Chartists,* p. 19 and n. 2.

39. Hansard, *Parliamentary Debates,* 3d ser., 47: 1027-28.

40. Russell, quoted in Mather, *Public Order in Age of Chartists,* p. 31.

41. Hansard, *Parliamentary Debates,* 3d ser., 47: 1027.

42. Ibid.

43. Egerton, quoted in Gatrell, "Theft and Violence," pp. 271-272.

44. Ibid., p. 272.

45. From speech published in the *Northern Star,* February 26, 1848, quoted in John Saville, *Ernest Jones, Chartist* (London, 1952), p. 27.

46. Mather, *Public Order in Age of Chartists,* pp. 75-82, 143.

47. Hansard, *Parliamentary Debates,* 3d ser., 42: 651.

48. General Napier, quoted in Mather, *Public Order in Age of Chartists,* p. 147.

49. Ibid., pp. 90-91.

50. Associations were formed at Monmouth and Pontypool; ibid., p. 91.

51. Ibid., pp. 91-92, 180.

52. Ibid., p. 84.

53. Stephenson, *London in the Age of Reform,* p. 186.

54. Stephenson quotes Sir Henry Ellis of the British Museum in 1848 "bewailing his lack of arms for his 200 Specials" and warning that if his request for muskets, cutlasses, and pikes went unfulfilled and the British Museum fell to rioters it would prove a fortress capable of holding 10,000 men; ibid., pp. 185, 189.

55. Saville, *Ernest Jones*, pp. 30–31.

56. W. S. Holdsworth, *A History of English Law*, 14 vols. (London, 1952), 13: 261.

57. Ibid., pp. 259–260, 279; J. J. Tobias, *Urban Crime in Victorian England* (New York, 1967), p. 199.

58. Hansard, *Parliamentary Debates*, 1st ser., 20: 296, 303; quotations cols. 297, 300–301.

59. 51 George III c. 39.

60. Holdsworth, *History of English Law*, 13: 266–268.

61. Quoted in ibid., p. 283.

62. 5 George IV c. 83.

63. A previous conviction, escape before serving the allotted time, or resisting arrest earned the culprit the title "incorrigible rogue."

64. Hansard, *Parliamentary Debates*, 1st ser., 16: 634–636.

65. Ibid., 17: 1174.

66. Ibid., col. 633.

67. David Philips, *Crime and Authority in Victorian England: The Black Country, 1835–60* (London, 1977), p. 47.

68. Hansard, *Parliamentary Debates*, 1st ser., 17: 1173.

69. Walter Bagehot, *The English Constitution* (1867; reprint, Boston, 1873), p. 355.

70. John Fielding, Esq., *A Plan for Preventing Robberies within Twenty Miles of London . . .* (London, 1755), p. 8.

71. Also see Joseph Ritson, Esq., *The Office of Constable: Being an Entirely New Compendium of the Law concerning that Ancient Minister for the Conservation of the Peace* (London, 1815).

72. For a brief history of the origins of the paid police force see Holdsworth, *History of English Law*, 13: 235–237.

73. Mather, *Public Order in Age of Chartists*, p. 137.

74. Ibid., pp. 110–111.

75. For this incident I am indebted to the account in Roy Ingleton, *Arming the British Police* (London, 1996), pp. 21–22.

76. Quoted in Mather, *Public Order in Age of Chartists*, pp. 121, 137.

77. Ibid., p. 137.

78. Gatrell, "Crime, Authority and the Policeman-state," pp. 255–256.

79. Ibid., p. 263.

80. Ibid., pp. 267–268.

81. Clive Emsley, *Crime and Society in England, 1750–1900* (London, 1987), p. 36. Taylor is skeptical of the official figures. See "Rationing Crime."

82. Even in the Black Country, the industrial regions of England's Midlands and northwest, where a higher level of violence than average might have been expected, a study found only 14 percent of committals were for violent offences, although this might have been affected by an increase in property crimes; Emsley, *Crime and Society,* pp. 36–38; Philips, *Crime and Authority,* p. 238.

83. Stanley Palmer, *Police and Protest in England and Ireland* (Cambridge, 1988), table 11.8.

84. I am indebted to Colin Greenwood, author of *Firearms Control,* for these figures.

85. Philips, *Crime and Authority,* p. 260.

86. See Emsley, *Crime and Society,* p. 35; Robert Sindall, *Street Violence in the Nineteenth Century: Media Panic or Real Danger?* (Leicester, 1990), p. 1.

87. This figure does not include Monmouth. E. A. Wrigley and R. S. Schofield, *The Population History of England: 1541–1871* (Cambridge, Mass., 1981), table A6.1, app. 6, p. 588.

88. Sindall, *Street Violence,* p. 1.

89. Ibid., p. 4.

90. Gatrell, "Crime, Authority and the Policeman-state," p. 292.

91. Gun Licence Act, 33 & 34 Victoria c. 57.

92. Hansard, *Parliamentary Debates,* 3d ser., 202: 855. Mr. Assheton Cross is paraphrasing the chancellor here.

93. 33 Henry VIII c. 6 prohibited those with less than £100 annual income from land from owning a handgun.

94. Hansard, *Parliamentary Debates,* 3d ser., 202: 852, 853, 856.

95. Ibid., col. 854.

96. Ibid., 203: 763–765, 766, 767.

97. Ibid., col. 765.

98. See *History and Proceedings of the National Rifle Association,* 1860, p. 28.

99. Hansard, *Parliamentary Debates,* 3d ser., 203: 768, 770.

100. A coroner from Newcastle-on-Tyne wrote the Home Office in 1886 to complain that revolvers were "far too cheap" and that "a splendid and well made weapon" could be bought new at any price ranging from 5 shillings upward. He suggested setting a minimum price on such weapons. See HO45/9605/A1842, fol. 46, Public Record Office, London (hereafter PRO).

101. Section 7(4) exempted a farmer carrying a gun on his own land to scare birds or shoot vermin from the need to get a licence. See 33 & 34 Victoria c. 57. A statute passed in 1831 repealed the highly restrictive game statutes and put hunting on a more modern basis. See 1 & 2 William IV c. 32.

102. HO45/9605/A1842, fol. 46, PRO. Wortley stated he wanted to stop the practice of carrying arms and asked if any further legislation was contemplated.

103. Ibid., notes on reverse of letter.

104. Ibid., fol. 47, November 25, 1886, R 26642.

105. Ibid., fol. 58.

106. Ibid., note of December 9, 1886.

107. Ibid., fol. 48, letter of January 1, 1887.

108. Other informants agreed that the instances in which persons who carried or used unlicenced revolvers were detected were "extremely rare." See, for example, ibid., fol. 50.

109. Ibid.

110. Ibid., fol. 57.

111. Hansard, *Parliamentary Debates,* 3d ser., 259: 746, 753.

112. Ibid., 760, 772.

113. Parliamentary Papers, 1887, vol. 2.

114. HO45/A1842/9605, fol. 66, PRO.

115. Act to Regulate the Sale of Poisons, July 1868, 31 & 32 Victoria c. 121. A copy of this statute was included in the papers on the subject. See HO45/A1842/9605, fols. 62, 67.

116. HO45/A1842/9605, fols. 62, 67, February 8, 1888.

117. "Reports respecting Laws in European Countries as to the carrying of Fire-arms by Private Persons," Parliamentary Papers, vol. 76.

118. In a letter to Asquith dated January 31, 1893, Herbert Gladstone at the Home Office judged that public opinion favoured strict controls. He noted that the Home Office had been pressed for years to do something. As for revolvers, he wrote, "the Act [1870] is a dead letter. The IR [Inland Revenue] have rarely prosecuted, and detection is extremely difficult. Moreover when boys are caught with revolvers, a solemn IR prosecution naturally breaks down"; HO45/9788/B3145A, PRO.

119. Ibid. The comment was initialled "W. H. C."

120. Hansard, *Parliamentary Debates,* September 12, 1893, 4th ser., 17: 1051, 1052–53, 1255.

121. The results are in ibid., cols. 1255–56 and 1660–61.

122. "Returns giving Particulars of Cases treated for Revolver or Pistol wounds in Hospitals during the Years 1890, 1891 and 1892," August 14, 1893, Home Office. See p. 11 of the report, p. 557 of 1893–94 session, vol. 73.

123. Some gun injuries were probably not treated in hospitals.

124. Hopwood cited these as figures that had been before the House during the 1893 debates; Hansard, *Parliamentary Debates,* February 27, 1895, 4th ser., 17: 1661. For the years 1878–1887 there were an average of only 5.5 cases of year of burglaries involving firearms. "Outrages by Burglars Carrying Firearms, 1887–1892," Parliamentary Papers, vol. 74, pt. 2. Also see Colin Greenwood, *Firearms Control: A Study of Armed Crime and Firearms Control in England and Wales* (London, 1972), p. 19.

Greenwood noted that a report in 1907 gave the total violent deaths for 1892 as 16,343, of which 217 were attributable to pistols (1.32 percent), and when the authors examined the number of accidental deaths due to pistols (16) they found this was just 3 more than deaths due to baby carriages. Poisons, then controlled by legislation, accounted for 400 deaths and vehicular accidents for 2,500. The Home Office did not present these figures to Parliament. See Greenwood, p. 22.

125. Hansard, *Parliamentary Debates*, September 12, 1893, 4th ser., 17: 1259.

126. Ibid., 30: 1657, 1667-68, 1674. I have found no evidence that the police pressed the government to pass such a measure.

127. Ibid., col. 1675.

128. Ibid., cols. 1657 ff.

129. In addition to the figures presented earlier in the text, in his sweeping survey of violence in Kent, J. S. Cockburn found that from 1880 on shootings comprised a mere one percent of homicides; "Patterns of Violence in English Society: Homicide in Kent, 1560-1985," *Past and Present*, no. 130 (February 1991), table 2, p. 80.

130. Hansard, *Parliamentary Debates*, 4th ser., 30: 1663, 1671.

131. Ibid., cols. 1670-71, 1672-73.

132. Ibid., cols. 1667, 1673, 1683.

133. Quoted in J. J. Tobias, *Urban Crime in Victorian England* (New York, 1967), p. 122.

134. Ibid. But see Taylor, "Rationing Crime," who argues that the official crime statistics were crafted to fit the budget of the police and prosecutors and did not reflect actual rates.

135. Tobias, *Urban Crime in Victorian England*, p. 123.

136. Ibid.

137. Sindall, *Street Violence*, p. 1. Gatrell found an increase in recorded woundings and assault in 1860-1864 associated with the garotting panic; "Theft and Violence," p. 290. But see Taylor, "Rationing Crime."

138. Tobias, *Urban Crime in Victorian England,* p. 125. For example, in 1896 the criminal registrar wrote: "The progressive amendment of the law tends to make the prosecution of criminals easier than it was, and consequently tends to make the number of prosecutions in any year a more accurate index to the number of crimes committed . . . There seems no reason to suppose that there is any growing reluctance on the part of private persons to prosecute . . . If, then, we find a steady diminution in the number of prosecutions, we may infer with tolerable safety that there has been, at least, a corresponding diminution in crime." *Criminal Registrar Report for 1896,* p. 13.

139. 5 George IV c. 83.

140. Thomas Macaulay, *Critical and Historical Essays, Contributed to the Edinburgh Review,* 5 vols. (Leipzig, 1850), 1: 154, 162.

141. James Paterson, *Commentaries on the Liberty of the Subject and the Laws of England Relating to the Security of the Person,* 2 vols. (London, 1877), 1: 441.

5. 1900–1953

Epigraph: War Cabinet report, quoted by Arthur Marwick, *Britain in the Century of Total War: War, Peace and Social Change, 1900–1967* (Boston, 1968), p. 78.

1. *Judicial Statistics for England and Wales, 1899,* Part 1: *Criminal Statistics* (London, 1900), pp. 36–37.

2. L. C. B. Seaman, *Post-Victorian Britain: 1902–1951* (London, 1966), p. 38.

3. Marwick, *Britain in the Century of Total War,* p. 34.

4. Martin Pugh, *State and Society: A Social and Political History of Britain, 1870–1997,* 2d ed. (London, 1999), p. 151.

5. There had also been a considerable expansion of the electorate. Until 1914 only six out of ten men and no women were able to vote in a parliamentary election. By 1917 virtually all men over the age of twenty-one were enfranchised, as were women over thirty who voted themselves in local government contests or were married to men who voted. As a result the

pre-1914 electorate of 7 to 8 million had been expanded to some 13 million men and more than 8 million women. See Pugh, *State and Society,* p. 178. Pugh notes that this huge expansion of the electorate placed limits upon the kind of policies the Conservatives felt they could pursue and that "in many ways it forced them to embrace the interventionist Edwardian social policies they had once criticized"; p. 182.

6. Ibid., p. 131. As one example of the growth of government, Pugh notes (p. 186) that in the early 1920s government expenditure accounted for 24–29 percent of the gross national product whereas before 1914 it was only around 12 percent.

7. V. A. C. Gatrell, "Crime, Authority and the Policeman-state," in *The Cambridge Social History of Britain: 1750–1950,* vol. 3: *Social Agencies and Institutions,* ed. F. M. L. Thompson (Cambridge, 1990), pp. 255–256.

8. The Pistols Act of 1903, 3 Edward VII c. 18. It did not apply to Ireland, where, according to the Earl of Onslow, "A person . . . can purchase and keep in his possession any number of pistols of any size or description, without even going through the formality of buying a gun licence." See T. C. Hansard, ed., *The Parliamentary Debates from the Year 1803 to the Present Time,* 4th ser., 120: 1016–18.

9. Colin Greenwood, *Firearms Control: A Study of Armed Crime and Firearms Control in England and Wales* (London, 1972), p. 30.

10. See Sir Archibald Bodkin, Chairman, "Report of the Departmental Committee on the Statutory Definition and Classification of Firearms and Ammunition," Cmd. 4758, in Parliamentary Papers, 1934, p. 878. The matter was raised in the House of Commons on four occasions in 1912 in response to two accidents in which children were killed with long-barrelled pistols. See Greenwood, *Firearms Control,* p. 32.

11. Greenwood, *Firearms Control,* p. 31.

12. There was no separate listing for this offence, but a parliamentary answer in 1911 gave these figures. See ibid., p. 32.

13. See Richard Munday, "The Right to Arms: Richard Munday

Considers the Implications of the Bill of Rights," *Salisbury Review,* Summer 1997, pp. 7–8.

14. For information on the proposed Prevention of Crime Bill of 1911 see Greenwood, *Firearms Control,* pp. 32–33. For official figures for 1900–1914 see V. A. C. Gatrell, Bruce Lenman, and Geoffrey Parker, eds., *Crime and the Law: The Social History of Crime in Western Europe since 1500* (London, 1980): for homicide offences (manslaughter and murder), table IV, p. 287; for offences involving felonious and malicious wounding, table A2, p. 348; for offences against property with violence, table 3, p. 352; for burglaries, breaking offences, and robberies (reports and trials), table 6, p. 364.

15. In July 1915 the home secretary, Sir John Simon, was reminded in the Commons about the number of instances in which police had been shot at, some of them killed, and of "the many deaths of civilians from the careless use of revolvers." Did he not think "the time is opportune for introducing legislation to restrict the carrying of pistols and to provide that no person may bring a revolver into the country"? Simon replied that the present time was "not opportune for dealing with a question which experience has shown to be very controversial." He reminded the member that Regulations 30 and 31 of the Defence of the Realm Act did not permit a firearm to be brought into the United Kingdom without a permit. See Hansard, *Parliamentary Debates,* 5th ser., 73: 2295.

16. The 1624 Infanticide Act, 21 James I c. 27, and Blackstone's reaction to it are discussed in Chapter 2. See also J. A. Sharpe, *Crime in Seventeenth-Century England* (Cambridge, 1983), p. 136.

17. The Defence of the Realm Act was passed on August 8, 1914, four days after the declaration of war, and extended six times.

18. Niall Ferguson, *The Pity of War: Explaining World War I* (London, 1998), p. 186.

19. The government justified the use of martial law on the

grounds that the Germans were planning an invasion. Apparently as late as 1915 they expected an attack on the south coast by from 70,000 to 160,000 German soldiers. See Egbert Kieser, *Hitler on the Doorstep: Operation "Sea Lion": The German Plan to Invade Britain, 1940*, trans. Helmut Bogler (Annapolis, 1997), p. 29. But see Ferguson, *The Pity of War,* p. 87, who points out that for several years before the outbreak of war British military and government experts had discounted the possibility of a German invasion. If this is true, than the government was merely using the fear of invasion to bolster its case for extreme measures. In 1915 some aspects of the Defence of the Realm Act were amended to restore the right to a civil trial. During the debate in the Commons on the bill to amend, Mr. Trevelyan claimed that the DORA had originally been passed because the Commons "in its patriotic anxiety to make everything easy for the Government in the time of crisis, abrogated its ordinary right of criticism." He claimed that responsibility for the act lay with the government, which "should have understood how serious the infringement of our ordinary liberties was in the Bill in its original form." He was pleased with the proposed amendments and noted: "What we ask, and want, is that so long as the ordinary Civil Courts are sitting Army officers shall not be the judges of our lives and liberties." See Hansard, *Parliamentary Debates,* February 14, 1915, 69: 301.

20. The Earl of Onslow, in introducing the Firearms Bill to the Lords, argued that the lower rate of armed crime during the war was due to the Defence of the Realm Act. See Greenwood, *Firearms Control,* p. 52.

21. Thomas Jones, *Whitehall Diary,* ed. Keith Middlemas, 3 vols. (Oxford, 1969), 1: 97.

22. Ironically, the first of these threatened strikes was that of the Metropolitan Police in August 1918. Police wages were so low that many officers' families were actually destitute.

23. In his notes the Cabinet secretary, Thomas Jones, made it clear he believed that the prime minister merely "played the role of taking the revolution very seriously." There were suspicions that the panic "was a War Office dodge for increasing the number of army recruits"; *Whitehall Diary*, 1: 99.

24. Emergency Powers Act, 10 & 11 George V c. 55 (1920).

25. Marwick, *Britain in the Century of Total War*, p. 150, notes that when the railwaymen struck in 1920 a state of emergency was declared and the home secretary appealed to citizens to join in the formation of "Citizen Guards" to combat the menace.

26. For information on this unpublished report I have relied upon Greenwood, *Firearms Control*, p. 36.

27. Ibid., pp. 38-39. The text of the proposed bill is reprinted on pp. 40-44.

28. Ibid., pp. 40, 44.

29. At a Cabinet meeting on February 2 Walter Long, then first lord of the Admiralty, said in reference to the Home Office bill, "A Bill is needed for licensing persons to bear arms. This has been useful in Ireland because the authorities know who were possessed of arms." But Shortt reminded the Cabinet of the difficulty of enacting such legislation: "in the past there have always been objections." See Jones, *Whitehall Diary*, 1: 100.

30. In his study of crime and the police in London from 1918 to 1929, Jonathan Lopian judged that robbery and housebreaking seem to have been the two offences that constituted the so-called crime wave after the First World War and that a small group of professional criminals was probably responsible for most of this. See Jonathan B. Lopian, "Crime, Police and Punishment, 1918-1929: Metropolitan Experiences, Perceptions and Politics" (Ph.D. diss., Cambridge University, 1986), pp. 139-142.

31. The *Times* article on the Commons debate reported that one reason given for the bill was the Arms Traffic Convention in Paris in 1919, "to which every country was a party, in common

with practically the whole civilised world, who had agreed to restrict the sale of arms as far as they could"; June 11, 1920, p. 3. The agreements were concerned with the flow of armaments in international trade. Nothing in them required a country to restrict the ability of its citizens to have guns. Gerda Richards Crosby, *Disarmament and Peace in British Politics, 1914–1919* (Cambridge, Mass., 1957), p. 103.

32. Ibid., p. 133.

33. Ibid., p. 134.

34. See Hansard, *Parliamentary Debates*, 1920, 5th ser., 130: 361–370, 655–686.

35. Ibid., cols. 364–365, 369.

36. Ibid., 133: 86.

37. Ibid., 130: 658–659.

38. Ibid., col. 663.

39. Ibid., col. 671; and see col. 674.

40. The small total number voting, 260, a minority of Commons members (the total after the 1830s reforms was 658), was probably attributable, as the government had hoped, to the lateness and suddenness of the debate on the bill.

41. An Act to amend the Law relating to Firearms and other Weapons and Ammunition, and to amend the Unlawful Drilling Act, 1819, 10 & 11 George V (1920).

42. This was a departure from the Blackwell Committee report, which had recommended annual renewal.

43. These penalties were much greater in Ireland, which was then in a state verging on civil war. Imprisonment could be for up to two years, there was no provision for appeal if a certificate was refused, and additional powers of arrest and search were conferred upon police constables in dealing with persons suspected of being in possession of guns.

44. Greenwood, *Firearms Control*, p. 55.

45. "Guidance from Home Office on Firearms Act, 1920," October 5, 1920, p. 3.

46. These directives from the home secretary to police chiefs remained classified until 1989.

47. "Guidance from Home Office on Firearms Act, 1920," p. 3.

48. Greenwood, *Firearms Control*, p. 56.

49. Colin Greenwood, "Armed Crime—A Declaration of War," *Security Gazette*, June 1983, p. 342.

50. "Criminal Statistics relating to Criminal Proceedings, Police, Coroners, Prisons and Criminal Lunatics for the year 1923," in Parliamentary Papers, Cmd. 2385, xxviii.63 (1925), p. 67.

51. Ibid., p. 8. A previous report of supposed cases of murder for England and Wales in 1912–1913 and 1920–1921 found a total of 390 cases in these four years. Eighty-three were suicides. The numbers of cases of supposed murders in England and Wales were as follows: 1912: 98; 1913: 100; 1920: 107; 1921: 85; "Supposed Cases of Murder in 1912–13 and 1920–21 (excluding Cases of Infanticide of Children under one year by Mother and Deaths from Illegal Operations)," December 1922, in Criminal Statistics, Parliamentary Papers, 1022 Sess. II, Cmd. 1787, iii, p. 745.

52. "Criminal Statistics," pp. 70–72.

53. Ibid., p. 8.

54. Greenwood, *Firearms Control*, p. 70.

55. Ibid., p. 243. On the same page Greenwood notes that police statistics for 1915–1917 show that on average fewer than sixteen people a year used firearms in connection with "all classes of crime" in London.

56. Sir Leon Radzinowicz and Joan King, *The Growth of Crime: The International Experience* (London, 1977), pp. 145–146.

57. Trade union membership during the years 1918–1933 reached a peak of 8.3 million in 1920, a year that also witnessed the highest number of strikes, some 1,607. From 1921 on the size of union membership and number of strikes declined. See Pugh, *State and Society*, table 12.1, p. 217.

58. Marwick, *Britain in the Century of Total War*, pp. 150, 155, 157–158.

59. Pugh, *State and Society,* p. 216.

60. Lucan, quoted in Greenwood, *Firearms Control,* p. 56.

61. Among these were naval, army, or air force personnel, members of approved rifle clubs, butchers, and persons running shooting galleries; Bodkin, "Report on Statutory Definition and Classification of Firearms and Ammunition."

62. Firearms Act, 1934, 24 & 25 George V c. 16.

63. Firearms Act, 1936, 26 George V and Edward VIII c. 39.

64. Firearms Act, 1937, 1 Edward VIII and 1 George VI c. 12.

65. *History and Proceedings of the National Rifle Association* (London, 1860), p. 28.

66. A. C. M. Croome, ed., *Fifty Years of Sport at Oxford, Cambridge, and the Great Public Schools* (London, 1913), p. 205.

67. *National Rifle Association Rules of Shooting and Programme, 121st Annual Meeting* (Bisley, 1990), p. 4.

68. Quoted in Susie Cornfield, *The Queen's Prize: The Story of the National Rifle Association* (London, 1987), p. 112.

69. "Memorandum for the Guidance of the Police," Home Office, Firearms Act, 1937. And see "Royal Commission on Police Powers and Procedure," 1929, Parliamentary Papers, Cmd. 3297.

70. See Kieser, *Hitler on the Doorstep,* p. 30.

71. Raymond E. Lee, *The London Journal of General Raymond E. Lee, 1940–1941,* ed. James Leutze (Boston, 1971), p. 106.

72. Kieser, *Hitler on the Doorstep,* p. 32.

73. Duncan H. Hall, *North American Supply* (London, 1955), p. 140 and n. 2. The request for weapons and binoculars was a private appeal with the consent of the British government. The British Civilian Committee for Protection of Homes, which launched the appeal, was based in Birmingham. It asked for weapons to defend homes, not for the Home Guard. The American Committee for Defense of British Homes was based in New York City. It ran an advertisement in *American Rifleman* seeking contributions. See *American Rifleman,* November 1940, p. 6. It is unclear what proportion of the do-

nated weapons went to protect homes and what went to the Home Guard.

74. Hall, *North American Supply,* p. 204.

75. Ibid.; parliamentary reply, March 20, 1945, quoted in Greenwood, *Firearms Control,* p. 71.

76. Despite this, for some reason *The Times* reported that a year after the founding of the Home Guard the War Office had exempted Home Guardsmen from the need to obtain firearm certificates; "News in Brief," August 29, 1941.

77. "News in Brief," *The Times,* December 4, 1941.

78. Lee, *London Journal,* pp. 429–430.

79. Philip Ziegler, *London at War, 1939–1945* (New York, 1995), pp. 176–177.

80. Ibid., p. 229.

81. Terrence Morris, *Crime and Criminal Justice since 1945* (Oxford, 1989), p. 34. This conclusion is based on a study of indictable offences known to police from 1938 through 1945.

82. See Ziegler, *London at War,* p. 232.

83. Greenwood, *Firearms Control,* p. 72. Roy Ingleton, *Arming the British Police* (London, 1996), p. 52, claims that the end of the Second World War saw ex-service weapons "available to the ill-intentioned" and that nearly every home had its souvenirs, including "improperly retained service-issue weapons."

84. Quoted in Greenwood, *Firearms Control,* p. 72.

85. *The Times,* January 16, 1948, p. 26.

86. *The Times,* January 13, 1951, pp. 3 f.

87. *The Times,* April 19, 1949.

88. See Greenwood, *Firearms Control,* p. 72.

6. 1953–2000

1. Eric A. Johnson and Eric H. Monkkonen, eds., *The Civilization of Crime: Violence in Town and Country since the Middle Ages* (Chicago, 1996), pp. 3–4.

2. Pat Mayhew and Jan J. M. van Dijk, *Criminal Victimisation in*

Eleven Industrialised Countries, Onderzoek en beleid, no. #162 (London, 1997).

3. Figures for rape are among the least reliable, since many victims never report the incident. American homicide figures are calculated very differently from the English system. The American figures include nonnegligent manslaughter and a substantial proportion of killings in self-defence. The result is to make the American number as high as possible without including attempted murder. The English system works to make the figure as low as possible by tracking every case of supposed homicide and removing any case in which the final verdict is not homicide. See R. I. Munday and J. A. Stevenson, *Guns and Violence: The Debate before Lord Cullen* (Brightlingsea, Essex, 1996), pp. 89–90.

4. Roy Ingleton, *Arming the British Police* (London, 1996), p. 16. It is well to be wary of police figures on crimes in which guns were involved, because the Home Office instructed police that every firearm stolen was to be listed as "involved in crime." If a country house was robbed by unarmed robbers who stole a collection of twelve antique pistols, the next year's statistics would count these as twelve guns "involved in crime." See Munday and Stevenson, *Guns and Violence,* p. 309.

5. Sir Leon Radzinowicz and Joan King, *The Growth of Crime: The International Experience* (London, 1977), pp. 3, 4. In 1974 there were 300,000 more crimes reported than in 1973, an almost threefold increase over the total number of reported crimes for 1901; ibid.

6. Nigel Walker, *Crimes, Courts and Figures: An Introduction to Criminal Statistics* (Middlesex, 1971), table 12.

7. From *The State of the Countryside, 2000,* report cited in *Daily Telegraph,* April 27, 2000.

8. Radzinowicz and King, *Growth of Crime,* pp. 5, 78–79.

9. See, for example, Paul Brantingham and Patricia Brantingham, *Patterns in Crime* (New York, 1984); Clive Emsley, *Crime*

and Society in England, 1750–1900 (London, 1987); Terrence Morris, *Crime and Criminal Justice since 1945* (Oxford, 1989); Robert Sindall, *Street Violence in the Nineteenth Century: Media Panic or Real Danger?* (Leicester, 1990); Nigel Walker, *Behaviour and Misbehaviour: Explanations and Non-Explanations* (Oxford, 1977).

10. Colin Greenwood, "Armed Crime—A Declaration of War," *Security Gazette,* June 1983, p. 342

11. See Shooting Sports Trust, *Firearms in Crime: An Analysis of Official Criminal Statistics for England and Wales for 1979* (London, 1980), p. 5; Munday and Stevenson, *Guns and Violence,* p. 133.

12. *Sunday Times,* October 22, 2000, online edition.

13. "Smoking Barrels: Is a Gun Culture Taking Root in Britain?" *The Economist,* July 29, 2000.

14. See Martin Pugh, *State and Society: A Social and Political History of Britain, 1870–1997,* 2d ed. (London, 1999), p. 274. And see pp. 269–273 and p. 275, table 16.2.

15. *The Times,* November 23, 1948, p. 5.

16. "Memorandum for the Guidance of the Police," Home Office, Firearms Act, 1937. A 1929 Royal Commission report on police powers affirmed that it had "long been the practice of the Home Office to issue circulars to Chief Constables on matters affecting Police work and administration and although these circulars are in the form of advice they have come to be treated virtually as instructions"; "Royal Commission on Police Powers and Procedure," 1929, in Parliamentary Papers, Cmd. 3297, p. 16.

17. "Memorandum for the Guidance of the Police," Home Office, 1964, p. 7; "Memorandum for the Guidance of the Police," Home Office, September, 1969, p. 22.

18. Munday and Stevenson, *Guns and Violence,* p. 136.

19. "The Control of Firearms in Great Britain: A Consultative Document," 1972–73, in Parliamentary Papers, Cmd. 5297.

Philip Rawlings finds this par for the course. He writes that Home Office civil servants were "able to govern through administrative rule making and the issuing of guidelines and advice, all backed up by inspections and fiscal pressure, rather than having to resort to the public exposure that legislation entailed." See Philip Rawlings, *Crime and Power: A History of Criminal Justice, 1688–1998* (London, 1999), p. 105.

20. N. P. Chibnall to R. G. Newnham, Esq., April 7, 1997, Royal Courts of Justice, Ref. 007030.

21. T. R. S. Allan, *Law, Liberty and Justice: The Legal Foundations of British Constitutionalism* (Oxford, 1993), p. 82.

22. Fyfe, in T. C. Hansard, ed., *The Parliamentary Debates from the Year 1803 to the Present Time*, February 26, 1953, 5th ser., 511: 2324.

23. Prevention of Crime Act, 1953, 1 & 2 Elizabeth II c. 14.

24. Hansard, *Parliamentary Debates*, 511: 2333, 2340, 2383, 2394, 2354, 2341–42.

25. Other government concerns than crime might have led to this step. There were worries about Communism and the recent Suez Canal fiasco, to mention but two. Home Office papers on this bill are not available, and the government's public pronouncements never directly explain its choice of tactics.

26. Hansard, *Parliamentary Debates*, 511: 2364, 2375, 2408.

27. Ibid., 513: 846, 848, 849.

28. Ibid., cols. 867–868.

29. Ibid., 181: 686, 690, 692, 693, 694. For the rest of Lord Saltoun's remarks see cols. 694–703.

30. Ibid., cols. 705–706, 712–713, 716, 717, 718, 723–725.

31. The amendment would have added a new subsection to section (1) that read: "For the purposes of this Act, any person suffering from bodily weakness or infirmity, whether caused by old age or otherwise, who carries a weapon for self-defence shall be deemed to have a reasonable excuse"; ibid., 182: 5.

32. Ibid., col. 13.

33. Ibid., cols. 214, 216.

34. Criminal Law Act 1967, Elizabeth II c. 58 sec. 3.

35. J. C. Smith, *Smith and Hogan Criminal Law,* 9th ed. (London, 1999), p. 257.

36. Julien (1969), 1 WLR 839, 2 A11 ER 856; quoted in Glanville Williams, *Textbook of Criminal Law,* 2d ed. (London, 1983), p. 505.

37. Williams, *Textbook of Criminal Law,* p. 507.

38. Carol Harlow, "Self-Defence: Public Right or Private Privilege," *Criminal Law Review,* 1974, pp. 537, 538.

39. Williams, *Textbook of Criminal Law,* p. 508.

40. Bradley v. Moss, in P. R. K. Menon, *Criminal Law Review,* 1974, pp. 430-431.

41. See Michael Supperstone, *Brownlie's Law of Public Order and National Security,* 2d ed. (London, 1981), p. 156.

42. Widgery, quoted in ibid., p. 157. See also Smith, *Criminal Law,* p. 447.

43. Frances Cowper, "London's Parallel to the Goetz Case," *New York Law Journal* 198 (October 20, 1987): 2.

44. Cadmus, "Arms for Self Preservation and Defence: Part II," *Guns Review* 35 (October 1995): 750. The Firearms (Amendment) Act, 1994, Elizabeth II c. 31, makes it an offence to have any firearm or imitation firearm "with intent—(a) by means thereof to cause, or (b) to enable another person by means thereof to cause, any person to believe that unlawful violence will be used against him or another person."

45. Peter Squires, *Gun Culture or Gun Control? Firearms, Violence and Society* (London, 2000), p. 2.

46. Smith, *Criminal Law,* p. 447 and nn. 5-11, 450.

47. Gail Tabor, "British Justice 'a Travesty'; Arizonan Won't Visit Again," *Arizona Republic,* November 10, 1991, pp. B1, B6.

48. Smith, *Criminal Law,* pp. 450, 447.

49. See Williams, *Textbook of Criminal Law,* p. 508. Oddly, the

courts have decided that intention is all-important. Therefore, whether the accused is guilty of carrying an offensive weapon does not depend on the "legality or illegality of [the accused's] ultimate purpose" but only on the intention to injure someone. This means that carrying implements for housebreaking is not a crime under the act, nor is the carrying of a knife originally intended for causing personal injury, once plans had changed and that possibility ceased to exist. See Supperstone, *Brownlie*, pp. 151, 156.

50. Williams, *Textbook of Criminal Law*, p. 508.

51. A. J. Ashworth, "Liability for Carrying Offensive Weapons," *Criminal Law Review*, 1976, pp. 726, 734.

52. Ibid., p. 735.

53. Williams, *Textbook of Criminal Law*, p. 507 and n. 7.

54. Ibid., pp. 507, 504.

55. Smith, *Criminal Law*, pp. 450-451 and nn. 20, 1.

56. "Royal Commission on the Police: Final Report," 1962, in Parliamentary Papers, Cmd. 1728.

57. Ashworth, "Liability for Carrying Offensive Weapons," p. 727.

58. For a brief discussion of the arguments about the wisdom of incarceration and the impact on prison population in Western Europe and America see Franklin E. Zimring and Gordon Hawkins, "Imprisonment as a Social Process: Rusche, Kirchheimer, and Blumstein," in *The Scale of Imprisonment* (Chicago, 1991), pp. 3-37.

59. The more modern approach to treatment of criminals goes back to the formation in 1894 of the Gladstone Committee, named for Henry Gladstone, then undersecretary at the Home Office. For information on their work see Rawlings, *Crime and Power*, pp. 107-109, 120.

60. Hansard, *Parliamentary Debates*, 5th ser., 449: 1236, 1237. The Criminal Justice Bill introduced in 1939 had set a minimum age for jurisdiction of courts at sixteen, which members hoped to extend to seventeen for appearance before courts of

summary jurisdiction and to reduce to fifteen for appearance before higher courts.

61. Ibid., cols. 1238-39.

62. See Criminal Justice Act, 1948, 11 & 12 George VI c. 58 sec. 17(2).

63. F. H. McClintock, assisted by N. Howard Avison, N. C. Savill, and V. L. Worthington, *Crimes of Violence: An Enquiry by the Cambridge Institute of Criminology into Crimes of Violence against the Person in London* (London, 1963), pp. 69-70.

64. See ibid., p. 134. The English practice still left its prison population greater than that of any other European countries. Of twenty European countries considered in a 1977 study, England and Wales had the sixteenth highest number of prisoners per 100,000 population. On the basis of the 1988 International Crime Victimisation Survey, however, England and Wales also had the highest rate of crime for the four offences considered. See Zimring and Hawkins, *Scale of Imprisonment,* table 6.6, p. 150; Mayhew and van Dijk, *Criminal Victimisation,* fig. 7, p. 35.

65. "Crime, Justice and Protecting the Public," Home Office White Paper, 1990, in Parliamentary Papers, Cmd. 965, pp. i, 7, 1, 3. Another policy along the same lines was the increasing use of recorded cautions and unrecorded warnings for offenders. See Home Office, "The Cautioning of Offenders," Circular Nos. 14/1985, 59/1990.

66. McClintock et al., *Crimes of Violence,* pp. 139-140. The 1991 Criminal Justice Act barred judges from imposing longer sentences on those convicted who had previous convictions or from punishing more severely a convicted prisoner who had harmed more than one person from a prisoner who had harmed only one. These provisions were repealed by the Criminal Justice Act of 1993.

67. See Langan and Farrington, *Crime and Justice,* p. 43.

68. "Crime, Justice and Protecting the Public," p. 8.

69. McClintock et al., *Crimes of Violence,* p. 150.

70. "Protecting the Public: The Government's Strategy on Crime in England and Wales," 1996 White Paper, in Parliamentary Papers, Cmd. 3910, pp. 1, 43.

71. Alan Travis, "London 'Is Safer than Most EU Capitals'" (Special Report: Policing Crime), *The Guardian,* May 4, 2001. The American imprisonment rate is 682 per 100,000.

72. Ibid., p. 46.

73. See Philip Johnston, "English Crime Rates Set to 'Overtake America,'" *The Spectator,* October 12, 1998, online edition.

74. For these figures on the risk of being caught see Langan and Farrington, *Crime and Justice,* p. 19, and graphs on p. 18.

75. James Q. Wilson, "Crime and Punishment in England," *Public Interest,* no. 43 (Spring 1976): 12; Farrington and Langan, "Crime and Justice," p. 19, and graphs on p. 18. The trend has continued. In 2001 the *Sunday Times* reported that for the year 2000 the police in England and Wales solved only 25 percent of the offences recorded, the lowest figure for a decade. See James Clark, "We Can't Stop Crime, Say Police," *Sunday Times,* May 13, 2001.

76. "Royal Commission on the Police: Interim Report," November 1960, in Parliamentary Papers, Cmd. 1222, p. 17. The police commissioners wrote: "The maintenance of law and order ranks with national defence as a primary task of government. We do not think that anyone acquainted with the facts can be satisfied with the state of law and order in Great Britain in 1960"; p. 4.

77. See Wilson, "Crime and Punishment in England," p. 13. In 1999 London police lost almost 800 officers; ibid., p. 11.

78. Jack Grimston and James Clark, "Alarm as Police Staffing Plummets," *Sunday Times,* April 2, 2000, p. 28.

79. Seventy of England's most rural authorities accused the government of "failing to give enough funds for the police and other public services in low population areas." See "Ministers

'Too Mean' with Case for Police," *Daily Telegraph,* April 27, 2000.

80. Michael Prescott and James Clark, "Territorial Police Force to Tackle Rural Crime Wave," *Sunday Times,* April 2, 2000, p. 7.

81. Charles Clover, "Fears That Undermine Blair's Rosy Image," *Daily Telegraph,* April 27, 2000.

82. Clark, "We Can't Stop Crime, Say Police."

83. This program appears to be going ahead. See Prescott and Clark, "Territorial Police Force to Tackle Rural Crime Wave," p. 7.

84. "Protecting the Public," pp. 2, 6. On August 15, 1999, *The Times* reported Home Office proposals to control an expected "huge crime wave" with measures that included more use of closed-circuit television, modernisation of the courts, and more prompt hearing of cases.

85. Mark Steyn, "In the Absence of Guns," *American Spectator,* June 2000, p. 47.

86. "Control of Firearms in Great Britain."

87. McClintock et al., *Crimes of Violence,* p. 49 and n. 1.

88. Ibid., p. 268 and table.

89. Munday and Stevenson, *Guns and Violence,* table 1, p. 323.

90. Lord Stoddart of Swindon, speech in Parliament, October 28, 1997. He inaccurately claimed it was .04 percent.

91. From 1968 to 1983 more than one-quarter of rifle and pistol certificate holders were eliminated through refusal to reissue certificates; Munday and Stevenson, *Guns and Violence,* p. 168.

92. Ibid., p. 169. A further increase in fees in 1979 was disallowed by the Commons. See Richard Harding, "Firearms Use in Crime," *Criminal Law Review,* 1979, p. 765 n. 6.

93. Two orders, in 1969 and 1970, changed the fees from those originally set by the Blackwell Committee to accord with inflation. After 1973 fees were raised yet again. See Munday and Stevenson, *Guns and Violence,* p. 169.

94. Ibid., p. 164. During the Commons debate in October 1987 af-

ter the Hungerford massacre (discussed later in the chapter) one member referred to the 6 million shotguns in legal circulation at that time. See Sir John Farr, in Hansard, *Parliamentary Debates*, 489: 51. The undersecretary of state for the Home Office, Douglas Hogg, referred to the 930,000 shotgun certificates in the country, many of which covered several weapons, and stated the government estimate that there were over 3 million shotguns in Britain; ibid., col. 66.

95. Munday and Stevenson, *Guns and Violence*, p. 164.

96. Ibid., p. 165.

97. Jenkins, quoted in *Daily Telegraph*, September 13, 1966. While it was claimed that shotgun offences had trebled since 1961 the figures were collected on a different basis every year since that date, and, as they included all "indictable offences involving shotguns," counted every sort of crime from armed robbery and poaching to the theft of old weapons. See Colin Greenwood, *Firearms Control: A Study of Armed Crime and Firearms Control in England and Wales* (London, 1972), chap. 8.

98. Munday and Stevenson, *Guns and Violence*, p. 166.

99. See Greenwood, *Firearms Control*, pp. 86–88, on the debate over Part V. Among the other facets of the bill was the abolition of the ancient distinction between felonies and misdemeanors, the requirement that jury verdicts in criminal cases be unanimous, the requirement for a full hearing of evidence at committal hearings, and the requirement for unrestricted press coverage of those hearings.

100. See a brief discussion of their debate in Greenwood, *Firearms Control*, pp. 86–87.

101. Lord Mansfield dubbed the first part of the measure the "Criminal Justice (Encouragement of Evildoers) Bill" and Part V the "Criminal Injustice (Harassment of Citizens) Bill"; ibid., p. 86.

102. In 1988 electrical stun devices would be added by the courts in the case of Flack v. Baldry, 1 A11 ER 673, to the longstand-

ing prohibition against defensive chemical sprays such as mace, which had been illegal since 1920.

103. See Munday and Stevenson, *Guns and Violence*, pp. 166-167.
104. See Greenwood, *Firearms Control*, p. 89.
105. "Control of Firearms in Great Britain." Harding describes the statistical base for the report's assertions as "defective . . . scientifically quite useless; the data are presented in a way which precludes objective evaluation by anyone else"; "Firearms Use in Crime," p. 772.
106. "Control of Firearms in Great Britain"; Harding, "Firearms Use in Crime," p. 765 and n. 6.
107. See Stewart Tendler, Andrew Morgan, David Sapsted, and Michael McCarthy, "Besieged Killer Shoots Himself," *The Times*, August 20, 1987, p. 2.
108. Munday and Stevenson, *Guns and Violence*, p. 170.
109. Hansard, *Parliamentary Debates*, October 26, 1987, 121: 671.
110. Munday and Stevenson, *Guns and Violence*, p. 128.
111. Douglas Hurd, secretary of state for the Home Office, in Hansard, *Parliamentary Debates*, October 26, 1987, 121: 65-66; October 27, 1987, col. 36.
112. Hansard, *Parliamentary Debates*, October 26, 1987, 121: 59, 50, 55, 46.
113. Hayward and McNail, ibid., cols. 42, 46.
114. See Hon. Lord Cullen, "The Public Inquiry into the Shootings at Dunblane Primary School on 13 March 1996," http://www.officialdocuments.co.uk/document/scottish/dunblane/dun01.htm.
115. See R. A. I. Munday, "Does the Level of Firearms Ownership Affect Levels of Violence? An Appraisal of the Evidence," in Munday and Stevenson, *Guns and Violence*, pp. 37-70.
116. See P. H. Jackson, J. A. G. Hawkins, A. R. Horrocks, and R. A. I. Munday, "Was the Dunblane Inquiry Misled?" November 9, 1996, ftp://ftp.islandnet.com/ForgeConsulting/res/crimstat.zip.

117. See Munday and Stevenson, *Guns and Violence,* pp. 33, 322–323, and table 1.

118. Lord Stoddart of Swindon, House of Lords, in Hansard, *Parliamentary Debates,* October 27, 1997, 582: 944.

119. See Cullen Report, "Inquiry into the Shootings at Dunblane Primary School," chap. 12, http://www.officialdocuments.co. uk/document/scottish/dunblane/dunblane.htm.

120. The Labour party had initially proposed to the Cullen Commission that single-shot .22 caliber handguns that needed to be reloaded after each shot should remain legal. Apparently public opinion polls persuaded them to go further. See Munday and Stevenson, *Guns and Violence,* pp. 31–35.

121. Firearms (Amendment) Act, 1997, c. 5.

122. Home Office press notice, November 3, 1997; Lord Stoddard, in Hansard, *Parliamentary Debates,* October 27, 1997, 582: 945.

123. Greenwood, *Firearms Control,* p. 238.

124. See Stevenson essay in Munday and Stevenson, *Guns and Violence,* p. 126.

125. *Firearms Certificates Statistics: England and Wales, 1991,* cited in ibid., p. 125.

126. Hansard, *Parliamentary Debates,* October 26, 1987, 121: 671.

127. See Munday and Stevenson, *Guns and Violence,* p. 127.

128. Home Office press notice, November 3, 1997. The original police estimate was just that, an estimate if a great overestimate, since the certificate system did not allow them to produce an accurate count of the number of weapons.

129. See Greenwood, *Firearms Control,* table 58, p. 235. For the information on the weapons surrendered between 1946 and 1968 see Greenwood, pp. 235–239.

130. Ibid., table 59, p. 236. The figures for the amnesties of 1946, 1961, and 1965 were adjusted to produce totals in round figures.

131. Ibid., table 60, p. 237.

132. Ibid., pp. 236-238.

133. Ibid. Of the 4,687 pistols surrendered in 1969, for example, 80 percent had never been subject to a firearm certificate.

134. Munday and Stevenson, *Guns and Violence*, pp. 131, 132.

135. James Clark, "Gun Law Takes Over in Gangland Drug Wars," *Sunday Times*, May 13, 2001, online edition.

136. Douglas Hurd, secretary of state for the Home Office during the debate on the 1988 Firearms Act, in Hansard, *Parliamentary Debates*, October 26, 1987, 582: 37.

137. Shooting Sports Trust, *Firearms in Crime*, p. 5.

138. John Briggs, Christopher Harrison, Angus McInnes, and David Vincent, eds., *Crime and Punishment in England: An Introductory History* (New York, 1996), p. 246.

139. Munday and Stevenson, *Guns and Violence*, pp. 133, 136.

140. Wilson, "Crime and Punishment in England," pp. 7-8. The continued truth of this statement is reflected in the annual crime figures released in July 2000.

141. For this approach see Sean Gabb, "Gun Control in Britain," Political Notes No. 33, Libertarian Alliance, London, 1988.

142. Greenwood, *Firearms Control*, table 62, p. 244.

143. See official government figures and Gabb, "Gun Control in Britain."

144. Mayhew and van Dijk, *Criminal Victimisation*, p. 6. The findings from this study are found on pp. 1-6.

145. David Povey, Judith Cotton, and Suzannah Sisson, "Recorded Crime Statistics, England and Wales, April 1999 to March 2000," Home Office, July 18, 2000. Also see Philip Johnston, "Muggings Add to First Rise in Crime for Seven Years," *The Telegraph*, July 18, 2000; "Straw Tries to Stop Pub Maimings," *The Mirror*, June 26, 2000, online edition.

146. Clark, "Gun Law Takes Over."

147. Steyn, "In the Absence of Guns," p. 46.

148. See Adam Luck, "Police Carry Pistols on Routine Street Patrols," *Sunday Times*, October 22, 2000, online edition.

149. Clark, "Gun Law Takes Over."

150. Mark Steyn, "Give Thanks It's Not the Old Country," *The Spectator*, November 28, 1998, p. 23.

151. Steyn, "In the Absence of Guns," pp. 46–47.

152. David Sapsted, "Farmer Who Killed Burglar Jailed for Life," *Daily Telegraph*, April 20, 2000, online edition. The following quotations are from this article.

153. Michael Higgins, "Start Fighting Back and Get the Criminals Running Scared: Bashing Burglars Is No Bad Thing," *Birmingham Post*, April 24, 2000, p. 13.

154. Terence Shaw, "Hague's Pledge on Self-Defence Means Reviving Old Reforms," *Daily Telegraph*, April 27, 2000, online edition; Andrew Sparrow, "Conservative Leader Accused of Adopting 'Lynch Mob Mentality,'" ibid.

155. Sparrow, "Conservative Leader Accused."

156. "Manslaughter Verdict for Martin," BBC News Online, October 30, 2001; "It Was Never Murder," *The Spectator*, November 3, 2001, p. 7.

157. J. H. Stephens, a highly respected legal expert, wrote in 1863, "If any person attempts the robbery or murder of another, or attempts to break open a house *in the night time*, and shall be killed in such an attempt, [either by the party assaulted, or the owner of the house, or the servant attendant upon either, or by any person present and interposing to prevent mischief], the slayer shall be acquitted and discharged"; *New Commentaries*, 5th ed., vol. 4 (London, 1863), p. 134. The *Daily Telegraph* investigated how the Martin case would be handled in other countries. In those mentioned as well as South Africa and Belgium Martin would not have been charged with murder. A test case working its way through the Belgium courts involves a jeweller who fired five shots from a revolver and ten from a hunting rifle from an upstairs window at a gang of thieves who were smashing their way into his shop. His arrest led to a petition for his release, and he is now out

on bail. See Toby Harnden, Christopher Munnion, Harry deQuetteville, and Toby Helm, "Wide Range of Laws on Defending Your Home with Force," *Daily Telegraph*, April 27, 2000, online edition.

158. A. V. Dicey, *Introduction to the Study of the Law of the Constitution*, 8th ed. (Indianapolis, 1982), p. 341.

7. More Guns More Crime or More Guns Less Crime?

Epigraphs: Gary Kleck, "Guns and Violence: An Interpretive Review of the Field," *Social Pathology* 1 (January 1995): 20; Lance Stell, "The Legitimation of Female Violence: Bias and the Law of Self-Defense," in *Justice, Law, and Violence*, ed. James B. Brady and Newton Garver (Philadelphia, 1991), p. 246.

1. *The Mirror,* June 26, 2000, online edition.

2. "Have a Nice Daydream," *The Mirror,* June 29, 2000, online edition. Also see Chris Gray, "Britain Is Capital of Crime, Says US TV Channel," *The Independent,* June 29, 2000. Jenny Booth, "Reporter Is Victim of London Thieves," *The Times,* wrote on the same day that the American newsman responsible for the report had twice had his English apartment burgled and might have had "a possible axe to grind"; June 29, 2000, online edition.

3. Mark Steyn, *American Spectator,* June 2000, p. 46.

4. *The Telegraph,* July 18, 2000.

5. James Clark, "Gun Law Takes Over in Gangland Drug Wars," *Sunday Times,* May 13, 2001, online edition.

6. Kleck, "Guns and Violence," p. 14.

7. Although offences involving firearms dropped after the handgun ban, from 5,209 in 1996 to 3,143 in 1999, the number of guns "used for violence against the person" rose from 1,206 in 1995 to 1,746 in 1999. A House of Commons report earlier in 2000 noted "a generally increasing trend in the misuse of

firearms." See "Smoking Barrels: Is a Gun Culture Taking Root in Britain?" *The Economist,* August 12, 2000.

8. There is no accurate count of the firearms in America. Consequently estimates vary, although 200 million is the figure most often used. In his study of firearms in America John Lott estimates there are between 200 and 240 million firearms, one-third of which are handguns; Lott, *More Guns, Less Crime: Understanding Crime and Gun Control Laws,* 2d ed. (Chicago, 2000), p. 1.

9. The murder rate, for example, per 100,000 population from 1992 through 1997 dropped from 9.3 to 6.8. From 1996 through 1997 alone the Federal Bureau of Investigation (FBI) reported that the murder rate had dropped by 8 percent. From 1973 through 1998 the overall rate of violent crime per 1,000 population aged twelve and over dropped from 48 to 39; aggravated assault fell from 13 to 9, robbery from 7 to 4, and rape from 3 to 1. See Anne Gearan, "U.S. Crime Rate Dips to 25-Year Low," *Boston Globe,* December 28, 1998, p. A3.

10. Thomas Farragher, "Experts Eye Rosy Trends in U.S. Crime," *Boston Globe,* January 10, 1999, p. A1.

11. Zimring, quoted in ibid.

12. See comment by criminologist Alfred Blumstein and figures in Lorraine Adams and David A. Vise, "FBI's Report of Falling Crime Greeted by Applause, Debate," *Boston Globe,* October 18, 1999, p. A8.

13. The decline in the American rate of violent crime began in 1991. The concealed-carry laws in thirty-two states are nondiscretionary, or "shall-issue"; that is, the licencing authority or police must issue concealed-weapons permits to all qualified applicants. Only eight states had such laws before 1985. Vermont has no statute on guns; law-abiding people may carry weapons without a licence.

14. This is not to imply that all those voting for a particular law,

such as the ban on so-called assault weapons, believe that less powerful firearms must be kept out of the hands of individuals. But these statutes are largely promoted by gun-control advocates, many of whom believe that all private weapons ought to be banned.

15. Convicted felons, however, cannot carry guns.

16. See Joyce Lee Malcolm, *To Keep and Bear Arms: The Origins of an Anglo-American Right* (Cambridge, Mass., 1994).

17. On March 31, 1999, U.S. District Judge Sam Cummings dismissed charges against a man on the basis that the federal statute involved violated his rights under the Second Amendment. The government took the case to the Fifth Circuit Court of Appeals. In a historic opinion the court found that the Second Amendment did protect an individual right to be armed. See United States v. Emerson, 207 F. 3d 203 (5th Cir. 2001).

18. See Robert J. Cottrol, ed., *Gun Control and the Constitution: Sources and Explorations on the Second Amendment* (New York, 1994), pp. xxiv–xxv.

19. The National Rifle Association had little political clout at this time. On the motive of the Roosevelt administration in opting for handgun registration see ibid., pp. xxvi–xxvii.

20. Ibid., p. xxx.

21. Overwhelming evidence that the Constitution protects an individual right to be armed has been presented in the past twenty years. Even leading liberal experts who formerly dismissed the Second Amendment as protecting only a collective right of the modern militia, the National Guard, have recognized the Second Amendment guarantee of an individual right to be armed. Like all rights, however, it is subject to reasonable regulation. See, for example, Lawrence Tribe, *American Constitutional Law*, 3d ed., vol. 1 (New York, 2000), pp. 894–903; Leonard W. Levy, *Origins of the Bill of Rights* (New Haven, 1999), pp. 133–149.

22. Patrick A. Langan and David P. Farrington, *Crime and Justice in the United States and in England and Wales, 1981–96* (Washington, D.C., 1998), p. 46. These figures are based on 1996 Home Office and FBI figures. For reasons that will be explained below such police figures are less reliable than the figures obtained from victim surveys. According to 1996 figures the English rate of murder from firearms was .09 per 100,000 while the U.S. firearm murder rate was 5.5.

23. These figures compare the 1995 victim survey in England and the 1996 victim survey in the United States; Langan and Farrington, *Crime and Justice,* p. 46. The English take a victim survey biannually while the Americans do so annually. These two surveys are the latest Langan and Farrington had at their disposal.

24. Even while violent crime was rising steeply in England and Wales, the murder rate in London, at 2.36 per 100,000, remained among the lowest of all European capitals. See Alan Travis, "London 'Is Safer than Most EU Capitals,'" Special Report: Policing Crime, *The Guardian,* May 4, 2001, online edition.

25. The figure for rape, the only other violent crime for which the American rate is higher, is more problematic, since reporting is erratic and until 1994 the English and American definitions of rape were very different.

26. Travis, "London 'Is Safer.'"

27. Eric H. Monkkonen, *Murder in New York City* (Berkeley, 2001), pp. 178–179.

28. Richard Maxwell Brown finds that Supreme Court Justice Oliver Wendell Holmes and other Americans believed that the right to stand one's ground and kill in self-defence "was as great a civil liberty as, for example, freedom of speech"; Brown, *No Duty to Retreat: Violence and Values in American History and Society* (Oxford, 1991), pp. 4–5, 36–7.

29. Lott, *More Guns, Less Crime,* p. 5.

30. For this analysis I am indebted to R. I. Munday and J. A. Stevenson, *Guns and Violence: The Debate before Lord Cullen* (Brightlingsea, Essex, 1996), pp. 89-91. The FBI instructs police: "Do not count a killing as justifiable or excusable solely on the basis of self-defense or the action of a coroner, prosecutor, grand jury or court. The willful (non-negligent) killing of one individual by another is being reported, not the criminal liability of the person or persons involved"; Munday and Stevenson, p. 90.

31. Ibid., pp. 90-91, 85.

32. Howard Taylor, "Rationing Crime: The Political Economy of Criminal Statistics since the 1850s," *Economic History Review* 51 (1998): 585, 586-587.

33. Ibid., p. iii.

34. Langan and Farrington, *Crime and Justice,* pp. 9, 11.

35. For English figures see Catriona Mirrless-Black, Tracey Budd, Sarah Partridge, and Pat Mayhew, *The 1998 British Crime Survey: England and Wales, Statistical Bulletin* no. 2/98, Home Office, fig. 4.3, p. 21, and pp. 11, ii.

36. I thank Patrick Langan for calculating this statistic for me.

37. Monkkonen, *Murder in New York City,* pp. 178-179 and fig. 7.6, p. 178.

38. Monkkonen has an interesting analysis of why the United States has been more violent than Western European countries, particularly England; ibid., chap. 7, pp. 151-179.

39. See U.S. Bureau of the Census, *Statistical Abstract of the United States, 1982-3* (Washington D.C., 1982), table 298; Lott, *More Guns, Less Crime,* p. 9 and n. 36; Munday and Stevenson, *Guns and Violence,* pp. 99-100.

40. Langan and Farrington, *Crime and Justice,* p. 44.

41. In 1995 Alfred Blumstein noted that the annual homicide rate for whites from 1976 to 1987 was 8.13 homicides per 100,000 and from 1987 to 1991 almost doubled, from 7.6 to 13.6. The annual rate for blacks more than doubled from 1987 through

1991, from 50.4 per 100,000 to 111.8. From 1984 to 1991 it tripled, from 32.0 to 111.8. See Blumstein, "Youth Violence, Guns, and the Illicit Drug Industry," *Journal of Criminal Law and Criminology* 86 (Fall 1995): 21–22.

42. Munday and Stevenson, *Guns and Violence*, p. 99. Blacks are 4.6 times more likely to be murdered and 5.1 times more likely to be offenders than are whites. See Lott, *More Guns, Less Crime*, p. 39.

43. Munday and Stevenson, *Guns and Violence*, pp. 99–100.

44. J. Q. Wilson, "Crime and Punishment in England," *Public Interest*, no. 43 (Spring 1976): 8.

45. Stewart Tendler, "London Gunmen Mostly Blacks," *The Times*, July 25, 2000, online edition.

46. Quoted in Munday and Stevenson, *Guns and Violence*, p. 101 and n. 43.

47. Dave Kopel, "Fatherlessness: *The* Root Cause," *National Review*, May 11, 2000, online edition.

48. Don B. Kates Jr., "Gun Control and Crime Rates," in *The Great American Gun Debate*, ed. Kates and Gary Kleck (San Francisco, 1997), pp. 9–10; Kleck, "Guns and Violence," p. 14.

49. A study of those who rescued crime victims or arrested violent criminals found that they were 2.5 times more likely to be gun owners than nonowners; Kates, "Gun Control and Crime Rates," p. 10.

50. Lott, *More Guns, Less Crime*, pp. 36–40. Of fourteen states with enough respondents to make state-level comparisons, the polls show that thirteen had more people owning guns, and six each had over a million more. Only Massachusetts saw a decline in gun ownership.

51. See Adams and Vise, "FBI's Report Greeted by Applause," p. A8. Lott notes that in 1993 cities with more than 500,000 people had murder rates that were over 60 percent higher than the rates in cities with populations between 50,000 and 500,000. Lott, *More Guns, Less Crime*, p. 39.

52. Munday and Stevenson, *Guns and Violence,* p. 100.

53. See Kates, "Gun Control and Crime Rates," p. 10.

54. David Huizinga, Rolf Loeber, and Terence P. Thornberry, *Urban Delinquency and Substance Abuse: Initial Findings* (Washington, D.C.: Office of Juvenile Justice and Delinquency Prevention, U.S. Department of Justice, 1995), p. 18.

55. D. A. Kairys, "A Carnage in the Name of Freedom," *Philadelphia Inquirer,* September 12, 1988, quoted in Kates, "Gun Control and Crime Rates," p. 11.

56. H. C. Brearley, *Homicide in the United States* (Chapel Hill, 1932), quoted in Gary Kleck, "The Frequency of Defensive Gun Use," in Kates and Kleck, *The Great American Gun Debate,* p. 152.

57. According to historians Lee Kennett and James LaVerne Anderson, three-quarters of the nation's newspapers and most of the periodical press support gun control. They point out that in the 1960s large urban dailies with mass circulation, including the *New York Times,* the *Washington Post,* the *Los Angeles Times,* and the *Christian Science Monitor* issued repeated calls for new and tougher laws and with few exceptions popular magazines agreed. They note that at one point the *Washington Post* published pro-control editorials on the gun issue for seventy-seven consecutive days, and in 1988, when a handgun referendum was on the ballot in Maryland, published pro-referendum editorials for nine consecutive days before the vote. See Kennett and Anderson, *The Gun in America* (Westport, Conn., 1975), pp. 237, 239, 312.

58. Craig A. Anderson, Arlin J. Benjamin Jr., and Bruce D. Bartholow, "Does the Gun Pull the Trigger? Automatic Priming Effects of Weapon Pictures and Weapon Names," *American Psychological Science* 9 (July 1998): 308–314.

59. Lott, *More Guns, Less Crime,* pp. 7–8.

60. Kates, "Gun Control and Crime Rates," pp. 11, 32; Lott, *More Guns, Less Crime,* p. 8.

61. Lott, *More Guns, Less Crime*, p. 8 and n. 32.

62. See Arthur Kellerman et al., "Gun Ownership as a Risk Factor for Homicide in the Home," *New England Journal of Medicine*, no. 329 (October 7, 1993): 1084-91.

63. For a quick analysis of the Kellerman study see Lott, *More Guns, Less Crime*, pp. 23-25.

64. See Norman B. Rushforth et al., "Violent Death in a Metropolitan County: Changing Patterns in Homicide (1958-1974)," *New England Journal of Medicine*, no. 297 (1975): 504-505.

65. Kates, "Gun Control and Crime Rates," p. 32.

66. M. A. Straus, "Domestic Violence and Homicide Antecedents," *Bulletin of the New York Academy of Medicine* 62 (1986): 454 and 457; and see Kates, "Gun Control and Crime Rates," pp. 32-33.

67. John Lott cites the testimony before the U.S. Senate of Captain James Mulvihill, who reported that the greater Los Angeles area had more than 1,250 known street gangs with a membership of approximately 150,000. These gangs were responsible for nearly 7,000 murders and thousands of injuries over ten years. See Lott, *More Guns, Less Crime*, p. 8 and n. 26.

68. Ibid., p. 54.

69. In 1991 230 children under the age of fifteen were killed in firearms-related accidents. Despite the growing concern such incidents have decreased by 55 percent since 1930 although there are now far more firearms in the country. The size of the private gun stock increased from the 1960s through the 1990s, especially for handguns. See Lott, *More Guns, Less Crime*, p. 36; "Guns: Triggering Safety in the Home," AMICA Insurance Company booklet, January 1999, p. 3; Kleck, "Guns and Violence," p. 13.

70. See Lott, *More Guns, Less Crime*, p. 9; Kleck, "Guns and Violence," pp. 29-30.

71. Kates, "Gun Control and Crime Rates," p. 6.

72. Father Drinan coined the expression "dangerous self-delusion" in his essay "Gun Control: The Good Outweighs the Evil," *Civil Liberties Review* 4 (1976): 3. See Kates, "Gun Control and Crime Rates," p. 6 and n. 12.

73. Kates, "Gun Control and Crime Rates," p. 6.

74. See Kleck, "Guns and Violence," pp. 17-18. Kleck cites a series of studies to this effect.

75. See Lott, *More Guns, Less Crime,* p. 3.

76. Kleck, "Guns and Violence," p. 18.

77. See Kevin O'Neal, *Indianapolis Star,* May 19, 2000; and Monica Scandlen, *Indianapolis Star,* May 20, 2000.

78. *New York Times,* September 7, 1995, p. A16, quoted in Lott, *More Guns, Less Crime,* p. 5, n. 17.

79. Even if defensive gun uses are reported to the police, the police do not keep a record of them or statistics on them. See Kleck, "Frequency of Defensive Gun Use," p. 185.

80. Ibid., pp. 159-160. On the difficulty of the figures in the various surveys see pp. 160-167. For problems with the NCVS see pp. 167-175. And see Lott, *More Guns, Less Crime,* p. 11 and n. 47.

81. In two Illinois surveys, even among respondents willing to report gun ownership 28 percent did not have the required Illinois licence; Kleck, "Frequency of Defensive Gun Use," p. 170. Kleck's own especially crafted National Self-Defense Survey, conducted in 1993 and involving 4,977 randomly selected respondents, found an estimated 2.1 to 2.5 million defensive gun uses a year; ibid., pp. 183-185.

82. See James D. Wright and Peter H. Rossi, *Armed and Considered Dangerous: A Survey of Felons and Their Firearms* (New York, 1986), p. 155.

83. Gary Kleck and Marc Gertz, "Armed Resistance to Crime: The Prevalence and Nature of Self-Defense with a Gun," *Journal of Crime and Criminology* 86 (Fall 1995): 180-181.

84. See Don B. Kates et al., "Guns and Public Health: Epidemic

of Violence or Pandemic of Propaganda?" *Tennessee Law Review* 62 (Spring 1995): 572–573. The number of guns in 1973 is an estimate, but the number added to it comes from domestic manufacture and imports.

85. Ibid., pp. 572–573; Munday and Stevenson, *Guns and Violence,* p. 104.

86. Lott, *More Guns, Less Crime,* pp. 12, 11.

87. *Richmond Times Dispatch,* January 16, 1997, cited by Lott, *More Guns, Less Crime,* p. 12.

88. See Lott, *More Guns, Less Crime,* p. 12.

89. *Charleston Gazette,* July 28, 1997, quoted in Lott, *More Guns, Less Crime,* p. 12.

90. See Wright and Rossi, *Armed and Considered Dangerous,* p. 146.

91. Lott, *More Guns, Less Crime,* p. 8; Wright and Rossi, *Armed and Considered Dangerous.*

92. David McDowall, Colin Loftin, and Brian Wiersema, "Easing Concealed Firearms Laws: Effects on Homicide in Three States," *Journal of Criminal Law and Criminology* 86 (Fall 1995): 193–206. They examined three counties in Florida, one in Mississippi, and one in Oregon.

93. "The False Allure of Concealed Guns," *New York Times,* October 6, 1995.

94. See, for example, Roger Tarling, *Analyzing Offenders: Data, Models and Interpretation* (London, 1993), p. 18. Tarling found that the peak age for all offences in England fell between fourteen and twenty.

95. Gary Kleck and E. Britt Patterson, "The Impact of Gun Control and Gun-Ownership Levels on Violence Rates," *Journal of Quantitative Criminology* 9 (1993): 249–287.

96. Lott, *More Guns, Less Crime,* pp. 51, 63, 181. Counties with a 37 percent black population, for example, experienced 11 percent declines in murder and in aggravated assaults.

97. Ibid., table 3.2, p. 46 and pp. 53–54. Lott also examined the impact of concealed-carry laws against general crime trends and

found that their impact was still important and that it increased over time.

98. In 1994 Alaska, Arizona, Tennessee, and Wyoming passed new right-to-carry laws, and Arkansas, Nevada, North Carolina, Oklahoma, Texas, and Utah followed in 1995.

99. In 1994 there were 279,401 federally licenced gun dealers; by the beginning of 1997 there were 124,286. See Lott, *More Guns, Less Crime*, p. 163.

100. Ibid., p. 83.

101. The Bureau of Alcohol, Tobacco and Firearms estimates that one percent of dealers sell guns illegally and that this percentage has stayed constant despite the decline in licenced dealers; ibid., p. 163.

102. See, for example, Wright and Rossi, *Armed and Considered Dangerous*, chap. 9 and table 9.3, p. 186. In 1996 Sarah Brady, for whose husband the Brady Act was named, claimed it had kept more than 100,000 felons and other prohibited buyers from purchasing handguns. But the General Accounting Office reported that in 1996 initial rejections were only about 60,000, of which more than half were for filing and other technical errors. Only 3,000 were for prior convictions. In June 1997 only four people had gone to jail for violations. Lott, *More Guns, Less Crime*, p. 162.

103. See Lott, *More Guns, Less Crime*, pp. 122–166. Since the second edition of his book was published other critics have emerged. M. V. Hood III and Grant W. Neeley, "Packin' in the Hood?: Examining Assumptions of Concealed-Handgun Research," *Social Science Quarterly* 81 (June 2000): 523–537, criticize Lott's use of counties as too large a unit and have studied the impact of a concealed-carry law on Dallas, Texas, on a zip code basis. From the profile of those who obtain the certificates to carry handguns they argue that those in lower-crime areas are more likely to have the certificates. In a 2001 article in the

Journal of Political Economy reviewed in advance by *The Economist,* Mark Duggan uses what the reviewer characterizes as a "high-powered proxy" for numbers of guns, the number of subscribers to a particular handgun magazine, to determine if states with higher magazine sales and a higher number of gun shows suffered higher or lower rates of gun-related deaths. Duggan argues that guns foster rather than deter such deaths. See "New Research Shoots Holes in the Idea That Guns in the Hands of Private Citizens Will Help to Deter Criminals," *The Economist,* January 11, 2001 online edition.

104. See John R. Lott and David B. Mustard, "Crime, Deterrence, and Right-to-Carry Concealed Weapons," *Journal of Legal Studies* 26 (January 1997). For Lott's discussion of what he terms "the political process" and his reply to critics see *More Guns, Less Crime,* pp. 122–158. He notes that although he approached 22 pro-control people asking for their comments on the essay above, upon which his book was based, only a young assistant professor accepted. Apparently pro-control people refused to comment because they didn't want to "help give any publicity to the paper." Once it got publicity anyway, they hurriedly asked for copies in order to be able to criticize it. See pp. 122–123.

105. For the comparison on rates of apprehension, conviction, and sentencing see Farrington and Langan, *Crime and Justice,* p. iv. For statistical purposes, the authors assume that those apprehended and convicted are guilty.

8. The Right Equation

1. John R. Lott, *More Guns, Less Crime: Understanding Crime and Gun Control Laws* (Chicago, 2000), p. 161.

2. T. C. Hansard, ed., *The Parliamentary Debates from the Year 1803 to the Present Time,* March 26, 1953, 513: 849.

3. See the analysis in Lance Stell, "The Legitimation of Female

Violence: Bias and the Law of Self-Defense," in *Justice, Law, and Violence,* ed. James B. Brady and Newton Garver (Philadelphia, 1991), p. 246.

4. William Blackstone, *Commentaries on the Laws of England,* 4 vols. (1765–1769; reprint, Chicago, 1979), I: 120, 125, 123.

5. Browne-Wilkinson L.J., in Wheeler v. Leicester City Council, 1985.

Appendix

1. Both Professor Gary Mauser and the author will be pleased to share the tables created by Neuburger that provide a detailed description of the variables included in his model.

Index